EARLE BIRNEY

CRITICAL VIEWS ON CANADIAN WRITERS

MICHAEL GNAROWSKI, *Series Editor*

1. *E. J. Pratt*
   Edited and with an Introduction
   by David G. Pitt

2. *The McGill Movement: A. J. M. Smith,
   F. R. Scott and Leo Kennedy*
   Edited and with an Introduction
   by Peter Stevens

3. *Archibald Lampman*
   Edited and with an Introduction
   by Michael Gnarowski

4. *A. M. Klein*
   Edited and with an Introduction
   by Tom Marshall

5. *Frederick Philip Grove*
   Edited and with an Introduction
   by Desmond Pacey

6. *Mordecai Richler*
   Edited and with an Introduction
   by G. David Sheps

7. *Ernest Buckler*
   Edited and with an Introduction
   by Gregory M. Cook

8. *Hugh MacLennan*
   Edited and with an Introduction
   by Paul Goetsch

9. *Earle Birney*
   Edited and with an Introduction
   by Bruce Nesbitt

Other titles in preparation

CRITICAL VIEWS ON CANADIAN WRITERS

EARLE BIRNEY

Edited and with an Introduction by
BRUCE NESBITT

McGRAW-HILL RYERSON LIMITED
TORONTO · MONTREAL · NEW YORK · LONDON · SYDNEY

EARLE BIRNEY

Copyright © McGraw-Hill Ryerson Limited, 1974

All rights reserved. No part of this publication
may be reproduced, stored in a retrieval system,
or transmitted in any form or by any means,
electronic, mechanical, photocopying, recording, or
otherwise, without the prior written permission
of McGraw-Hill Ryerson Limited.

ISBN 0-07-077364-5 Hard Cover
      0-07-077788-8 Soft Cover
Library of Congress Catalog Card Number 74-10172
Printed and bound in Canada
1 2 3 4 5 6 7 8 9 10   JD   3 2 1 0 9 8 7 6 5 4

Every reasonable care has been taken to trace ownership
of copyrighted material used in this book. The author
and the publisher will welcome information that will
enable them to rectify any errors or omissions.

Author's Note: Original conventions of style in reprinted
selections—except for elisions indicated and unless
otherwise noted—have been retained. The author is
grateful to Mrs. Jean Sangwine of the Library of
Simon Fraser University, for assistance during early
research; to Earle Birney, for a fascinating tennis match;
and to the archivists of the University of Toronto Library.

For Mrs. Susan

CONTENTS

INTRODUCTION 1

1. ONE SOCIETY: Poetry, 1937-1948

Two Reviews of *David and Other Poems* (1942)
    NORTHROP FRYE   39
    E. J. PRATT   41

JOHN SUTHERLAND: Earle Birney's "David"   43

ROY DANIELS: Earle Birney   47

Three Reviews of *Now Is Time* (1945)
    E. K. BROWN   54
    M. H. MARTIN   55
    WATSON KIRKCONNELL   57
    EARLE BIRNEY, Letter to the Editor   58

Six Reviews of *The Strait of Anian: Selected Poems* (1948)
    ROY DANIELS   59
    DOROTHY LIVESAY   60
    L. A. MACKAY   61
    TIMES LITERARY SUPPLEMENT   63
        LIONEL MONTEITH, Letter to the Editor   65
        "Our reviewer writes"   65
    GUSTAV DAVIDSON   65
    A. G. BAILEY   67

2. LINES FOR A PEACE: Fiction, 1949-1955

A Review of *Turvey: A Military Picaresque* (1949)
    MALCOLM LOWRY   73

D. J. DOOLEY: The Satiric Novel in Canada Today: *Turvey*   76

EARLE BIRNEY: Creativity Through Fiction   80

GEORGE WOODCOCK: Introduction to *Turvey*   85

EARLE BIRNEY: Turvey and the Critics   90

D. J. DOOLEY: The Satiric Novel in Canada Today: *Down the Long Table* (1955)   95

    ARNOLD EDINBOROUGH: A Review of *Down the Long Table*   97

    GEORGE WOODCOCK: Earle Birney: *Down the Long Table*   99

3. ONE WORLD: Poetry, 1949-1965

Two Reviews of *Trial of a City and Other Verse* (1952)
    NORTHROP FRYE   101
    SIMON PAYNTER   104

W. E. FREDEMAN: Earle Birney: Poet   107

EARLE BIRNEY: The Writing of a Poem: Compulsion and Suppression   115

PAUL WEST: Earle Birney and the Compound Ghost   119

    ROBIN SKELTON: A Review of *Ice Cod Bell or Stone* (1962)   129

    EARLE BIRNEY, Letter to the Editor   131

Three Reviews of *Near False Creek Mouth* (1964)
    A. W. PURDY   132
    MILTON WILSON   133
    A. KINGSLEY WEATHERHEAD   136

4. SELECTED POEMS 1940-1966

A. J. M. SMITH: A Unified Personality: Birney's Poems   141

MILTON WILSON: Poet Without a Muse   150

HAYDEN CARRUTH: Up, Over, and Out   157

A. W. PURDY, Letter to the Editor   163

JOE ROSENBLATT, Letter to the Editor   164

GEORGE WOODCOCK: Turning New Leaves   166

5. WEED BED: New Directions

BP NICHOL: Introduction to *Pnomes Jukollages & Other Stunzas* (1969)   171

Five Reviews of *Rag & Bone Shop* (1971)
    CARL BALLSTADT   173
    FRED COGSWELL   175
    ANDY WAINWRIGHT   177

LIONEL KEARNS   179

JUDITH COPITHORNE   182

EARLE BIRNEY: Preface to *Four Parts Sand* (1972)   185

D. G. JONES: The Courage To Be   187

EARLE BIRNEY: Madness and Exorcism of Poetry   196

EARLE BIRNEY: The Writer-Creator in Today's World   203

EARLE BIRNEY: Epilogue   206

SELECTED BIBLIOGRAPHY   219

INTRODUCTION

Earle Birney's work both reflects and summarizes the ambiguities of writing in Canada over the past five decades, but it is scarcely for that that he will continue to be acknowledged as Canada's finest poet. He is one of very few Canadian men of letters whose work has substantially altered our literary perception of ourselves. Another, Northrop Frye, reviewed his first volume of poetry, and opens this collection of responses to Birney's poetry and fiction. As Frye predicted in 1942, Birney's intuitive apprehension of themes central to the Canadian literary imagination promised an increase of fertility: to date, twenty-three volumes of poetry, fiction, criticism, anthologies and editions, as well as nearly 100 short stories, pamphlets, essays, reviews and articles. Yet as the review also suggests, Birney's poetry presented a curious difficulty which Frye found exemplified in Birney's "searching for the basis of his own attitude" to nature. He reveals both "stereotyped oratory" and "spiritual truancy . . . which refuses to oversimplify the imagination". Equally strangely, he writes one poem easily accessible to the "common reader" and another influenced by techniques a millenium old. Birney was, in short, a highly talented poet so eclectic as to cause quizzical puzzlement, and for others a figure of controversy so unpredictable as to be a thoroughly disturbing element.

The controversy is not over. His politics, his personality, his writing, his influence, his reputation: all have been subject to jaundiced scrutiny or wry acceptance rarely seen in Canadian literary history. Major John Richardson, best known for his nineteenth-century novel *Wacousta,* was openly shot at by his enemies; Birney continues to attract more than his share of literary snipers. During the 1960s he found that he was reinvigorated (he said "goosed") by the new movements among young Canadian writers, and his latest work is received enthusiastically by university students at readings throughout the country. On the other hand, balanced judgements of Birney's work—indeed, thoughtful assessments of any length—are relatively scarce despite the volume of criticism and reviews of his books. For this reason I have chosen to structure this collection as a variety of dialectic, both to gather together the most valuable critical commentary on Canada's most important poet, and to imply as well the shifting preoccupations of literary criticism in Canada since his first book was published. To attempt to include criticism of all his writing and editing would extend the length of this book beyond practical considerations, and so I have consciously limited the material covered to his eight main volumes of poetry and two novels published before 1973. Similarly, in the comments which follow I have attempted only to offer a cursory background perspective on the verbal documentary presented here, and to indicate some directions in his poetry as it was revised and brought together in his major work, *Selected Poems*. Anything more would have tempted me to expand this introduction into a separate book, for despite two short monographs recently published, no full critical study of Birney has yet been written.

Perhaps it is fitting that the juxtaposition of opinions in the collection occasionally yields ironies I had not anticipated. For of all twentieth-century Canadian poets, Birney is the master ironist, even having written his Ph.D. thesis on Chaucer's irony. In an article published a year after the University of Toronto had accepted his thesis in 1936, he reluctantly put forward a definition of irony which he knew to be slightly pedantic. Only after I had finished reading all available criticism of his work did the appropriateness of the definition strike me:

> An illusion has been created that a real incongruity or conflict is non-existent, and the illusion has been so shaped that a bystander may, immediately or ultimately, see through it and be thereby surprised into a more vivid awareness of that very conflict.[1]

As an entry into his poetry—and Canada itself—his statement still stands.

In retrospect, critical preoccupations in assessing Birney's work have remained remarkably constant throughout three decades. Frye's review of *David and Other Poems* (1942) noted that Birney as lyricist is "an artist in vignette", while "satire makes him relapse into an idiom more suitable for prose". But already disagreement on Birney's technical mastery is implied in Frye's comment on Birney's run-on lines—particularly in "David"—"which have nowhere in particular to run to". For E. J. Pratt, on the other hand, Birney's cunning use of "rove-over" lines was "admirable", and

---

[1]Earle Birney, "English Irony before Chaucer", *University of Toronto Quarterley*, VI (1937), p. 540.

he was particularly struck by the "ironic foreshadowing of the catastrophe" in the poem. Six years later Birney would dedicate *Strait of Anian* to Pratt, just a year after Pratt wrote Birney privately about a discussion at one of his parties in Toronto on "the future of Canadian poetry. I claimed as I have maintained for some years, that you were our white hope, that no one, particularly in the Montreal 'faction' . . . was even within light-years of your constellation".[2] Pratt's reference to a Montreal "faction" is significant in light of John Sutherland's comments on Birney's "David" ("of all our young modernist poets he is the only one who has made consistent use of a Canadian landscape"), for as other collections of documents by Michael Gnarowski, Louis Dudek and Peter Stevens have made clear, the issue of "modernism" as opposed to "Canadianism" was at the centre of a major critical debate throughout the 1940s.[3] Birney was an obvious new source of data for the controversy through his straightforward narrative "and the incorporation in it of a Canadian environment", which marked him off from other "modernists". Roy Daniells, however, found in "David" a different level of significance; it was quite simply "le meilleur poème de longeur qui ait jamais été écrit au Canada", and from a broader perspective, the poem "peut bien être considéré comme le *Shepheardes Calendar* des lettres canadiennes".

Both *David* and *Now is Time* (1945) won the Governor General's Award; to all appearances his reputation was established and not merely promising. Yet as E. K. Brown's review demonstrates, Birney's "social idealism", his tendency to write elegies, and the bitter tone of several poems resulting from his experiences in the Depression and Second World War were a matter of some unease. Even as late as 1945, Canadian literary critics were not wholly prepared to acknowledge social injustice as a fit subject for poetry, especially when (as Brown put it) Birney's poetry suffered from "his summary unconvincing presentation" of the masters of the poor. His "bitterness", that is, tended "to destroy a touch of reality". M. H. Martin, at least, had the critical sense to distinguish the essential difference in tone between *David* and *Now is Time* as a sense of "implacable nature" in the first and of man's implacability" in the latter. He spoke, moreover, for those who challenged the

[2]University of Toronto Library, Manuscript Collection 49, Birney Collection, E. J. Pratt to Earle Birney, 30 September 1947. Hereafter cited as *BC*.
[3]Louis Dudek and Michael Gnarowski, eds., *The Making of Modern Poetry in Canada* (Toronto: Ryerson, 1967); Peter Stevens, ed., *The McGill Movement*. (Critical Views on Canadian Writers series; Toronto: Ryerson **1969.**)

equation of optimism with merit, seemingly an ineradicable assumption of Canadian literary criticism since the early nineteenth century. Others were less sure that poetry of social protest was even desirable in postwar Canada, much less poetry of "metaphysical modernity", as Watson Kirkconnell's review in the *Canadian Poetry Magazine* makes bluntly plain. Birney himself—presumably one of Canada's "clique of Leftist poseurs"—would shortly thereafter assume the editorship of the journal. That he would later resign in protest against what he called in 1946 a "clique of Rightist flaneurs" writing in the journal seems only just.

The appearance of *Strait of Anian* in 1948 posed a difficult series of questions to critics both in Canada and elsewhere. For some Canadian critics like Roy Daniells, this volume of selected poems demonstrated Birney's increased technical competence, "mellowness", and "greater maturity of outlook". Others, Dorothy Livesay in particular, found him "the only poet who sees Canada whole", or like Louis MacKay felt obliged to comment on "the profoundly Canadian quality of his inspiration": "invariably, whatever the theme, he is at his best when his feet are on his native soil, or not far removed from it." It was precisely this aspect of literary nationalism which interested the *Times Literary Supplement*'s reviewer, for he saw flowing from Birney's Canadianism "a tendency to fall now into manly rant, now into manly sentimentality". Lionel Monteith's prompt response to this patronizing generality brought a reply from the reviewer even more curious than his original statement: "in young societies masculine energy is less tempered than in old societies by feminine scepticism". Despite the absurd critical assumptions underlying the reviewer's comments, his reply illustrates some of the problems Canadian poets have been forced to expect when their work is read by reviewers unfamiliar with two centuries of Canadian literature. Gustav Davidson, writing in the United States, was at least familiar with some of Birney's other work, and despite one notable lapse (he considered "Anglosaxon Street" to be "avant-garde" whimsy) attempted a fair evaluation. To Alfred Bailey, by contrast, Birney's "Canadianness" was not an issue to be debated, but simply accepted. Observing that *Strait of Anian* was divided into two sections, "One Society" and "One World", he suggested that "the two problems, national and œcumenical, are ultimately the same, because they spring from the more fundamental predicament that confronts humanity as a whole in the face of what appears to be a brutish and indifferent universe". At the same time Bailey noted that Birney was not a "modernist" in the sense that his more recent work revealed him moving "through the realm of metaphysical symbol to one of action in time and space". That Bailey's review article would remain until 1960 the longest and most considered assessment of the first decade of Birney's poetry is a fact scarcely to the credit of Canadian literary critics.

By the end of 1948 Birney had published seventy-nine poems, four of them juvenilia from his days at U.B.C., and three from the 1930s. During the next decade he published only twenty-two more, and in 1957 wrote privately that "at the moment I am interested in writing poetry only as a medium of drama".[4] The period was far from unproductive, although several critics were surprised to see Birney as the author of two novels and a verse drama, and the editor of an anthology, *Twentieth Century Canadian Poetry* (1953). That the most perceptive review of his first novel, *Turvey* (1949), was written by his friend Malcolm Lowry for a journal of limited circulation is another reflection on the state of literature reviewing in Canada. Lowry considered three aspects of the novel to be particularly important: the nature of Birney's satire and humour, his narrative attitude, and the symbolic significance of Turvey himself for Canadians. One of very few reviewers to place *Turvey* within the context of Bunyan's *Pilgrim's Progress* and Hasek's *Good Soldier Schweik,* Lowry was also careful to distinguish the peculiarly Canadian perspective which gives the novel its special element of "ribald and paradoxical miracle". He refutes possible criticism that the novel is sentimental, and suggests that Birney's heteroplastic method of bringing together disparate elements in the experiences of his innocent rogue is essential to Turvey's retaining his own integrity at the conclusion of the book. D. J. Dooley, however, found many of these same qualities to be vital weaknesses in *Turvey*. Arguing from a particularly narrow definition of "picaresque", Dooley maintained that the book is neither a satire of a military system nor "a dramatic conflict between the little man and the impersonal system", that Birney puts comic effect ahead of satire, and that even the portrait of Turvey is inconsistent: "evidently the author has not decided what kind of book he is writing". As Lowry anticipated, "people will doubtless lose their tempers over Turvey", but the premises underlying Dooley's comments have not been uncommon in the history of Canadian criticism. Dooley implies that a "first-rate" Canadian

[4]*BC*, Earle Birney to Desmond Pacey, 4 February 1957.

novel should be disciplined; a book which is neither fish nor fowl is necessarily something inferior to both; and consistency of characterization and narrative view are important if the Canadian novelist is to avoid his "usual difficulties with plot" and his "usual interference of things read with things imagined or seen".

In this context, it is useful to consider the author's own observations on what he wrote, rather than what he should have written. (The informality of Birney's discussion of *Turvey*'s genesis stems from its origin as part of a series of radio broadcasts given in 1965, and revised for publication as *The Creative Writer* in 1966.) Three points emerge almost as a partial answer to Dooley's criticisms: that Birney took great care in revising his novel until it took the shape and style he had intended; that he deliberately chose the character of Turvey as a crystallization of several kinds of military experience, including his own broad personal knowledge; and that the humour of the novel had a peculiar Canadian twist which made it alien to both British and American publishers. More basic is his assertion that the writing of fiction, like the writing of poetry, consists in exorcizing ghosts; the creative impulse behind both is very similar, and hence the twentieth-century author can be compartmentalized by critics as "poet" or "novelist" with increasingly less validity. While George Woodcock does consider *Turvey* to be essentially a "poet's novel", nevertheless he establishes his grounds for doing so. The most acute analysis of the novel yet written, Woodcock's introduction to *Turvey* shares with Lowry's review— both make remarkably similar points—an emphasis on the benign qualities of Birney's humour. The humour is indeed more than Canadian, just as Turvey is not an *"ersatz* Schweik", but "natural man triumphant". On the other hand, if *Turvey* is the satirical fantasia Woodcock claims it to be, and the episodes rather than psychological development are at the centre of the novel's interest, then Birney's humour is far darker than any critic has yet suggested. The war, in effect, becomes a metaphor for all human activity. That *Turvey* should have been produced on the stage as a musical comedy is perhaps an example of terminal irony. Birney too was disturbed by much of the criticism *Turvey* had attracted, and in 1966 undertook an assessment of his assessors. What emerged is a thorough indictment of the provincialism and ignorance of Canadian newspaper and radio reviewers, and a more muted response to some of his academic critics. From one viewpoint, Birney has adopted a ritual pose in "Turvey and the Critics", but the seriousness of his broodings should not be underestimated. Media reviewers do exert considerable power, however irresponsibly used, and any instruments which detach the artist from his audience also diminish the artist's ability to survive as part of his chosen community.

Birney's second novel, *Down the Long Table* (1955), presented critics with a far different problem. As one of very few novels concerned with the political milieu of the 1930s in Canada, it forced many readers into wholly unfamiliar territory: a portrait of the young man as political activist, and Trotskyist at that. The *ad hominem* proclivities of Canadian critics were unleashed in ignorance, and Birney himself stood trial as a self-indulgent autobiographer or confused apostle of American realism. That Birney was politically active in both Canada and England during the 1930s is a matter of public record. Interviewer of Leon Trotsky, part-time political organizer in England and full-time in Canada, visitor to Nazi Germany (where he was assaulted when he failed to show sufficient enthusiasm for saluting) : only Birney's autobiography could reveal the full influence of much of this period immediately before he began some of his most important creative work. When *Turvey* appeared, many critics could write with some personal assurance of the realism or otherwise of the events faced by Private Thomas Turvey. Few understood the atmosphere in Canada engendered by political infighting and criminal syndicalism laws, as Birney experienced them in the Depression. Writing to a friend in 1934 he described some of his summer activities:

> The Socialist Party of Canada is much more respectful of my position now and actually made me guest speaker at their open forum last week. I spoke, of course, under a new name—the Stalinites would have got wise if I had used my old pseudonym and would have organized hoodlums to break up a "Trotskyite" speech. . . . Another ubiquitous problem is the *agent provocateur*. He's getting smarter, has stopped hanging around doorways like a private detective, and is joining workers' organizations and penetrating into all revolutionary circles.[5]

D. J. Dooley's comments on *Down the Long Table* properly emphasize the irony and satire in the novel, although the character of Gordon Saunders, the academic being investigated by a Senatorial Committee, is clearly uncongenial to the critic who expects Saunders to apologize for his past activities rather than mock them. Arnold Edinborough chose a safer course, suggesting that both the

[5]*BC,* Earle Birney to S. Angleman, 20 July 1934.

framework and technique of the novel are "old-fashioned" while praising Birney's gift for dialogue. But like Dooley earlier, whose comments can be balanced by those of Woodcock later, Edinborough speculates that Birney does not seem to have decided what kind of novel he is writing, one about the 1930s or the 1950s, while he laments the relative absence of satire. In the opposing observations of these critics lies yet another dilemma for the student of both Birney and Canadian literary criticism. However much literary judgement is a by-product of scholarly understanding, that understanding itself must first be weighed on an infinitely variable set of scales.

Literary judgement, in any case, must weigh with both eyes open, while justice is blind. Perhaps it is no coincidence that the structure of Birney's only verse drama, "Trial of a City" (later the "Damnation of Vancouver"), is also that of a public hearing. Already calling Birney one of Canada's two leading poets (the other was Pratt), Northrop Frye began his review of *Trial of a City and Other Verse* (1952) by asserting "the existence of a Canadianism in Canadian poetry". He found in the dialectic implicit in "Trial of a City" two elements central to that Canadianism: problems of communication, and a radical conservatism opposed to mercantilist Whiggery. The former in Birney is reflected by his unique virtuosity of language, and the latter in the characters of the drama. For the first time in criticism of Birney, and as one of very few instances in Canadian literary history, the issue of "Canadianism" was raised in strictly literary terms. Simon Paynter, however, sees only at the centre of the play "the old British-Columbian standby of landscape and nature"; for him Birney's verbal distortions are meaningless or irrelevant, particularly when compared with Christopher Frye's work. The distinction between the criticism of Northrop Frye and Paynter in 1952 is that between a maturing sense of Canadian literary criticism with its own referents and a retrogressive colonial pandering to imaginary standards through limited knowledge. A midpoint between the two is represented by W. E. Fredeman's essay on Birney, written in anticipation of a *Selected Poems* which was to be published in 1960 but which did not appear. The issue of Birney as a Canadian poet had to Fredeman "no critical validity"; indeed, "it may be that Birney has won more fame in Canadian letters than he might have realized in a more competitive intellectual climate, but certainly he would be regarded as a serious poet in any country." As only the second attempt in two decades to offer a critical overview of Birney's poetry, Fredeman's essay should not necessarily be discounted because of one footnote. His stressing of "Trial of a City" as a thematic summary of Birney's poetry is valuable, but the relative brevity of his analysis of the poems themselves (compared with his discussion of "the problem of evaluation") is a certain indicator of the margin-straddler.

During the late 1950s Birney's creative impulse was once again beginning to find expression in poetry, and at a steadily increasing rate. In the two years following *Down the Long Table* he published only two poems; from 1958 until the appearance of *Selected Poems* eight years later, 87 poems were published in literary magazines throughout the world. "It's only by our lack of ghosts we're haunted", he has written, but his growing compulsion to exorcise "the fearful ghosts of my separateness" may be one explanation for his return to poetry. Whatever the reason, as a reflection of the process of subconscious purging his description of the circumstances prompting him to write "Bushed" is a revealing introduction to Paul West's essay on *Ice Cod Bell or Stone* (1962), Birney's first collection of poetry in a decade. "Earle Birney and the Compound Ghost" mirrors, in a sense, a new direction in Canadian literary criticism, for West's points of comparison are frequently other Canadian poets and Birney himself; his call for more of the "home image" in Birney's poetry suggests his concern for an evolving literary tradition in Canada, and the poet-novelist's place in it. The didactic assumptions behind West's criticism are obvious: Birney has a unique talent for creating a particular kind of poetry lacking in Canada; why, then, does he not turn his talent to creating that sort of poetry when he writes about Canada, rather than demonstrating his abilities in poems about other nations and peoples? Yet to Robin Skelton, Birney's mastery of techniques is merely clever, and the book itself is simply another indication that "some poets show a consciousness of the 'Canadian problem' which mars their work." Skelton too appears to believe that Birney ought to be writing a different kind of poetry (presumably less "aggressively avant-garde"), but the violence of his phrasing surely deserves Birney's irritated response to the editor of the journal which published it. With the publication of *Near False Creek Mouth* in 1964, critics were forced to concede that his earlier book was not simply "a bit of a poet's holiday", as Paul West put it, and that they were dealing with a poet at the height of his powers, revitalized by contemporary poetic modes. For Al Purdy there were two Birneys: the relatively impersonal poet of the early poems and the more recent poet "inside" his work; a shift in voice, he implies, marks the transition. Purdy shares with Milton Wilson a fascination with the change in Birney's sensibility and voice over twenty-five years, although Wilson is more confident in drawing out some thematic affinities between the early and later work. Interestingly enough, neither comments extensively on the title poem, the main focus of A. Kingsley Weatherhead's review.

The full significance of Birney's contribution as a poet over a quarter-century of writing in Canada only becomes apparent in his *Selected Poems* (1966). Despite clear differences in emphasis, review articles by two of Canada's most influential critics and anthologists remain as essential reading for any student of Birney because of the underlying consistency of their responses. Both A. J. M. Smith and Milton Wilson devote excessive space to lamenting Birney's "typographical gimmicks" and "notational idiosyncrasies"; both comment creatively on the emergence of his individual poetic personality; and both find in his work confirmation for some of their own critical preoccupations. Each of their responses, moreover, is an implied commentary on the state of conservative Canadian literary criticism in the mid-1960s. Smith considers the poems on Mexico, Peru and the Caribbean islands to be Birney's finest, without qualification; unlike Paul West, Smith feels no need to tell the poet what he ought to write. Birney's imagery and diction are part of an excellent "northern style" rooted in a native tradition, and "November Walk" is both emotionally and rationally satisfying in its orientation of poet, place and time. Wilson's more tentative and scholarly "notes towards an unwritten revised portrait" of Birney gloss the chronology of the poems in an attempt to evaluate his development in relation to his contemporaries, and are particularly useful for their hints at the Chaucerian nature of his irony. In comparison to the balanced assessments of Smith and Wilson, the appalling triviality of Hayden Carruth's review of *Selected Poems* ought not (it might be urged) to be included in this collection. Nevertheless it is essential to understanding Birney's critical reception, for the editor of *Tamarack Review* consciously chose an American poet to review the book, and then consciously chose to print that review. The journal is one of Canada's leading literary periodicals, and most readers might agree with Al Purdy and Joe Rosenblatt in their letters to the editor. Others who share Carruth's biases, particularly non-Canadian readers, may well feel on the side of the gods, for Birney's work has not until recently been widely circulated outside Canada. Is our principal poetic swan therefore a goose the moment he crosses Canada's boundaries?

Even praise can have its dangers, for well over half of George Woodcock's review is not concerned with Birney's poetry as such, and his conclusion—that Birney is "one of the four most maturely vital poets writing in Canada today"—begs at least five separate questions. What four, and who are the others? Mature in what sense? What is vitality? Are better Canadian poets writing outside Canada, or non-Canadians in the country? And why "today", or is it "writing today"?

Commenting on Birney's statement in his preface to *Selected Poems* that "in my next work I'm thinking of pasting my poems on mobiles", A. J. M. Smith assumed that Birney was making a "frivolous joke". Smith profoundly underestimated Birney's commitment to new forms of poetic expression, as a mobile version of "Like an Eddy" hanging in the poet's apartment and the *grOnk* issue of *Pnomes Jukollages & Other Stunzas* (1969) both demonstrate. bp nichol's introduction to *Pnomes* suggests how much of Birney's "return to the ear" may have its origin in his Chaucerian scholarship and sensitivity to dialect and accent, and also anticipates the confusion of some readers faced with *Rag & Bone Shop* (1971). Carl Ballstadt notes in his review that "what bp nichol and his generation have done is to stimulate certain tendencies which are deeply rooted in Birney's career", a point echoed by Fred Cogswell. Yet both are unhesitating in their judgements that his concrete "shapomes" are of ephemeral interest, or more often failures than successes. Neither gives any hint of the bases for his judgement. Andy Wainwright attempts a justification for agreeing with Ballstadt and Cogswell, but betrays the young critic's penchant for arguing from dicta toward poetry, the source of his highly arbitrary conclusion. Two more sympathetic reviewers, Lionel Kearns and Judith Copithorne (both involved in expanding the linear frontiers of Canadian poetry), coincidentally choose the same poem as an example of Birney's continuing lyrical gift, while acknowledging the strengths of what he has called "magic picturetraps": "poets need the lost freedom to make speechsigns as varied and tough and cunning as football*player*faces . . . wordball."[6]

The serious game of poetry which Birney has been playing under new rules since the mid-1960s has placed many of his spectator-critics at a disadvantage, especially those unfamiliar with contemporary experimentation in stretching the boundaries. The central question resolves itself into who determines those boundaries, the

---

[6]Earle Birney, *Four Parts Sand* (Ottawa: Oberon, 1972), p. 2.

critic or the poet? If the critic, then Birney is clearly a weird bird, or as his young New Zealand friend has it in "kiwis", a "weed bed". Scholar that he is (many of his academic articles are mandatory reading for any serious Chaucerian), Birney well knows the association of "weird" with "fate", from the Old English *weordhan*, to become. Anglers know how many hooks can be lost in strange waters. Any critical overview of Birney's poetry faces the same hazard, an explanation perhaps for the rarity of any extended critical work on Birney since the publication of his *Selected Poems*: two short monographs and two essays, one of them part of a full-length thematic study of Canadian literature. The extract from D. G. Jones' *Butterfly on Rock* forms part of an extended argument based on Northrop Frye's critical theories, among others, and takes its title from Paul Tillich's philosophical work *The Courage to Be*. Birney's poetry, Jones suggests, is essentially life-affirming in its vigorous defiance of a destructive universe. To the extent that Birney proclaims stoic courage rather than Christian acceptance in the face of death, he has posed a clear answer to the question of Job: what shall man do when faced with Leviathan? Whether Jones is correct in describing Birney's view of man as frequently sardonic is secondary to his main argument, and to our assessment of it. By insisting on man's individualism, Birney's poetry suggests that swallowing Leviathan, collective anti-humanism, is an essential step in preserving man himself. A recent essay by W. H. New begins with this suggestion, and attempts to explain the tension between "humane optimism and ironic dismay" as a symptom of "the divided character of the Canadian soul".[7] The opposites, for New, demand a resolution as much as they did for Jones, and Birney's irony does not provide a necessary mode to solve the poet's dilemma. The answer lies in confronting death by reconciling history and myth, by abolishing time through the discovery of a "sense of co-existent mythic and empirical realities".

The issues raised by Jones, ironically, are precisely those discussed by Birney in *The Creative Writer*: obliquely in his memory of the circumstances leading to the creation of "The Bear on the Delhi Road", and more specifically in his analysis of the process wich resulted in "Aluroid". In the end, Birney's wryly apocalyptic claims for the writer-creator demand the preservation of the artist's independence as a sign of man's willingness to save himself. And

[7]W. H. New, "Maker of Order, Prisoner of Dreams: The Poetry of Earle Birney," *Articulating West* (Toronto: New Press, 1972), p. 259. This essay was not available for inclusion here.

as he also observes, "We must know ourselves before we can better ourselves". Enhancing that self-knowledge is the critics' primary task and principal justification. From this perspective, the critic in Canada is also charged with the responsibility of charting the course of his nation's cultural life, and the stakes are high for the unwary navigator. The discovery of *ultima Thule* is his fondest hope, and his failure to identify it, his constant despair. Birney's *Selected Poems*, the major work of Canada's major poet, is just such a goal.

Birney's poetic reputation is secure in his *Selected Poems*, a volume which can reveal more than his individual collections taken together because of the ways it bears the imprint of the poet's active imagination, consciously shaping much of his life's work. Unlike a comprehensive final collection, it serves a vital interim purpose: not that of the gravestone, a static monument to accomplishment finished, but of living belief, the testament of a poet conscious of judging himself, shaping a syncretic vision which demands to be articulated. As an embodiment of this vision, *Selected Poems* also reflects Birney's poetic process, for with few other Canadian poets is it as important to understand the movement of the poet's mind. His aesthetic is a function of expanding time and place as much as of literary history and biography, and it is toward understanding the evolution of an aesthetic-in-process that Birney's poetry urges his audience.

The casual reader might judge the structure of *Selected Poems* to be embarrassingly simple-minded: the six sections group together poems about travel generally in the eastern hemisphere; travel in the United States, Mexico, the Caribbean and South America; poems from the Second World War; on Canada; on man's future; and, seemingly as an afterthought, a verse drama about a fictional trial of the west coast city with which Birney has come to be associated. Even to the careful reader considering the whole of Birney's poetry, beginning with the revised work as it stood in 1966, his poems do appear to be principally concerned with a limited number of recurring themes. And so some literalists and poetic illiterates have led themselves into perverse by-ways of generalization on Birney' "Canadianness", or to speculate that his best work ignores Canada (or his roots, or his craft), or that his fiction (or criticism, or essays), have little to do with his poetic sensibilities. Yet in much of Birney's work an evolving process is the meaning and merit, just as his phrasing, his notation and the typographical shape of his poetry are crucial to a complete appreciation of his directions. That he has more recently turned to non-linear, non-print modes of expression is a further reflection of his own concern with poetry as process. In the past, Birney has been chiefly valued—and undervalued—for his rhetoric; his reputation in the future will be reinforced by a clearer apprehension of his aesthetic-in-process, the interpenetration of craft and craftsman.

Central to all of Birney's poetry is his definition of man's place in a world blind to the ironic consequences of the simultaneity of time. His verbal and dramatic irony have long been remarked on; less explored is his irony of manner as it is expressed by his shifting sense of voice; his profoundly personal sense of philosophic irony; and his care in constructing poems and books whose very structure is ironic. "The Bear on the Delhi Road", one of his best poems and the title poem both of the first section of his *Selected Poems* and of the first British edition of his poetry, in many ways represents a distillation of his whole aesthetic.

The ambiguity of the poet-narrator's position is obvious from the two opening stanzas, which carry the only directly observed action, two men attempting to control a dancing bear. Yet they also begin with the observer's impulse to raise the moment to a complex level of generalization. The remainder of the poem is an extended comment on the significance of the incident by an authentic tourist, the person who travels because of some personal necessity, but who may find himself in any given place for wholly accidental reasons. The Delhi road, in this instance, is merely a way between two significant points of interest, the capital of India and the Vale of Kashmir. At the same time the place carries its own irony, for the tourist is on the same route as the two men he observes, and is thus identified with them. Nevertheless he is *on* the road in a car while they are *by* it on foot, and his nominal superiority is maintained throughout the poem by his objectively affirmative statements.

Birney's verbal irony, less forcefully evident here than in many of his poems, is operating even in the opening words of the poem. The situation for the narrator as tourist is indeed "unreal", one beyond his own reality, despite the episode's happening in front of him; he responds to the unexpected by unconscious colloquialism, or by denying it. That the bear is for him "tall as a myth", furthermore, implies a leap of the imagination important to the construction of the poem, if a myth is the story of men acting at the limits of human desire. The bear, then can be *Ursus major,* permanently with us. Or is the spectacle simply a tall story, and the bear a gigantic figure from legend? Both are clearly present, for it is a bear from earth's highest mountains, the Himalayas, whose story, we now suspect, is intricately involved with the narrator, the two men around him, and all men. The trainers, after all, are also "bare", sharing with their bear the crooked arms of locusts, even if they are a plague upon him. And as Birney will demonstrate throughout the poem, their actions are onomatopoeically suited to the poem's diction when they leap like locusts or pull or flick, when the bear's eyes are rolling, or his arms beating. By the end of the initial scene, in any case, the bear is victim, and his spindly masters control him by the force of nose-ring and stick, viciously through his most sensitive parts. However spindly, they are in fact masters of physical control because of their knowledge; something as tall as a myth can be controlled because of their will.

Birney having established the place of the actors, the rest of the poem flows from the first instant of vision. He shares his knowledge of the "clamorous" world with the two bear-masters, a world "alien" to him as tourist, to the men as Kashmiris, and to the bear as Himalayan from the "fabulous" hills, hills of fable, perhaps legend and possibly myth. The burning Gangetic plain, by contrast, is both bald and alien. Despite their ostensible violence, the two men are simple dance-masters, peaceful, we are told, and "spare" not because they are superfluous, but because they are poor without the bear, their means of living. The plains are bald like the bear because some natural features have to be eroded away if man is to survive in the world of men. Yet the dance-masters are dancing, dancing galvanically, as if they were frogs on Luigi Galvani's hooks, objects of an experiment to prove something beyond their existence. Who controls whom? The bear, significantly, retains his "tranced wish", his memory *and* his will, simply to be himself, a four-footed bear not forced to walk on two feet as a dancer for the entertainment of the aliens.

The men, however, are aliens in more ways than one. First, they are themselves foreigners to the hot dust of the plains. Then they are in danger from the sharp claws of the bear; they themselves become the ants which the bear usually eats. More obliquely, the poet himself shares in their predicament as master-victim. If the bear is "tall as a myth", moreover, and "it is not easy to free/myth from reality", both the bear and the trainers can be seen as victims of a system which requires man and animal to be forced from their own environment simply for some men to survive. The bear could exist on his own, "four-footed in berries", but the trainers could not; they depend on him, and without the bear might perish if they fail "to rear his fellow up", to make him walk unnaturally for the entertainment of other men. Both they and the bear have been forced to dance, and with all men are in a trance, hypnotically lurching toward death.

Birney's choice of "The Bear on the Delhi Road" as the title for the first section of his *Selected Poems* should thus serve as a warning to readers approaching Birney for the first time. The traveller whose experience dominates many of his poems is no ordinary tourist, as his satire on the Twenty-third Psalm makes obvious. The ostensible object of his satire is the poet himself, the aging ram wryly musing in Hawaii on apparently impossible desire. But the ram's horn is also the *shofar,* the instrument whose voice brought down the walls of Jericho; Birney's psalm is an ironic hymn of praise for the new god of profit whose power we will find personified in P.S. Legion, counsel for Vancouver in "The Damnation of Vancouver". Hawaii, Captain Cook's Sandwich Islands, has prostituted ritual for commerce, green pastures for the valley of the shadow of death. This theme is echoed ironically in Birney's following poem on Cook himself, the archetypal traveller whose life is bracketed by two flashes of light: the toss of a South Seas shilling which prompted Cook's curiosity as a boy, and the glint of the spear which pinned him forever in Hawaii. Neither act has any significant motivation, yet each defines one extreme in the life of a man for whom discovery was the sole justification for existence.

For all men, too, discovery can annihilate time by forcing a simultaneity of vision. What the tourist discovers, as in "Honolulu", is not simply the coexistence of elements of Hawaii's Polynesian past and their assimilation (and perversion) in the present, but the perspective of the observer who sees as a kind of blessing the young Hawaiian girl's asking her mother whether electric catfish can kiss. The irony is in the juxtaposition, but it also results from the tourist's new consciousness of potential. As in all possibilities of human love, symbolized in "Wind-Chimes in a Temple Ruin":

> Who is the moving
> or moved is no matter
> but the birth of the possible
> song in the rafter

Nevertheless at another level the traveller's journey is one into confinement because he is a stranger in a strange land, alienated from his new environment by language, assumptions and sheer physical size. Escape can come by immersing himself in the trivia of "Wake Island", where the transients have "scarcely time to think —/since here's our coffee still to drink", or by attempting "to build a moral" or "parable" ("A Walk in Kyoto"). Here the traveller is a castaway, Gulliver in a Lilliput of ambiguously discrete sexuality. At the same time he is penned like the flailing carp who stare at him while he stares at them. Imaginative release comes when the two aspects of the parable he has tried to construct coalesce: the drawing together of the significance of the masculinity celebrated on Boys' Day and the necessary constraint implied by a coming-of-age. The sudden sight of a boy's giant carp-shaped kite, huge as Gulliver and himself, thrusting phallically up, seems to integrate the poet and the symbol, and lifts him too "into the endless winds of the world".

But even this symbiosis cannot deny time, as "Bangkok Boy" dramatically demonstrates. All men carry the seeds of their own destruction within them, and the joy of the skipping, prancing young Thai boy becomes a desperate plea to postpone death, the counterpoint to the boy's dancing. The world around him beats to the corruption of Hong Kong strippers, and despite his father's "Buddha smile", he will inevitably become part of other boys' ashes under ten thousand Buddhas. The dancer has been caught in the poem much as temple dancers of the past have been immortalized in a stone frieze, but the observer remains a tourist, pacing out his own "grave measure", plodding with the others "to their funeral music". The Bangkok boy, doomed to "slide lethewards / on choleric canals", is still in his own environment, continuing and projecting the history of his own place. Thus his dancing is "forever", and his "first / last cry / of joy" is another aspect of the coexistence of past, present and future.

The tourist's most difficult movement, backward into the myths of the past, offers only a partial escape from isolation, for the true traveller is the true alien, and we must discriminate between escape from loneliness, the cause of the journey, and the discovery of oneness, journey's end. And so the poet lingering in "Tavern by the Hellespont" knows that the myth of Hero and Leander cannot be recreated for him, that he is not looking "to see / love swimming naked toward me out of myth". Nor is he Byron, "better poet longer swimmer"; art is essentially the creation of the man conscious of his oneness, even through the ultimate privacy of death ("Plaza de Inquisición"). Greek drama has been reduced to gimmickry and a sanitized six-week season for tourists ("Epidaurus"), not the vital acting out of a culture. The contemporary artist, in a sense, is trapped by his own craft. With the crucifix-maker in "El Greco: *Espolio*" his first responsibility is to his work, not its social consequences. Yet that way lies death, or the pretentiousness of the poseur in "London Poetry Pub". To deny his place in time and accept total introversion, on the other hand, invites madness and silence, even though much of the power of his vision has its origin in non-rational dream and in his ability to articulate all men's wheeling fears and flowering delights ("Introvert"). The time of myth is gone, and "St. Valentine is past". Is the act of silent coupling man's only remaining response to his mutual solitude, or can the act of poeming break both the silence and the loneness through love?

If so, perhaps the contemporary poet is now our last true explorer, discovering not new lands but new relationships among man and land, order and dissolution, time and ultimate destruction. What Birney discovers in North and South America suggests that the tranced dancing of men on the Delhi road leads to unexpected places. In "Ellesmereland I" we find Canada's far north not as it was before the settlement of man, but before his evolution. The fish remain cod, the ice wears away the stone into sand and soil, and the harebells flower briefly. Man is so alien to the environment that he has not yet begun to evolve from the sea. Thirteen years later "there is talk of growth" indeed, but not of man as a higher form of life. Social order and civilization have brought only one Mountie and a colony of warders, themselves prisoners of the environment. The hills are already infected by the disease which man always carries: himself. Now there can be no talk of making fish or flowers from man, and explorers must set off for new discoveries.

A second interrelated group of poems, arranged as "Transamerica" in *Selected Poems,* expands several aspects of Birney's philosophic irony through his exploration of various metaphors for death in contemporary North and South America. His irony of manner in presenting the narrator as a tourist continues to reinforce his sense of ironic juxtaposition as deftly as before, although here a more subtle sense of dramatic irony is revealed, particularly in his four longer poems. The new world, "this sometime garden", has "grown sick / with man" ("Transcontinental"). But man is also sick, trailing in Canada's face "the dark breath of her dooming". She won't die, but will grow old too quickly:

> old with us—
> nor have we any antibodies for her aid
> except our own.

Man, then, is both death-dealer because of his hostility to the metaphor of the land, and healer through his anti-body, his consciousness of his destructive power. Equally importantly, he is man *in* the land rather than *of* the land as much as Mr. Chubb is inside his bomb shelter "beneath his personal hill in Minnesota". Canadians have accrued no special virtues simply by living in Canada because they have consciously denied identification with their environment. Explorers all in the beginning, they are exploiters of all in the end. And as Mr. Chubb learns, the security he seeks against his own weapons leads inevitably to the death of his wife's love and his own isolation. He shares the objects of his terror with the husband of the lady with a diaper: "SEPRTISTS and BEATNIKS", "Z-BOMB and GREASERS and PINKOS". Their fear is real, but it is essentially a terror of words, the rhetoric of politics, American nationalism and commerce. Two remedies exist for this diarrhoea of rhetoric: either a "soft white disposable diaper of *s i l e n c e*", or a recapturing of the union man once had with his other more fertile gods.

Far from being expelled from Eden, however, man has driven himself away from the parks he has created. Animals have been "barred", and the moon becomes a "bright noose" when organized by man ("Leaving the Park"). Only one old man retains his identification with the trees which mark his age as he

> Stands in a whimsical wait for any young
> hunter of fuel to duel him down

("Oldster")

He created the young, and they will inevitably consume him. For them, there is no more choice between the old man and the trees than between

> say like trees and billbores lessa course
> wenna buncha trees is flattint out inta
> BILLB—

"Billboards Build Freedom of Choice" between two unacceptable options, "between two a de same": the TRUWAY. The environment, in this context, becomes an amoral intrusion on the necessary course of commerce. Man's success in ordering his world, as "Campus Theatre Steps" suggests, has blinded him to the fact that he has lost contact with the forces prompting him to that success. Cripples cannot wheel themselves up stairs to see *The Miracle Worker,* as illusion and entertainment conquer reality and necessity. "The eye", Birney notes in "Looking from Oregon", "is all out of proportion", and "the earth is not holding"; cormorants dive, sealions devour, and fishermen hook, all from the same water which washes Vietnam's Gulf of Tonkin, the American illusion which was to swallow the Vietnamese reality. Even God is served by illusion and the true way, by the "bag bloo sheikelgetting Ayes" of Aimee Semple McPherson. The prophet's profit allows few losers and little loss; "mamomma" is mammon.

Birney's poems written from his experiences in Mexico present verbal ironies slightly more ambiguous than the punning and fragmented colloquialisms of his American poems. As he observes in "State of Sonora",

>   boys   like chestnuts   naked skip
>   or stricken
>   wither to death across adobe sills
>
>
>   By puma-colored crossroads
>   with names dry and implacable
>   as locusts—
>   Chirriones   Bacarac
>   Los Muertos

The Dead, the definite consonants and extended vowels: these are the observer's entry into the layers of a society far more complex and far poorer than his own, and which demands a complete suspension of alien preconceptions. The corrupt sensuality of expatriate *gringo* life in "Ajijic" is easily accessible; less so are the triple ironies of "Sinalóa". The narrator, a Mexican speaking to a tourist, is apparently a clear-headed realist, brushing aside the guidebook beauties of the country to call for industrial development: a breakwater, bulldozers, wheat elevators, tractors, irrigation canals. And yet for Mexico itself he utters a litany of death and hate: to "take hax to them jeezly palmas", "shoot all them anarquista egrets", "bugger the pink flamingos", "chingar [fuck] those cute little burros", and "defecar [shit] on those goddam guidebook". His response, identical to that found on the TRUWAY, denies history and aesthetics: in short, an authentic capitalist ethic in a country whose governing political party is the Party of Institutional Revolution. The second irony is that he calls on the tourist to supply the tools for industrial development, inviting exploitation from outside in a nation intensely nationalistic. Finally, he is an outsider in his own country, part of a small but influential middle-class élite. His brother was sent to Québec to "learn to be padre", despite the secularization of Mexico, and he himself is an utter racist, eager to leave the food which attracts the tourist to "Indios, solamente". All else is to be exported for the profit of his class.

Another side of the peculiarly Mexican metaphors for death Birney finds in Pachucan among the silver miners. Although his mythic reference to Orpheus is obvious, it is Eurydice who holds our interest, principally because of another poem, "Six-Sided Square: Actopan". That the *gringos* inhabit Olympus and that the miners assert their masculinity in tequila and song is not unexpected. With both her "snakes Toltecan" and her crucifix, however, Eurydice takes on aspects we later see can be

> more hex-
> agon and more extraordinary
> than even you, dear lady, or than Egypt's queens.

The six sides of Actopan's plaza are defined by answers to the female tourist's six simple-minded questions, all of which reveal the coexistence of cultures, times and sexes in one place. It is Actopan's women who determine the patterns reflected in the shape of the square. The pattern, Birney suggests in "Irapuato", has been determined by massacre and its consequent mixing through time: Toltecs, Mixtecs, Aztecs, Spaniards, Americans and Mexicans. The symbol, like that of the hexagramatic piles of fiery chillies in Actopan, are strawberries, "small clotting hearts". In a continuous culture all symbols are part of a continuum, whether it is the aging bourgeoisie attempting to reactivate their glands in Moctezuma's hot springs ("Hot Springs"), or all classes in Manzanillo waiting passively for their determined futures ("Late Afternoon in Manzanillo"). From this perspective "Sestina for Tehuantepec" can be read as one of Birney's most careful exercises in ironic counterpoint, a deliberate reflection of a tourist guidebook's attempt to distill a civilization into "six claims to fame". Each stanza elaborates progressively on the town's six aspects, and each by its contrapuntal repetition leads to the concluding question containing all six.

A final irony of Birney's Mexican poems is his metaphor for Mexico itself in "Memory No Servant", the title poem for his first collection to be published outside Canada. The narrator stumbles over the usually unforgettable tourist concerns, the minor pleasures of travel for which memory serves as a pleasant filter. Only one image remains with him eight years later, his accidentally running over a turtle on the highway:

>   Looking back:—
>   the untouched head
>   ancient   stretched   and still
>   moving

He has crushed its body ("The sound   a crushed carton") just as Mexico has suffered so many invasions by other strangers. For him, the memory is no servant "but a stubborn master": his recognition that the turtle's qualities are precisely those which have allowed the country to survive all foreign incursions. That the turtle has come up from the Gulf of Mexico is not accidental, for it suggests that nations, like man, survive biologically by evolving. The natural armour may fail, but the instinctive will must inevitably persist. Survival, after all, is the only alternative to death.

As for nations, so for every individual: a connection Birney examines with particular force in his West Indian and South American poetry. Off the coast of Panama, for instance, he is at one level a flying fish himself, flashing "into alien air", always conscious of being gauged by the "gleaming calipers" of the dolphin's jaw. The original conclusion of the poem when it was first published in *Now Is Time,* however, was rather more pessimistic for the manfish:

>   Spirals to a sudden spray
>   now our graceful Nemesis;
>   rising to His gladsome peak
>   cometing Jehovah leaps.

The voyager out of his element, that is, must be eternally conscious of the ease with which he can be struck down by forces to whom no place is alien. It is possible for the traveller to move elementally in an environment made familiar by the enfolding and protecting love of others:

>   in the gardens
>   in the castles
>   of your skins
>   ("For George Lamming")

The prominent West Indian novelist's castle, of course, is the colour of his skin; the tourist can have no such home when threatened.

Perhaps self-deprecating humour is the only acceptable response, retrospectively, to the ultimate terror of facing a violent and needless death ("Meeting of Strangers"). Conversely, slightly swaggering sexual braggadocio is a not inappropriate response to the generosity he experiences on another island ("Curaçao"), and for the same reason. Each man carries his shell with him. Similarly he can maintain his role as ironic observer by emphasizing the elements of play involved in the deadly economic game of capitalist exploitation symbolized in "Barranquilla Bridge". Young boys fish out of a Colombian river produce that has been thrown away or accidentally lost in the market upstream, and their activity is innocent. Their throwing the worst culls back into the river to be fished out once more by yet smaller boys suggests a more sinister allegory; that one of the smallest boys then gathers up the remaining culls and throws them back into the river upstream "to be hailed snared and rejected / all over again" is far more than

> the sort of rough justice
> the weak can perform on powers above

A more direct level of economic satire permeates "Caracas", where the underlying metaphor is that of evolution; taken together, both poems have the same object. The Liberator, Bolívar, is buried beneath an increasing tomb of concrete and skyscrapers erected by Galician immigrants while the owners of Venezuela's 1000 Cadillacs circle the Capitol "where 1 declaration of independence / is said to lie". Even that phrasing has a special irony, however, for the poem's more or less careful measuring of quantities makes Birney's point clear. From 206 bones of Bolívar, his body when alive, has come the single declaration of independence; round that swim the 1000 sharks, moving up through the "shoals / of Galicians" and the seven million other "lesser organisms" to the atolls lapped by the "bright bloodsmell/of dollar$$$". The lust for profit, whether from the market or hotels on atolls, provides the stimulus for the same highest form of economic survival. The only other option, as we have seen before, is another form of death. Both poems also depend on a movement from water to air, for the border between sea and land through Birney's evolutionary metaphor is the border between man and not-man, the line which contracts time and orders chaos.

It is not accidental that the four longer poems in this group centre in four kinds of art—song, poetry, rhetoric, and architecture—for each is a defiant assertion of human values against those of capitalism, while each gains its dramatic irony by counterpoising those values with the demands of the market. "Transistor" depends for its patterning on the characters in the poem: the narrator, a Jamaican engineer, his secretary and her boy friend, and an old woman, caretaker of an isolated mountain guesthouse, the singer. The engineer is the catalyst, prompting the old woman to sing, to become

> the toughened reed
> vibrated still by the singing dead
> by the slaved and the half-free

The engineer's rum prompts her to sing for the narrator "in the grave high rhythms of the Victorians". The following silence reveals a counter bass in the background, the steno and her boyfriend listening to a country and western singer for Puerto Rico on a transistor radio on the porch:

> I suppose they'd been listening to him
> as exclusively as I to her
> and out of just as much need
> to exchange our pasts

But the exchange is impossible if we accept the accretive force behind "our" pasts. The exchange is between people and instruments, rather than between two people. The engineer keeps the old woman singing in the same sense that the battery keeps the transistor working, and just as the radio is effectively neutral as a transmitting medium, so the old woman is authentically a caretaker of her people's vanished past.

The pattern of "Cartagena de Indias" is far more deliberately ironic. In the first part of the poem, each memory from the past of this historic Colombian city conjured up by the narrator is met by the reality of a twentieth-century equivalent, from cigarette hawkers to shoeshine boys. Beyond the tourist circuit he confronts successively in the Indian market (where he is regarded as an evil demon) a diseased *mestiza,* and a "slit-eyed savage" who offers him his sister:

> Somewhere there must be another bridge
> from my stupid wish
> to their human acceptance
> but what can I offer

Except for pesos, the answer is flatly nothing. He is the total alien, "routed" and "guiltily wakeful". But the sudden discovery of a monument to the poet Luis Lopez allows him to build a one-way bridge to the city which reluctantly, but proudly, chose to erect a symbolic and splendidly ironic monument to the man who hated the city's "rancid disarray", and who finally accepted his own birthplace. The poet, himself "seldom read by my townsmen", can only envy Lopez, who has been read even by the taxi driver:

> See here this sonnet
> always he made hard words
> Said we were lazy except to make noise
> we only shout to get money
> ugly too, backward . . . why not?
> It is for a poet to write these things

The brotherhood fostered by poetry has for once brought together "the whole starved cheating / poetry-reading lot of you", and for once the poet can walk among strangers with love.

Birney's "Letter to a Cuzco Priest", on the other hand, is an extended meditation not only on the direct power of rhetoric, but also on the nature of belief. The precise form of the poem is that of a litany, addressed not to God but to a young Peruvian priest whose condenmation of the Government—"only / an armed front for fifty Families"—resulted in the death of two of his Inca parishioners marching with his words on a banner. Two-thirds of the thirty who followed them were jailed. Whose then is the guilt? In the response the priest is asked to forgive himself, to worship himself; is told that the guilt is not his, or that he spoke; and is beseeched to

> forgive all men if you must
> but only in despite of god
> and in Man's name

The structure of many of Birney's poems is that of assertion and comment; here the letter appears to be an agnostic cry on behalf of "the martyrdom of the gullible", while the letter-writer is himself gullible, believing not in God but "in the wild unquenchable God / flaming within you". With the Incas, he believes in the man who has nearly become God himself, a creator whose essence can exist in all men who persist in their humanity.

Persistence and its subsequent miracle of survival are at the centre of the dialectic of time embodied in the movement of "Machu Picchu". The stubborn and obstinate ruins of a civilization in the high Andes, Machu Picchu, the Holy City of the Incas, remained hidden from the Spaniards of the Conquest, only to be discovered four centuries later by "a believer in myth". Its rediscoverers, four contemporary tourists, similarly feel themselves growing "bodily back into legend". If a distinction can be made between myth and legend, the latter lies in the impulse of the tourists to people the Holy City, to feel themselves part of it as it was before the Conquest. The myth, however, is the force that resides in its bare stones, all "human leavings" gone, "brain and blood gone forever", "picked clean of writhing vine or man". For Machu Picchu is a monument to the worship of the sun, and even the faithful have joined "the attrition / of continents perishing itno the sea". The myth, in a sense, is that man's presumption may dare to claim a permanence for his works, and the myth transcends legend, the story of those presuming men who are also us. The irony lies in the poet's recognition that even the Holy City will sooner or later "finish dying", as will all men. And so the city becomes a metaphor for a world beyond man, immune to the travesties of physical conquest, and an acknowledgement that man's act of creation is one stage in the act of dying.

The final irony of these poems, then, is that survival is no alternate to death, but part of it. If so, is Birney's concept of time simply absurd? For if all acts are part of dying, how can the simultaneous perception of past, present, and future offer man any consolation to justify his presence as anything other than a transitory excrescence on a decaying planet?

Part of the answer, implied in "Letter to a Cuzco Priest", lies in the persistence of belief, usually manifested through reciprocating hope or despair, in the poetry resulting from Birney's experiences in the Second World War. "Hands" establishes one part of the process (for if belief is not part of a process, it is absolute, and absolute belief—in creeds, systems, groups—perverts man). The central metaphor, that the hands of trees are those of man, is relatively straightforward. Other complexities lie in a word like "manumission", the freeing of hands, of *man*us, with the further association of *ita missa est,* it is finished. None of Birney's words can be overlooked. The progress of the canoeist from tree-lined inlet to the dead wood and telephone poles of the city emphasizes more than the transformation of nature. Trees die and nourish their successors; trees are killed and serve man's commerce. Man dies and withers away; man is killed and serves the death-dealing anti-humanity of other men.

"Yet we must speak", man proclaims in "Vancouver Lights", despite the "primal ink" of death and (ironically) the blackouts of wartime. Man created both light and dark:

> No one bound Prometheus   Himself he chained
> and consumed his own bright liver

He is his own glory and damnation, capable of creating descendants, annihilating his planet, or ravaging it so that it is suitable only for the beast. War is the highest form of the beast, proclaiming bloody survival by no law save that of the fittest to kill. Birney's sense of the potential of war and destruction as implicit in peace and harmony is clear in the imagery of "Dusk on the Bay". The rain cooling English Bay in Vancouver is also the shrapnel of war; distance hazes the sex of bathers as bombs obliterate the sex of soldiers. From the "whitening ribs" of a raft, divers flash into the water and are "quenched"; the bay's lamps are "regimented", and Venus—goddess of love and the first star of evening—is "an arrested rocket" (not merely stopped, but imprisoned). Peace is simply another aspect of war, an interim strategy for the tactics of certain destruction. The three Fates of "In this Verandah" knit man's destiny as inexorably on a Toronto verandah as they once knitted the socks of Roman legionaires preparing for their conquest of Britain. Only the sun, that "beautiful bright coyote" and source of life, will outlast man's urge to destroy himself; warm stocks and asbestos breasts are little comfort or protection against the infinitely resourceful enemy.

With this close association of a single act through time, the alliterative measure of Old and Middle English poetry is an appropriately contemporary form through which to explore civilian life in time of war ("Anglosaxon Street"). In the face of the Hun, the prejudices, eating, diversions and lovemaking of the English are little different now in their essentials from those of the Celts faced with the Germanic Angles, Saxons and Jutes progressively invading England in the fifth and sixth centuries. One eventual result of the invasion and settlement was a new language, the same tongue now spoken by a majority of Canadians (There'll Always Be an Angleland). The poem's movement is that of a day, from "dawn-drizzle" to moonglow. The dawn, however, is the dawn of peace ("world-rise"); in the meantime the sleeping civilians as the third party to the conflict wait for the milkman-milkmaid. Theirs cannot be a lawyer's watching brief, but merely a "waiting brief". "Caterwaul and clip" will, in the end, present the closing case for survival.

Dawn and spring are not unusually negative in Birney's poems from the war; at the outbreak "our roots are in autumn and store for no spring" ("Hands"). For Canadians, as well, the title poem of the third section of *Selected Poems* clearly indicates that in the metaphoric winter of man's "woedealing", war and peace are not conditions to be confined to one place or one nation ("War Winters"). The world is one, and the position of the sun is no longer determined by latitude and place or months and time. The earth is the sun's "lifecrusted satellite", and is equally the "lackey" of a peace which our stupidity has changed to a "sucked wafer". That failure of perception, in turn, also implies man's impulse to judge causes, assign motives, and impute blame. The bitter responses of "Joe Harris, 1913-1942" are among Birney's strongest statements on our need for self-justification. That the Shortened Service for the Burial of the Dead offers consolation for those who die "in the Lord" is of no moment to Joe Harris, already dead. He fought for a principle, one which mercilessly indicts those who had only consolation to offer the victims of the previous decade. Although Joe Harris does not mention the word, for most western Canadians it was The Depression, not a depression.

> Those seven years on the go, they were not my life, surely. The ceaseless palsy of boxcars, the graceless gingerly handout .... Then that jail-in-woods, the winter relief camp. ...

"*He fleeth as it were a shadow and never continueth in one place*"; Joe Harris's participation in the war had only one justification:

> It is neither flight nor roaming foot that sent me, but the need to stand against those who would make us forever rootless.

His stand against those who profit, the "fat and unheeding" idolaters and moneychangers, inevitably resulted in his willing sacrifice to redeem the living, for he had asserted his most precious right, his ability to choose:

> These deaths we died as we lived our lives, not by desire but by choice, as against a worse life and a meaner death.

Any other options are untenable; "to walk two-footed" transcends heroism and sanctity.

Joe Harris's death, in the end, was meaningless, although he lost his life fighting for the essential element of his humanity. The grotesque arrogance and blindness of the leaders of "mildewed

Canada" and the world have denied him his ultimate choice, to stay alive:

> There is no fog but in the will
> the iceberg is elective
> ("Conference of Heads")

But the *Titanic* has sunk, and the political titans offer the tatters of the "migrant Must" and "blasted Shall" of "Lines for a Peace". To cure this madness only electric shock therapy is left:

> now is time
> to bed the beast and with the pain
> of love shock him to the brain—
> then certify the future sane

"Sane", that is, if love is merely a palliative for arbitrary normality.

To the poet in "This Page My Pigeon" and "The Road to Nijmegen", however, love is no instrument of obliterating therapy but memory and sanity itself. An alternate "creed" to madness, it can lead to the future, "the wide light / that will be"; at the same time it remains a baseline from which to measure the writer's sanity by the standards of the world he has left and is in peril of forgetting in "the blasted Now", the shattered present of bones, stumps and graves. Love, in other words, is essential to re-create the present, reinforce the continuity of the past and capture the potential of the future.

From another perspective, and despite the shelter proffered by the idea of love, time poses a more immediately agonizing problem for the survivor of war. To deny the "blasted Now" is to fall off the edge of his collapsing singular world. Charting that one world in "Mappemounde", Birney has outlined his original intentions:

> Think of the speaker as a man, ancient or modern, saying goodbye to his girl before setting out across an ocean or some other bigness of space. But really, he's more concerned with the map of time for it's the years, not the miles, that makes lovers forget. Time's the enemy of us all, the beast that catches up with any world that's willing to set aside loving for voyages into seas of hate.
>
> However, the poem is intended not as moral allegory so much as Hardyean irony.[8]

That irony of fate, in which the Canadian forces leaving England as well as their English girl friends would forget their pledges to

---

[8]Earle Birney, *The Cow Jumped Over the Moon* (Toronto: Holt, Rinehart and Winston, 1972), p. 86.

each other, again depends on the ambiguities of time. The soldiers of "Young Veterans", for instance, find themselves part of a montage of behaviour and events shaped by a frozen past, a present reality determined by their own experience, and the necessity to forget both past and present in a world determined to obliterate the previous years. Forgetfulness is, paradoxically, the key to the future for the veterans. Because of their willingness to forget, moreover, the future will be a part of the same mystery which

> bemused that fatal pliant fish
> who first forgot the sea.

Unknown to the veterans, however, the consequences are determined, and the forces are beyond their control. Through Birney's evolutionary metaphor, they are the fittest simply because they have survived, like the men in "Ulysses". The "phony lords" who grew fat at home, the suitors wooing wives, Penelope-Canada, Time twitching his tail on the dungpile: all remain to be encountered as challenges. The main trial is momentarily over, but a failure to act on the home front with their special knowledge of other tests implies an inexorable dilution of the qualities that led Joe Harris to his death, and an inevitable repetition of the past in the future. To return home unseeing is to leave the recounting of the consequences to the last remaining observer, whether he is the blind poet Homer or the blinded Cyclops. Spring has finally returned after the war winter, but time demands a repetition of all seasons.

Canada, Birney's Ithaca, can also be characterized through a journey of return, although an east-to-west geographic focus (the order Birney has adopted in *Selected Poems*) is the least unified among the works so far discussed. Nevertheless such a progression yields an essential case history of the country as compiled by one concerned and experienced observer: a record of impressions through time, and all part of a synthesizing vision. Perhaps one of Birney's best known titles, "Canada: Case History" has in its three published versions concluded with an increasingly definite prognosis for the nation's future:

> will he learn to grow up before it's too late? (1948)
> is this a highschool land
> or a premature senescent? (1969)
>   this youth we fear has moved from adolescence
> into what looks like permanent senescence (1972)

Despite the witty satire of each of these versions (a fourth, Birney notes, remains unpublished), his Canadian poems taken together offer subtly different perspectives from those set elsewhere. Man can still be considered a tourist in Canada, but he is no longer completely an alien; the environment is not wholly accessible to him, but his movement is gradually toward integration with it. Conflict is clearly evident, but it is more a lover's quarrel than the deathgrip of armed conflict. Most importantly, his evolutionary metaphor assumes a far greater significance as the organizing focus of his philosophic irony:

> Come then trailing whatever pattern
> of gain or solace and think no more than you must
> of the simple unhuman truth of this emptiness
> that down deep below the lowest pulsing
> of primal cell
> tar-dark and dead
> lie the bleak and forever capacious tombs of the sea
> ("Atlantic Door")

For Canada's returned soldiers, the implications are obvious, as they are in the military images of "Maritime Faces". But there too the implacable sea battles, bellows and smashes the maritime shore, much as glaciers once wore down rough maritime rock formations into the "old laconic resourceful hills"; "something of this in the maritime faces".

This interpenetration of man and land implies two further relationships: between man and his social environment, and among all three. In Canada, significantly, nature's moral neutrality in any human context becomes a potent emblem for society's response to individual human activity. But if collective humanity is morally indifferent to every individual, what possible meaning is left for any man? And even if the symbolic equation is admitted, must nature's amorality—the absence of right and wrong—supplant *amor*-ality, our capacity to suspend judgement through compassion? In "AR-RIVALS Wolfville", "the hand that caught in me" is far different from the "legend / no conquistador hooked even / his mailed finger into" of "Machu Picchu". The agents of death are fishermen in both cases, although the worth of the catch depends on the nature of the death. The Inca died for belief. The lawyer from Halifax is killed accidentally. Nevertheless the blizzard that obscured the railway track is "sudden as a beast"; the diesel that hits the car has a bland "face"; the car lies "like a beetle battered by catspaw", its engine ticking as it cools, "something live under the snow", and the destination is *Wolf*ville. In the face of death man must rationalize the irrational by creating predators. Neither the storm nor the machines are hostile or benign, yet the driver is dead. That he is a lawyer reinforces the irony of the poem, for his career of pleading has failed to result in a verdict. Even for him it is no final judgement beyond reason; it simply happened. Nor can guilt exist, in the sense that the passengers on the train are no more guilty than the train itself, or the blizzard, or the train tracks. The only possible judgement is that the train from Halifax is thirty minutes late.

Perhaps it is as much a comment on Canada as it is on the poet that Birney has written so little about Quebec (only two poems in *Selected Poems*, and both relatively early). Twenty-five years after its first publication the title of "Québec May" is ironic, as are the multilingual puns ("last sick isle of ice on *lac*"), sentence structure, and intimations of *franglais*. As an exercise in extended metaphor, "Page of Gaspé" can be contrasted with the sensuousness of a poem published only two years earlier, "From the Hazel Bough". There the humorously direct identification of woman, bird, fish and trees, together with a definite rhyme and imperative rhythm (inspired, Birney has said, by the ballad "Casey Jones"), belie the ambiguous sense of loss suggested at the conclusion.

Away from his native west, Birney's impulse to capture "the welling and wildness of Canada" is best seen in the transcontinental sweep of "North Star West". The airplane passengers are vulnerable to the "sealed Fates in the ship's brain", and yet their ascent empowers them with a peculiar strength of vision, holding briefly "the fling of a nation". They have literally become for a moment higher forms of life.

With "The Ebb Begins from Dream", Birney's evolutionary metaphor merges with the "one pelagic motion" of life. Human activity has its source in dream, that full tide which allows us to deny our rootlessness by acknowledging our roots in the sea, reaffirming our connection with "all the globe in swaying water". We awake into nightmare, the utter negation of that connection in the blunt "DEAD END" of "Way to the West". Rotted semen ejaculates from the smokestacks of Sudbury, testimony to the impotency of free enterprise dislocated from the source of its power. The river route of the *voyageurs* has become the Trans-Canada Highway, on which "phallic Calvary" is merely a diversion into Hell. Man has chosen to be foresaken by God, succumbing to the temptations of the technological wilderness so completely that he perpetuates it.

And if man alone can despoil the Garden, then he will have to be prepared to face the utter silence of the land of "North of Superior", completely unassimilated imaginatively and wholly dominated in his mind by negatives: no myth, no legend, no people, and finally, "no world" except the land and waning waves.

In such an environment, Canadians can easily lose their benchmarks, those signs of earlier surveyors whose measurements both allow and define man's present existence. Freed from their chrysalis of a farmhouse by the passing of a winter storm, the moth-family of "Winter Saturday" move almost by instinct to the nearest town, only to discover that it is "less than its glow", a cold flame, and "time is false". Their time is with the waiting snow, whose melting will be the source of their prosperity in the spring, but which is the form of their isolation in the winter. To attempt to escape it too early is to deny the cycle which will allow them to awake later to the real sun. At least they have avoided the hazards of the village in "De-Composition". The static prairie towns of Saskatchewan (itself shaped like a tooth) are rotting, and their inhabitants are now only deadened nerves, serving the parasites of a decayed commercial society. In this light, the relief of "Holiday in the Foothills" is a "trance" among the activities of nature wholly indifferent to roads, farms, faces and factories. That the natural environment acts in its languid way as if it were human is equally a statement of the opposite, that man when freed will adopt its rhythm and emotions. The definition is that of the foothills, not man's. As the young boy in "First Tree for Frost" recognizes, "Some things my loving never has convinced"; trees, like people, need to go their own way however desperate the need to keep alive. The metaphor for man is scarcely concealed. In love, motives are never enough to preserve or justify the love itself.

Two of Birney's best-known poems, "Bushed" and "David", offer a further expansion on the complex interrelationship between man and his natural environment. Although informed commentary on both appears elsewhere in this collection, one aspect of Birney's vision deserves emphasis. In much of Birney's work nature is animistic, or is allowed to assume a positive moral function (whether for good or ill), only *after* a failure of perception by man in that environment. Much has been written on the connotative shift of imagery in "David", lending strength to the essentially human focus of the poem as a work exploring initiation, not euthanasia. The Fall of Man was necessary for him to know good and evil, and thus to be truly human. After David's fall, the mountains become alive and hostile, and only the sky remains indifferent to the boy who has become a man. Perhaps it is significant that a related process is traced in "Bushed", where the first line of the poem suggests a mysterious failure, a dream "invented", and so destroyed. The man's growing madness is progressively reinforced as he discovers his surroundings to be more and more threatening, until finally his self-created enemy, in his mind, is about to destroy him. He had attempted at first to be aboriginal man with "quills on his hatband"; thus it is an appropriate irony that it is he, not the winds, who has shaped an arrowhead, and it is he who draws the metaphoric bow. "Biography" describes the identical movement, natural images successively reflecting both the growth of a man and his perception of his outer life and society. When the man is forty, his *nunatak,* a pile of stones serving as a marker for his future trail, is also a warning of passing time. "Later", however, he loses sight of of the marker not simply because of a shrill wind, but because he allowed the wind, some event in his life, to turn him away from the marker. That done, his efforts to rediscover it are "without might"; his nerve is gone, and forgetting the forks in the trail, he can only wait for inevitable death, "the ice knuckling his eyes" like a fist.

That nature without man can be animistic is obvious from "Takakkaw Falls"; the significance of the sexuality of the waterfall lies in its cyclic self-perpetuation, for only man has the capacity to destroy the integrity of nature's own life. In "Climbers", ostensibly a celebration of man's ability to persist in the face of an antagonistic environment and propelled by his need to climb, the peak is "pointless": "there is nothing to say / and no time". The climbers' escape from "the long pigs of the cars squealing" has been futile, because by seeing their surroundings in animistic terms, they find at the top of the mountain only a reflection of the human condition below them. Read differently, "the beginning of space" at the top obviates the need to talk and annihilates time. But they are too much part of the world below in their need to return, as by a deadline, to the squeal of "the long pigs of cars." "Long pig", ironically, is a term once current in Melanesian pidgin for cooked human flesh. Man is indeed a cannibal, satisfied with consuming not only himself but the "pacifist fir" as he crawls like bacteria with his multiplying machines over "the browning / pulp of the peeled world" ("Images in Place of Logging"). He has lost even the grace of the foodward quest of "Slug in Woods" and the instinctual violence of "Aluroid". Part of the answer, perhaps, lies in recapturing the significance of dogwood flowers behind a prickly hedge of holly ("Haiku for a

Young Waitress") or more importantly, in recapturing a sense of man's evolutionary origins, to

> Trail the laggard fins of your flesh
> in the world's lost home
> and wash your mind of its landness
> ("Gulf of Georgia")

"November Walk Near False Creek Mouth", Birney's longest poem, is also his most extensive meditation on man's "landness". Yet "November Walk" has received curiously little critical attention. While this is not the place to undertake a substantial analysis of a poem nearly 300 lines long, it is worth stressing the importance of the poem as a syncretic view of many of Birney's concerns and techniques. The structure is patterned by the poet's walk along the sea edges near False Creek, a small inlet in urban Vancouver now encrusted with industries, but the place matters less than the mood (it is, in fact, an amalgam of the poet's experiences along several parts of Vancouver's disparate waterfront leading to Second Beach). The central pattern is the progression of nine interrelated and italicized stanzas defining the "time" of the poem, its theme, and the beat of the sea. The beat becomes the rhetorical focus, while time reappears at the end to introduce the concluding section which fuses beat and theme. The physical shape of the poem is obviously intended to be an integral part of its significance. As the walker moves along the beach, his direct observation is frequently distinguished from meditations, glosses and dreaming by Birney's indenting the latter, particularly when he reaches back to myth and legend.

Most important, however, is the process of the poem, from beginning of sunset to dark; from the walk through dream to arrival; and especially from "the common explosion of time" down to "the dense unbeating black unapproachable / heart of this world" and the evolution back up from the "dead centre" to the "sunblazed living mud". Implications of potential nuclear destruction cannot be avoided, nor can the evolutionary metaphor associating man with fish, the first of the vertebrates. The walker returns eventually to his "brief night's ledge", his transitory place on the shifting scale of ascent. Higher still is the penthouse in his apartment block, a play on man's assumption that height ("pylons marching over the peaks") is development. For if that is accepted, "on the highest shelf of ever" lies only "unreachable nothing".

The poet's passage, perhaps, is not far different from that of Sir

Francis Drake attempting to find the Strait of Anian and a shortcut back to England: "but his Mariners finding the coast of Nuoa Albion to be very cold, had no good will to sayle any further Northward".[9] Men are "only joined by long endeavour to be joined", much as Birney suggests the essential similarity of entering Canada through the nearly identical conclusions of "Atlantic Door" and Pacific Door":

>Come then on the waves of desire that well forever
>and think no more than you must
>of the simple unhuman truth of this emptiness
>that deep down below the lowest pulsing of primal cell
>tar-dark and still
>lie the bleak and forever capacious tombs of the sea
>   ("Pacific Door")

The sea is the source of life; it also symbolizes the end of the devolution of a species bred, apparently, with the unique ability to disappear without having to wait for the discriminations of natural selection. Man has selected himself as the least fit to survive.

"Letter to a Conceivable Great-Grandson" offers at least the hope that man will survive, but the irony lies in "conceivable". If man does not sterilize himself with automated nuclear weapons, his heirs will be mutations. In any case, as the visitors from outer space observe, the end of man is inevitable, either cataclysmically or slowly, over "a few milennia" ("Remarks Decoded from Outer Space"). In the meantime he has the potential to be a wind, roaring free with the strength of his will (". . . Or a Wind") or a snow

>that cracks
>the trees' red resinous arches
>and winters the cabined heart
>   ("Man is a Snow")

So long as we fail to recognise our interdependency, each child taught

>first of itself alone
>will conjure back the Belsen breath
>and raise a world of bone
>   ("Each Lie", formerly "Status Quo")

The choices are unavoidable:

---

[9]Thomas Blundeville on Drake's first voyage to the Indies in 1594, cited as part of the headnote to *The Strait of Anian* (Toronto: Ryerson, 1948), p. ii.

> O men be swift to be mankind
> or let the grizzly take
>
> ("Time Bomb")

Although some of Birney's own comments on the compulsions which result in poetry appear elsewhere in this collection, little of his poetry is a direct rhetorical statement on the way ordered words contribute to a revived world, one made live and human again. As he has written, "The artist-writer is on life's side nevertheless, and essential to its victory". Thus it seems appropriate that he chose to conclude the poetry in *Selected Poetry* with five poems centring in the power of words. "Answers to a Grade-School Biology Test" represents man's answers to his final examination; rats will endure beyond man, once men "have cleared themselves" and cats, their predatory pets, from the earth. "A superior order" better adapted to survival waits to take over when man loses by default. It is to the credit of whoever wrote the examination that he has presumably passed, but that it is a child is scarcely reassuring. Success in this test is a clear recognition that mankind has failed.

Birney's four translations from Attila József and Mao Tse-tung, on the other hand, offer more direct statements on the function of poetry in a revolutionary world. The northern vision of Mao's "Snowscape from a Plane" recalls the literary abilities of former Chinese emperors, necessary for dynastic founders in the past. Because China's mountains and rivers are constant, now all the people have the potential to be great poets:

> We must now in the arrogance of our knowledge
> Uproot our scented careers.
> Fingering mountains only, and rivers,
> To hold poetry alive in our minds,
> We will use for manure
> Those bygone dreams of ten-thousand-household fiefdoms.
>
> ("Midstream")

This, not emperors, will decree "the rise, the fall". The curses of five poor Hungarians in József's "Five Poor Men Speak" are ineffectual against a landlord's agent, but they are one stage toward the political action to be prompted by the poetry of the people:

> Words on the poet's lips are a clatter,
> yet it's he who engineers
> this world's magics and enchantments;
> he forsees mankind's career;
> constructs a harmony within himself
> as you shall in the world's sphere.

In the end, perhaps no more appropriate metaphors could serve to describe Birney's own contributions to Canadian literature.

B. N.

West Vancouver
December 1973

1. ONE SOCIETY: *POETRY, 1937–1948*

TWO REVIEWS OF *DAVID AND OTHER POEMS* (1942)

NORTHROP FRYE

This is a book for those interested in Canadian poetry to buy and for those interested in complaining that we haven't got any to ignore. Anyone who follows Canadian verse at all closely will be very pleased to see Mr. Birney's fugitive pieces gathered into one volume, and anyone who read the title poem when it first appeared in the Forum will be keenly interested in finding it again in a published book as part of a larger collection.

The people who are familiar with the conventions of modern poetry, who can grasp its difficult language and place its recondite illusions, now form a specialized cult largely confined to universities. "David" will get the full approval of this audience as being on its own merits a touching, beautiful and sensitively written story. But a large reserve of intelligent readers, not in the cult but willing to listen to a poet who has a real story to tell and who tells it simply and honestly, will also like this poem. The more blasé will take a while to recover from their surprise at seeing, in a volume of contemporary verse, a straightforward narrative cut to fit the "common reader," without flounces of fake symbolism, gathers of atmosphere, tucks of philosophic rumination, or fullness of garrulous comment. But they will like it too. "David" is the best thing of its kind that I have seen in current poetry—and for some benighted reason its kind is rare.

The other poems are uneven, but frequently reach the high level of the title piece. As a lyrical poet, Mr. Birney is chiefly an artist in vignette, a sharpe and humorous observer. His humor on the whole is best when least directly satiric: satire makes him relapse into an idiom more suitable to prose. But he utters "conceits," or deliberately strained images, with exactly the right kind of deadpan delivery, and his meticulous study of a slug, which should now be famous through its inclusion in Gustafson's Pelican anthology, is

From *Canadian Forum,* 22 (1942), p. 278. By permission of Northrop Frye.

a shimmering rich texture of poetic wit from beginning to end. This indicates that he is not, in spite of the simplicity of "David," a naive poet, and there are some brilliant flashes of imagery, of the kind that come from short-circuiting associations, notably in the briefer lyrics, such as "Monody on a Century" and "European Nocturne." A tendency to a rather facile animism, of the "grassy hair of old hobo ocean" variety, is the only weakness of an important virtue.

Quizzical and ironic imagery is frequent in North American poetry: the source of it is usually the fascinating stare of an indifferent Nature which was here long before man and could very well get along without him. In such a poet as Robinson Jeffers, whose Pacific symbolism Mr. Birney occasionally recalls, this develops into a philosophy of tragic nihilism; in such a poet as E. J. Pratt, the immense debauchery of Nature, its gigantic appetite for life and its incredible waste of it, is transmuted into strange visions of submarine souses, pliocene Armageddons, and maddened savages with a "viscous melanotic current" coursing through their blood. The former results in slick, portentous, stereotyped oratory; the richer humor and greater subtlety of the latter is a spiritual truancy . . . which refuses to over-simplify the imagination. In searching for the basis of his own attitude, Mr. Birney gives us an example of each tendency. "Dusk on English Bay," a vision of a spinning world at peace and at war, comes to a simple time-marches-on conclusion which seems to me rather frivolous: "Vancouver Lights," ending in a tone of quiet resistance, is far more impressive.

The most obvious technical influence on Mr. Birney's work—he has gone somewhat out of his way to underline it—is the alliterative line and kenning of Old English. This is frequently claimed as an influence by modern poets, though many of them end up by producing imitations of Gerard Manley Hopkins, who, along with William Morris, started a vogue in the last century for bumping over offbeats, babbling bastard "Beowulf." Here the influence is genuine, but the technique is difficult, and easily gets out of hand. It does so, for instance, when the alliteration becomes part of an over-elaborate pattern of repetition—the rhymes, for example, are sometimes harsh and insensitive—and it does so when the use of kennings and compound words makes the diction sound rather spiky and self-conscious. The rhythm also could sometimes be more fluent: there are too many run-on lines, especially in "David," which have nowhere in particular to run to. I mention these details because this is not one of those impeccable and immaculate first volumes which "promise" nothing but more of the same. Just as a pregnant woman is in too interesting a condition to win a beauty contest, so the many and remarkable virtues of these poems are accompanied by faults which guarantee an increase of fertility. In case you didn't get the point the first time, for those who care about Canadian poetry this book is good enough to buy, not to borrow or get from a library.

E. J. PRATT

The hearty acceptance of this volume by literary critics and general readers is not only a deserved tribute to the author but a reflection of the growing good taste on the part of the public. The enjoyment of the poems is primarily based, as it should be, on the artistry by which humour, satire, wit, and tragedy are made the vehicles for the emotional responses.

"David," the title poem, is a masterly piece of work fashioned out of simple material. It has the directness and spontaneity of musical speech—the traditional hall-mark of lyricism—combined with the strength and stride of good narrative. It has the authority of a personal experience. It is always gratifying to a reader to feel convinced that a writer has first-hand contact with the raw stuff on which he imposes the technical resources of his craft. The science of mountain climbing is here in detail and principle made subject to the art of poetry. The vast stretches, the towering peaks, the frozen "ocean of rock," the glaciers and skylines, the bighorns across the moraines, the prints of the grizzlies, are all woven into a beautiful tapestry against which a human story is poignantly related. The rhythms, pauses, bursts of speed, retardations, and the cunning use of the "rove-over" lines are admirable, but the most impressive feature of the poem is the ironic foreshadowing of the catastrophe by the references to the Finger "crooked like a talon," to the "splayed, white ribs" of a mountain goat, to the "silken feathers of kites," to the robin wing-broken, and then by the abrupt switch to the wider canvas—"the glistening wedge of giant Assiniboine, heedless of handhold." This is in the finest manner of tragic poetry leading up to the conclusion—a story of youth (to use Professor Sedgewick's phrase) "stabbed into age by a sudden and unintelligible agony."

The shorter poems give variety to the collection. Some of them

From *Canadian Poetry Magazine,* March 1943, pages 34-5. By permission of Mrs. E. J. Pratt.

suffer by too much condensation—a cryptic virtue which may so easily pass into a mannerism, but on the whole the level of expression is extraordinarily high as in "Reverse on the Coast Range," "Hands," and "Vancouver Lights." Canadian poetry has been truly enriched by the appearance in 1942 of *David and Other Poems.*

EARLE BIRNEY'S *DAVID*

JOHN SUTHERLAND

W. E. Collin, the author of "White Savannahs", discussing the aims of "The Montreal Poets", Scott, Smith, Klein and Kennedy, tells us that these writers reacted to the materialism of the city, "but no, decidedly no," did not turn back to the country-side. Not only did they not return to the country of the Victorians, but they tended to let country landscape disappear altogether from their poems. What is true of them is even more emphatically true of those recent writers who have a kinship with them. P. K. Page, in a discussion of Canadian poetry in "Preview" (a witty summary rather than a criticism), complains that the prizes go to those who write of "the first trillium on the hills." "Hitch-hike to the towns", she advises young Canadian poets, "and forget the country of your own head." P. K. Page writes out of personal experience and she describes her own poetical development. She wrote for years of almost nothing but the first trillium on the hills, and then new circumstances and a new environment, the impact of other forces, worked a complete change in her poetry. She, in common with the majority of our modernists, has come to regard the country as too insignificant for inclusion. They have developed an antipathy to the country landscape on the basis of its meaning and importance, but there are also reasons of style that cause them to disregard it. Recent poetry has been affected in greater or less degree by the stream of consciousness technique. The rhythms may not move swiftly, but the manner of passing from one concept to another gives an impression of speed. The poetry does not stop long enough over one thing to give us those images of description that are recognizable as the landscape of a particular country. Further, it does not employ the kind of detail that would allow it to describe landscapes of this kind. It may make a brutal descent into fact, giving us truth in the hardest, crudest terms (often with a salutary effect). But average facts concerning the flow and shape of the landscape, the well-worn facts that are handled by everyone, are regarded as homely and out of date. The country may occasionally appear, but it is always curiously transformed.

Earle Birney, in employing the mountains and scenery of the

From *First Statement,* No. 9 (n.d.), pages 6-8. By permission of Mrs. Audrey Sutherland.

Pacific coast, is in no danger of reverting to the first trillium on the hills. Of all our young modernist poets, he is the only one who has made consistent use of a Canadian landscape. "David", with its sparseness of language, its unpretentious rhythm acting like an understatement, brings the mountains so near that they hover and press upon the mind. In "Vancouver Lights" the night-time city and the ocean beyond it are spread before us like a great carpet on which a drama of human thought and emotion is acted out. A poem like "Hands", almost in spite of its heady images, gains a real beauty because it draws in factual details of a familiar landscape. All the best work in this volume—"David and other Poems" —makes use of the Canadian environment.

There is some comparison, I think, between "David" and the narrative poems of Robinson Jeffers. Both writers take the mountains of the Pacific coast for their setting. A blood-pact between two young men is struck by the full weight of a force of evil. The picture of David after his fall on the mountain presents a paradox of the good and the bad such as fascinates Jeffers:

> . . . He lay still, with his lean
> Young face upturned and strangely unmarred, but his legs
> Splayed beneath him, beside the final drop,
> Six hundred feet sheer to the ice.

David holds the evil force imprisoned in him, but, (as Jeffers would have drawn him), wears an innocent face. The problem raised by the fall—whether to preserve David as a permanent cripple, with an uncertain hold on life, or to end his suffering at once—is the kind of problem that absorbs Jeffers.

Birney, however, may not have been influenced by Jeffers, except as he is influenced by the tradition of narrative poetry and its best modern examples. His poem has a warmth and intimacy and a personal note that do not appear in Jeffers. It is not as deliberately abstract as Jeffers', and does not have a structure of the same proportions. The initiative to write factual narrative comes, perhaps, from Dr. Pratt's poetry, if it has any immediate source. More important, in any case, than the discussion of literary influences, is the fact that Birney, by his use of a straightforward narrative medium and the incorporation in it of a Canadian environment, establishes a distinction between himself and those younger poets with whom he has a kinship in style.

"David" has that curious rhythm with which the readers of Birney's poems have grown familiar. The conversational manner of modern poetry is present here, but in a positive, more emphatic sense. It widens its scope and gains in freedom and yet shows a tendency to be in some manner formalized. It becomes almost a creed and a belief, and is an expression of something basic in the author's mind and personality. The conversational style, one supposes, has developed partly as a result of modern life growing in complexity and pressing its weight against the poet. In Birney this fact is taken for granted, either consciously or subconsciously: not only that, but the obstacles are now invited, and the difficulties are enticed into the poem as desirable factors. The characteristic rhythm is the frank admission of complexity, and it derives from a belief in the power of the spirit to absorb it. It widens in scope, it includes more of thought and emotion, as life in general and modern life in particular press and bear against it. It catches and holds all the complex elements in a great net. Since nothing is lost in this way, only patience and time are required to set the thought or subject in its proper focus, and to clothe it in the right frame of words. The rhythm has a recuperative power. It invites falls and lapses, because strength is developed out of them, and more than the initial progress is made. It moves slowly and patiently, with eyes like a microscope, and comes gradually in contact with the living substances.

In "David" it is a pedestrian rhythm without any pretension. It seems inevitable for the description of mountain-climbing:

> ... At an outthrust we balked
> Till David clung with his left to a dint in the scarp,
> Lobbed the iceaxe over the rocky lip,
> Slipped from his holds and hung by the quivering pick,
> Twisted his long legs up into space and kicked
> To the crest. Then grinning, he reached with his freckled wrist
> And drew me up after.

It makes poetry from a prose event like picking raspberries:

> ... The woods were alive
> With the vaulting of mule-deer and drenched with clouds [all]
>   the morning,
> Till we burst at noon to the flashing and floating round
> of the peaks. Coming down we picked in our hats the bright
> And sunhot raspberries, eating them under a mighty
> Spruce, while a marten moving like quicksilver scouted us.

But the style can rise to the greater force and vividness of the last section:

> ... At last through the fanged
> And blinding seracs I slid to the milky wrangling
> Falls at the glacier's snout, through the rocks piled huge
> On the humped moraine, and into the spectral larches,
> Alone.

    The title poem on the whole is characteristic of the other poems in this volume. Space and air are admitted into our contracted modernist poetry. The scope is widened until factual event and intelligible emotion are included, but without the loss of imagery. The knotted complexities of style are unravelled and the power of phrasing remains. "David" is an important poem, and Birney's book is a significant contribution to Canadian literature.

EARLE BIRNEY

ROY DANIELLS

Une des qualités qui manquent à l'art canadien[1], comme à la vie canadienne d'ailleurs, c'est le fini, signe d'une perfection indiscutable. On trouvera difficilement, dans notre peinture et dans notre littérature, l'art scrupuleux d'un Cézanne, d'une Virginia Woolf ou d'un de la Mare. Notre vie intellectuelle a trop manqué d'unité, elle a été trop rudement interrompue par les nécessités de la vie pionnière, par les grandes distances, par l'instabilité de la population pour permettre la possibilité d'une tradition littéraire au mécanisme parfaitement établi et qui fournirait à un nouveau poèt comme un fond, une source où il trouverait des exemples et une inspiration. Des pages de Hansard au journalisme de Vancouver, du plan de la ville de Winnipeg à l'architecture de Halifax, partout le même fait alarmant nous saute aux yeux: nous avons peu ou pas de subtilité dans nos lettres.

En poésie, dans le domaine de la technique justement adaptée et réglée, il est facile de remarquer un manque de forme fraîche et réussie. Parmi nos poètes les plus vénérés, nous en trouvons plusieurs dont l'habileté technique est considérable, mais qui sont incapables de dépasser un mélange tennysonien dans lequel il entre un rhythme régulier, un choix musical des mots et une sympathie intime entre le paysage et les émotions humaines. Même parmi les plus jeunes poètes, parmi ceux qui se lancent dans des expériences poétiques audacieuses, il est rare de trouver un rhythme qui ait quelque subtilité, un style qui soit assez original pour qu'on puisse le reconnaître dans le monde de ses semblables. *The Wind our Enemy,* œuvre qui mérite par ailleurs la louange, est décevante sous ce rapport. Les vers ne sont pas amenés par une nécessité indéniable du génie, ils ne vibrent pas de cette ferveur que l'on sent dans un vers inspiré et qui est nécessaire pour qu'un vers entre en nous et y vive une vie émouvante. Même Pratt, qui est sans doute le meilleur représentant que nous ayons de la poésie cana-

From "Earle Birney et Robert Finch," *Gants du Ciel,* 11 (1946), pages 83-90, 95-96. By permission of Roy Daniells.

[1] Il est inutile de faire remarquer que, dans cette étude, chaque fois que nous disons « canadien » nous voulons dire « canadien anglais » ; on nous pardonnera cette liberté qui n'a été adoptée que pour simplifier les choses.

dienne classique, ne tire pas sa force des subtilités de son style. S'il avait des qualités de cet ordre, il ne pourrait guère être ce qu'il est, c'est-à-dire un poète qui excelle dans le mouvement épique, dans la conduite d'une action héroïque, dont le vers a l'énorme palpitation des mers houleuses et des événements orageux qu'il évoque. Nous voyons donc que la poésie canadienne dans son ensemble, dans sa forme la plus caractéristique et la plus classique—car nous avons déjà nos classiques et notre tradition—ou bien continue la tradition anglais du XIXe siècle, ou bien s'en échappe, mais sans alors atteindre la finesse de la forme poétique. Et je ne m'intéresse pas en ce moment à d'autres sortes de réussites, quelque heureuses qu'elles soient.

Nous ne sommes pas seuls à être dans cette position. Les poètes américains montrent les mêmes tendances. *Western Star* de Stephen Vincent Benét, au rhythme trop évident et au contenu mince, ne réussit pas mieux à résoudre le problème que Randall Jarrell dans ses poèmes de la *Partisan Review,* poèmes qui se distinguent par une effusion mal contrôlée et aventureuse. Quelles que soient les réussites de ces deux poètes et d'autres poètes de la même famille, ils n'ont jamais atteint la perfection d'une forme scrupuleuse, qui est le fruit d'une travail long et attentif et en même temps le don du génie. Les poètes anglais, si toutefois nous pouvons trouver dans les poèmes du *Penguin New Writing* des exemples typiques, sont plus heureux. Eliot a toujours été un artiste attentif à la forme, et les deux poètes les plus acceptés parmi les plus jeunes poètes, George Barker et Dylan Thomas, sont, si l'on en excepte leur difficulté et même leur obscurité volontaire, d'habiles artisans qui connaissent leur métier littéraire. Celui qui lira ces lignes pourra dès maintenant se révolter et se préparer à défendre ses poètes canadiens favoris, mais pourra-t-il vraiment discuter ce point général, c'est-à-dire la rareté de perfection technique dans la poésie canadienne, perfection de chaque vers et de chaque strophe? Il se peut même qu'il veuille accepter sans discussion—discussion qui serait trop longue pour le cadre de cet article—que la facture d'une vers ferme est devenue une matière de plus grande importance pour les poètes contemporains, dès le moment où le relâchement du vers libre sans discipline et l'ébullition de la clameur marxiste sont devenus choses du passé. L'attention toujours plus grande qu'Auden donne à une forme toujours plus serrée peut être considérée maintenant non seulement comme symptomatique mais aussi comme représentative. Que ceux qui considèrent Auden comme un poète sans discipline, essaient de reproduire la forme de son *Stage Manager to the Critics.*

* * *

Le meilleur poème de Earle Birney et, sans aucun doute, le meilleur poème de longueur moyenne qui ait jamais été écrit au Canada, est *David.* Je vais l'examiner en détail et je renvoie le lecteur qui ne le connaît pas au *Book of Canadian Poetry,* édité par A. J. M. Smith et publié par Gage. *David* est une étape dans l'histoire de la culture canadienne, aussi indéniable que *The Shepheardes Calendar* dans l'histoire de la culture anglaise. On y trouve une fusion tout à fait satisfaisante du thème et de la forme, quelque chose de parfait en son genre. Et le fait que sette sorte de perfection est très rare au Canada lui donne d'autant plus de valeur.

Il y aurait beaucoup à dire au sujet de *David,* mais ce qui m'intéressera ici ce ne sera qu'un de ses maints aspects, c'est-à-dire son mouvement ininterrompu, sa fermeté de texture. Earle Birney emploie ici la strophe de quatre vers de forme pentamétrique. Les cinq pieds contiennent un nombre variable de syllabes, les syllabes surnuméraires contribuant à donner au vers plus de flexibilité.

> Our first was Mount Gleam. We hiked in the long afternoon
> To a curling lake and lost the line of the faceted
> Cone in the swell of its sprawling shoulders. Past
> The inlet we grilled our bacon, the strips festooned
>
> On a poplar prong in the hurrying slant of the sunset.

Les avantages qu'a ce vers sur un pentamètre conventionnel sont évidents. Il est frappant de voir comme ce nombre variable de syllabes dans le pied apporte de variété dans l'adaptation du son au sens. Dans le dernier vers cité, nous avons, avant la césure, deux pieds, l'un de trois syllabes, l'autre de deux; qui rendent la simplicité de la chose décrite et suggèrent sa forme définie, petite, utilitaire. Après la césure, nous avons trois pieds, un total de dix syllabes dont les cinq premières rendent admirablement le sens de la chose exprimée par le son de leurs voyelles légères.

Un second moyen que le poète emploie pour obtenir une continuité flexible est l'enjambement. Nous en avons déjà un exemple dans le passage cité ci-dessus. On en trouvera un exemple encore plus frappant dans les vers suivants:

> Down through the dusty
> Skree on the west we descended, and David showed me
> How to use the give of the shale for giant incredible
> Strides. I remember, before the larches' edge,
> That I jumped a long green surf of juniper flowing
>
> Away from the wind, and landed in gentian and saxifrage
> Spilled on the moss.

Du troisième au quatrième vers, le lecteur fait le même saut que le poète : le genièvre déborde par-dessus la fin de la première strophe et se répand sur la suivante ; les fleurs de montagne sont renversées dans le dernier vers. Le procédé est simple, clair et charmant.

Un autre procédé qui aide à la continuité du mouvement est la rime non-chantante. « Faceted » rime avec « past ». Chaque rime est sifflante et dentale, mais la longueur différente de la voyelle a introduit une variation. « Incredible » et « Edge » contiennent des e correspondants et, de plus, il y a, pour les yeux, un rapport entre les d qui les suivent. « showed » et « flowing » ont la même voyelle accentuée et de plus le même nombre de syllabes, la seconde syllabe contenant une nasale dans les deux cas. Ces sortes de correspondances partielles, de rimes déformées volontairement ou de rime non-chantante, persistent, avec des variantes, à travers tout le poème. Elles servent à ponctuer les fins de vers et à produire une musique subtile et fuyante, et ne donnent pas le son clair, le retour prévu et facile qui finit un vers et ferme une strophe ; au contraire elles leur laissent une possibilité de nouvel envol. Ce poème—en ceci contraire à la technique traditionnelle, à la forme classique de Spenser par exemple—ce poème entraîne adroitement l'œil et l'oreille d'un vers ou d'une strophe à l'autre sans aucune pause nécessaire. Vous me direz peut-être que le poète emploie parfois la rime chantante ou répète le même mot dans deux vers successifs pour donner à la chose exprimée plus de force. Je vous répondrai que le poète se sert très rarement de ces procédés, et que ceci ne doit pas affaiblir la constatation générale que je viens de faire.

Un quatrième procédé qui assure la continuité rapide du poème est l'emploi de l'allitération et d'autres correspondances de sons moins évidentes, et ce procédé est employé de telle façon qu'il ne suggère jamais une fin, mais entraîne sans cesse l'oreille prête à une nouvelle découverte.

By the forks of the Spray we caught five trout and fried them
Over a balsom fire. The woods were alive
With the vaulting of mule-deer and drenched with clouds all the morning.

Avant que l'effet produit par les f successifs ne cesse, la succession continue des « i » a saisi l'oreille. Et dans cette succession d'allitérations « mule-deer », « drenched », « morning » intervient la plus subtile correspondance de sons « vaulting » et « clouds ». Ce n'est pas tout. Cette analyse n'épuise pas les possibilités contenues dans ces quelques vers.

Pour passer de la mécanique du vers au décor du récit, nous voyons que ce décor est surtout celui de la nature et nous y remarquons aussi la prépondérance de formes qui, littéralement ou psychologiquement, suggèrent un mouvement en avant ou en haut. « Les pins se jettent vers les étoiles »; « le genièvre coule »; « des lames d'eau descendant d'une falaise »; « les chaînes de montagnes marchent en rangs »; il y a un martin qui « bouge comme le vif-argent », et ainsi de suite. Et il y a d'autres phénomènes naturels qui suggèrent le mouvement sous forme de menace, des phénomènes qui sont individuellement minuscules, mais qui, pris collectivement, sont de mauvais augure. « Le crâne des blanches côtes écartées d'une chèvre » apparaissent; le pin est « cicatrisé par l'éclair »; on remarque les grandes traces d'une ours grizzly; une rouge-gorge « tournoie dans l'herbe, l'aile cassée ». Et même cette petite phrase jetée au hasard: « Se déroulant au loin vers l'Est, la prairie étrangère luisait » est pour un lecteur de la Colombie Britannique extrêmement suggestive: pour un Canadien du Pacifique, l'Est n'est pas, comme pour l'Européen, un pays de chaleur et de richesses, d'où sortent la sagesse et la vérité salutaire; il est plutôt hostile, froid et mystérieusement menaçant. Il n'y a ni salut ni sympathie venant du dehors.

De plus, les événements de l'ascension, distincts des observations accidentelles des alpinistes, annoncent par eux-mêmes, et avec une force extrême, ce qui va venir, dans les exploits comme dans le désastre. Jusqu'au Mont Gleam, le voyage est relativement peu mouvementé. Sur le Mont Rampart, les alpinistes sont en danger pendant une heure. Une autre ascension oblige David à se suspendre au-dessus de l'abîme avec son piolet. Ensuite, après cette accumulation d'événements que préparent un cataclysme, vient le faux pas fatal sur le Finger. Tout ceci n'est pas, cependant, aussi raide et mécanique que je veux bien le dire. Les courts récits de l'ascension de l'Inglismaldi et de la Forteresse accentuent la continuité, le récit de l'ascension de la Forteresse en particulier servant d'intermède idyllique: la calme avant la tempête.

Par le retour constant des images, dans l'histoire d'ascensions toujours plus hasardeuses, dans le pressentiment d'un malheur, si habilement suggéré que l'ombre surgit avec la menace elle-même, le poème avance avec la continuité tendue et tordue d'un câble qui rattache à un quai le poids immense d'un lourd navire. Cependant le lecteur ne sent jamais qu'on a employé injustement des moyens mécaniques, qu'il a été pris par le poète comme dans une trappe où il aurait été forcé à des émotions qu'il ne souhaitait pas. Il ne se détache pas du poème pour rentrer dans la vie réelle, comme il le ferait après avoir lu un poème ou une histoire de Poe. Ceci est dû partiellement au fait que le but réel de l'écrivain est aussi ambigu que celui de Melville, avec cette différence cependant: tandis que dans *Moby Dick* on voit que l'acquisition du summum bonum inclut d'un façon terrifiante le désastre, ici la catastrophe purifie complètement le lecteur et le laisse dans une état d'extase et de joie lumineuse, car il a fait la connaissance d'une grande âme. « David m'a appris cela » est aussi une remarque que le lecteur, non pas seulement l'écrivain, fera.

La continuité donc qui a conduit le lecteur à la fin du poème avec une telle variété de procédés techniques et un entrelacement si intime de l'accidentel et de l'essentiel, de l'épisodique avec l'action principale, cette continuité ne l'arrête pas là. Il est conduit à « ce jour, le dernier de ma jeunesse sur la dernière de nos montagnes », mais aussi au commencement de l'âge mûr, au moment où l'on se dirige par ses propres moyens, la fin de la soumission à un maître et le commencement d'une vie indépendante qui perpétueront et illustreront les leçons qu'on aura apprises du héros mort.

David, grâce à sa forme fraîche et impeccable, grâce à ses qualités originelles et sa vitalité, peut bien être considéré comme le *Shepheardes Calendar* des lettres canadiennes, la preuve indiscutable du « Et in Arcadia ego ». Avez-vous des doutes ? Placez *David* à côté de n'importe quelle Eglogue du *Calendar* et vous serez convaincus.

* * *

Comparées avec la technique de Birney—qui, dans *David*, est vigoureuse et tendue, les formes de l'art de Finch peuvent apparaître plus faibles, mais cela est dû dans une grande mesure à leur intention délibérée. Elles ne se développent pas et ne se déplacent pas dans une mouvement en avant. Elles restent dans leur propre monde d'artifice, un monde brillant, qui est hors du temps. Le secret de leur création nous est caché. Il est cependant une chose sûre, c'est que la joie du métier, la joie de voir des mots justes placés dans l'ordre juste, nous donnent une réponse partielle à nos qustions.

* * *

Une défense du point de vue exprimé dans ce pages est probablement inutile pour ceux qui sont d'accord avec moi et peu convaincante pour ceux qui ne le sont pas. En tout cas, le problème consiste réellement à maintenir un équilibre entre les deux éléments nécessaires dans la poésie et pourtant en conflit: la matière et la manière. Malgré l'argument apparemment convaincant, que « soul is form and doth the body make », les limitations humaines sont telles que nous trouvons en la matière et la manière des desiderata, dont l'un est atteint aux dépens de l'autre. Nous avons supposé dans ces pages que la littérature canadienne a souffert dans le passé de trop peu d'attention à la forme et que les poètes qui montrent d'excellentes qualités de forme devraient être examinés avec un respect tout spécial à ce moment de notre histoire culturelle. Cette idée est supportée par l'affirmation suivante exprimée récemment par un critique éminent : « Je considère comme auteur celui pour qui le métier d'auteur est le premier art et le plus important, qui met exactement autant de poids sur le style que sur le contenu, et dont l'œuvre demande donc pour être comprise, un sens du style aussi développé que la faculté de comprendre le contenu. »[2]

[2]T. S. Eliot, « Forfattaren och Europas Framtid » (*Bonniers Litterara Magasin*, Jan. 1946, pp. 23-8.)

THREE REVIEWS OF
NOW IS TIME (1945)

❧ E. K. BROWN

Between Mr. Scott's poems and those of Mr. Earle Birney's second collection, *Now is Time,* there are many resemblances. Mr. Birney professes the same belief in mind, speaking with respect of a "map of a reasoned future"; his counsel to a World Organization is that "the iceberg is elective" for the dangerous fogs are projections only of our wills and thus are under our control. A social idealism, the same in final aim, animates him. He has almost the same pleasure in the precise vision, the firm touch, with him a harder touch.

Perhaps the essential differences are that Mr. Birney is more dramatic, and more bitter in temper. There is no narrative in this collection to remind us of *David;* instead we are given elegies. One of these is already widely known: "Joe Harris 1913-1942." This is in a highly successful poetic prose, and is intended, as its biblical captions emphasize, to be not only a lament for an individual and an account of his life and death, but a generalized accusing picture of the plight of a generation of poor Canadian boys upon whom a cruel necessity forced first a depression and then a war. "For Steve," in long stanzas with a curious and stirring effect of assonance, recounts a story which is much the same, but told with even less concentration on the individual, and a more wide-ranging concern with the Canadian economic and social problem,

> the human fissures
> that cleave the lanky land from which we grew.

"Man on a Tractor" belongs with the elegies, in the framework of thought at least, although in this poem the individual survives the worst that depression seconded by war can do against him. The poor of the tractor-man's generation (which is also Joe Harris's and Steve's, and roughly speaking is the generation following Mr. Birney's) had in the thirties an exceedingly raw deal. Mr. Scott is aware of this; it haunts Mr. Birney. His poems are packed with references to the plight of the unemployed. He speaks of the "ceaseless palsy of boxcars," the "slammed doors," the "graceless gingerly

From *University of Toronto Quarterly,* 15 (1946), pages 272-3. By permission of *University of Toronto Quarterly.*

handout," the "stale handout," the "kicks in the rump or three day hungers," the "yardbulls ahead," the "pinched slumboy." The poor people, rural or urban, have been ridden mercilessly and smugly by the rich, "fat and unheeding":

> sprouting thicker than wheat are the towers
> of its traders, shining more than the headstone
> his father saved from a lifetime's farming.

What Chesterton called "the impudent fatness of the few" is never far from Mr. Birney's mind. The rich are on high either in their towers, or as hawks circling over the helpless flocks, and when they descend it is always to hurt. Their life is seen from below angrily, and without any real sense of motive. The dramatic quality in Mr. Birney's poetry suffers by the contrast between his ever-ready sympathy with the poor, a sympathy grounded in understanding, and his summary unconvincing presentation of their masters. His bitterness of mood forces its way into almost everything he writes, sometimes to give it greater energy and vigour, but often to weaken a note of delight or triumph, or to destroy a touch of reality.

❦ M. H. MARTIN

An author's second book always seems to fall too much in the shadow of the first. If we have called the first work promising, there is the temptation to write the second volume off the ledger as a promise fulfilled, to substantiate our case with some strenuous adjectives, a quotation here and there, and feel that justice has been done. In *Now is Time,* the new book of Earle Birney's poetry, there is much to discourage this kind of attitude, but there is also much to carry us back to the earlier *David* for reflective comparison. We find at once, in the longer poems like "Man on a Tractor," "Joe Harris," and "On a Diary" the same dramatic power as in the David poem, and the same instinct for vivid and significant detail. But there is a difference. In the title poem of *David* an implacable nature was a stage for the action and in a sense its protagonist. Now it is man's implacability, the war and its tragedies, and a sense of responsibility is involved. There is in "Man on a Tractor," for example, a profounder sense of social values, more specifically expressed than in any of the earlier work.

From *Canadian Forum,* 25 (1946), pages 292-3. By permission of *Canadian Forum.*

> Could he know that the crops from these smoking furrows,
> the ache in his back, the smile of his bride, were lines
> in the map of a reasoned future . . .
> then could he sit resolute on this tractor as once in a tank,
> and the bones of his brother have meaning.

In the other two poems that we have mentioned, Birney simply states the tragedy for what it is worth, in the life and death of a man and in the new life of a woman, and leaves us with our own conclusions.

By far the larger part of the collection is made up of short poems, various in mood, tone and significance, bits of the kaleidoscopic pattern of yesterday, today and tomorrow in the war years. In most of these the thought is simple, the common property of humanity, and the heritage of the truly original poet. Beyond this there is the sense of a common drama and destiny, that comes out most strongly in one of the best poems in the book.

> The soldiers merge and move with all of us
> toward whatever mystery
> bemused that fatal pliant fish
> who first forgot the sea.

I do not feel that the blurb-blazoned phrase about originality is an adequate summary of the good that is in *Now is Time*. It may be that in Canadian poetry, vigor and optimism are the symptoms of revolt from the established tradition, and in that sense original. Beyond this the phrase has little meaning. His speech, it is true, is strongly individual. In a poem like "Skeleton in the Grass" he sets his vivid images to a technical counterpoint as new and startling as they deserve. Yet in what he has to say there is strength and often great depth of meaning, but seldom the metaphysical brilliance that the critics lead us to expect.

Optimism is a word that smacks strongly of the poets' corner in a Sunday supplement, or calls to mind the kind of theatrical robustiousness that we associate with Whitman. Certainly Earle Birney is too much a poet, and too much a man of his age to fit into either of these classes, yet I feel that a considered, mature optimism is the background of the most serious, and the best poems in this book. There is no self-deception implied in the word as I would have it understood. No one could read *Now is Time* and not feel the square-set honesty of the writer's mind. When a poet can write at the end of a book that deals vividly and frankly with the tragedy and the futility of war

> The compassed mind must quiver north
> though every chart defective;
> there is no fog but in the will,
> the iceberg is elective

then something has been said, not only for the critics, but for the nation.

❧ [WATSON KIRKCONNELL]

This is Major Birney's first volume since the prize-winning *David* (1942). The achievement of his earlier work sends one to this new harvest with eager anticipation.

The result, on the whole, is disappointing. The intellectual power is as evident as ever, but the style has gone to seed in contortions of metaphysical modernity. Our clique of Leftist poseurs will rejoice, but others will regret the self-frustration of obvious talent. There is no single poem with the straight-forward objectivity of "David." With the exception of the superb "Road to Nijmegen," most of the present volume is only semi-intelligible, as the result of a perverse striving after allusiveness and novelty. Thus a young girl's diary says:

> This is the steady wind of trivialities,
> of lady prohibitions and normalities
> from muffin-mouths that howled away Eustacia,

and only the reader who recalls a phrase in Chapter VII of Hardy's *Return of the Native* has the key to the passage.

In general, the mood is one of intense bitterness. Thus his "Remarks for the Part of Death," associates even the alternative of religion with softening of the brain:

> Continue to grow, if you wish,
> Your dusty bushes of bombs
> or suck the shell's dug in your mouth
> —or come with paresis and psalms.

Some of his figures, however, are rich in suggestiveness:

Within these caverned days, ears cocked
for breathing minotaur, our palms
read a pied Braille of rock.

From *Canadian Poetry Magazine,* 9 (March 1946), pages 35-6. By permission of Watson Kirkconnell.

EARLE BIRNEY, LETTER TO THE EDITOR
OF *Canadian Poetry Magazine*

Dear Sir:—

When a magazine publishes an anonymous review, it presumably takes editorial responsibility for its viewpoint. I am therefore asking you to allow me space in answer to an unsigned review of my "Now Is Time" in your March issue.

It is one thing to damn a book; it is another to misconstrue the context and misstate facts in order to damn it. When your reviewer excepts only one poem from his charge that my volume is "only semi-intelligible", he is making a statement which he could not sustain in semi-literate company. If he finds my "Man On A Tractor" or "Joe Harris" only semi-intelligible, he betrays either an inability or refusal to understand poems which have been clear to every reader and reviewer of them I have encountered.

Two of the three quotations cited by the reviewer are admittedly not as clear as some nursery rhymes, particularly when robbed of their true context and a false context supplied by the reviewer. Thus, in an attempt to make a poem look ridiculous, three lines are quoted as if I had put them into the diary of a young girl, where an honest reviewer would have indicated that the lines were *the author's comment* on the material of the diary. Again it is not honest to ascribe *to the poet* a philosophy contained in a dramatic monologue where an allegorical character, Death, is presumed to be speaking. It would be extremely easy to make any poet who has ever written sound unintelligible by the methods used by your reviewer. In view of the amount of sentimental doggerel which your journal continues to publish, I am not surprised that you would employ a reviewer who is eager to attack any poetry which strikes him as being in any sense allusive or novel, or tainted with "metaphysical modernity". That is your privilege. It is my privilege to write as I please and to be attacked because I do so, both by the "clique of Leftist poseurs" with whom the reviewer seeks to link me, as well as by the clique of Rightist flaneurs which seems to have taken possession of the Canadian Poetry Magazine.

Yours faithfully,
Earle Birney

Unpublished letter to the editor of *Canadian Poetry Magazine* in reply to an anonymous review of *Now Is Time,* (March 1946). By permission of Earle Birney.

SIX REVIEWS OF *THE STRAIT OF ANIAN: SELECTED POEMS* (1948)

ROY DANIELLS

Wider variety, greater maturity and increased technical competence are the marks of this new book of Earle Birney's. It is true that the publishers, instead of keeping in print *David and other Poems* and *Now is Time,* have chosen in the annoying fashion now all too familiar to readers of poetry to mix recapitulated material from the older books with new poems; nevertheless, three-fifths of *The Strait of Anian* is new and the reappearance of "David" as part of a sequence covering the physical and cultural width of Canada (from "Atlantic Door" to "Pacific Door") is not without enriching advantages.

Variety is apparent in the swift change of critical attitudes and descriptive approaches as we traverse the enormous and differentiated terrain which is this country. The Atlantic is appropriately the "old whalehall," the historic and much-navigated ocean. Cultural and political criticism of Canada as an entity follows. An acute analysis of Montreal and French-Canadian values is succeeded by an evocation of the landscape of the Canadian Shield with its terrible beauty and inhumanity. Then a day in Toronto, the tide of multifarious humanity flowing down into the city and ebbing home at night. Two prairie scenes, winter and autumn, are beautifully realized and we are led on to a cluster of British Columbian poems,—the running historical and ethical comment culminating in the reminder

> that there is no clear Strait of Anian
> to lead us easy back to Europe,
> that men are isled in ocean or in ice
> and only joined by long endeavour to be joined..

Greater maturity of outlook is evidenced by an almost complete absence (except in "New Brunswick") of the note of angular querulousness which was not infrequent in the earlier volumes. Here the critical thrust is made with poise and dexterity; large ideas are moved without strain; tangled issues are presented without confusion. There is a marked gain in mellowness and ease without loss of strength.

From *Canadian Poetry Magazine,* 11 (June 1948), page 48. By permission of Roy Daniells.

Only after repeated readings does the technical skill of the sequence become fully apparent. The long verse-paragraphs predominantly semantic in rhythm which are Birney's specialty, are varied by a sonnet with Anglo-Saxon adornments; by lyrics that make the mouth water; by a "prairie counterpoint" of conversational realism and delicate nature description; by the long striding stanzas of "David" and a deft light stanza quite new in style:

> Come where the seal in a silver sway
> like the wind through grass
> goes blowing balloons behind him.

All this comprises less than half the book, the second part being sufficient of itself to make a noteworthy publication, containing as it does many previous pieces (including the best of the war poems), a dozen new pieces and "Man on a Tractor" which in a hundred lines of honest writing leads us through the mind of a post-war Canadian and is by itself worth the price of the book.

❧ DOROTHY LIVESAY

On the old maps used by Sir Francis Drake "The Strait of Anian" was marked as a northwest passage to the Pacific Coast through the continent from the Atlantic. No one ever found this passage, though many sought. Today, Earle Birney uses it as a symbol of his search for Canada. Having found her, his aim is to relate her to the world.

What makes this British Columbia writer important for Canadians is the fact that he is the only poet who sees Canada whole. Too often, in the past and present generation of lyric writers, the voices have been regional. However delightfully and meaningfully they described Tantramar or Ottawa, our poets never seemed to be able to fly from their narrow home and see the country in its entirety.

Earle Birney, standing between the old and the very young, is as close to the earth as a traditional poet like Lampman, but he is also one with the jacks and jills, the young farmers, workers and veterans restlessly searching to find a name for the future. For them Birney points out the pitfalls, gives warning of the darkness, urges hope.

In the present collection appear the strongest poems from

From the *Vancouver Sun*, Magazine Supplement, 1 May 1948, page 4. By permission of Dorothy Livesay.

"David" and "Now is Time," now out of print. Added thereto is a new section which, although brief, is well worth having. For in these new poems, Birney has integrated his feeling about his country—building up, if not a symphony, at least a suite for full orchestra. He opens his theme with "Atlantic Door," the necessary ocean that must be crossed:

> ... through hiss and throttle come
> where the great ships are scattered twigs
> on a green commotion
> and the plane is a fugitive mote
> in the stare of the sun ...

This prelude is followed by a series of pictures of Canada, done with a dry ironic hand reminiscent of W. H. Auden. Passing the Maritimes and Quebec to "Laurentian Shield" the deeper music prevails.

But it is when he reaches the prairie that Earle Birney moves with a new stride. "Prairie Counterpoint" is the most interesting poem in the book because it contains human drama behind the poetic assimilation of the land. The style here is of a different cut, a refreshing interlude before we reach the Rockies, the charming lyric "Gulf of Georgia" and the finale, "Pacific Door."

There are new poems also in Birney's more philosophical sections; although he never quite reaches the emotional heights of the earlier "At the Bay" and some of his war poems, he is still able to jolt the reader out of blindness and complacency. Most moving poem of this group is "World War III" in which the poet castigates, but still offers hope for man ...

> Can love bend the earth to his will,
> can we kill only that which drives us to kill,
> and drown our deaths in a Creed?

If Birney rarely answers his own questions, at least he poses them in a forceful, thought-provoking way. No one can ask more of a poet.

❦ L. A. MACKAY

Earle Birney's "Strait of Anian" includes, along with much newer work, the best of his earlier volumes, now out of print. This volume

"Canadianism of Earle Birney Is Both Subtle and Intense", from *Saturday Night*, 63 (24 July 1948), page 18. By permission of L. A. MacKay.

gives further indication of the individual quality which most markedly distinguishes Mr. Birney among his Canadian contemporaries—his ability to handle a large-scale pattern. Only one other Canadian poet in our time has shown outstanding ability in the organization of large themes. That is, of course, E. J. Pratt, to whom this book is dedicated.

Mr. Birney's dedication and his performance suggest the hope that he may also develop from shorter poems to a more ample movement. There is about the long poem, when it is handled as Pratt handled it in *Brébeuf,* an amplitude, a magnificence, and a solid satisfaction such as the most accomplished performance on a smaller scale can never yield. It would be a terrible thing if all our poets took to composing at great length, but it is a good thing that some should, and Mr. Birney seems to have the necessary qualities.

He is capable of concentration, but he is also capable of expansion; he does not tire easily, nor exhaust the attention of his readers by a too minute intensity, a too ruthless restlessness. Of many gifted contemporary poets it may be said, as Macaulay said of Seneca, that to read them in bulk is like dining on anchovy sauce. Some have claimed that a fragmentary approach is an accurate reflection of the modern world; but they seem to have overlooked, as the novelists have not, one of the outstanding characteristics of the modern age, the sheer magnitude of its constructions, whether physical or social.

Mr. Birney's rhythm is sufficiently flexible to maintain an extended movement. His choice of words shows an accurate estimate of the degree of remoteness from common speech that makes for poetic freshness without sacrificing intelligibility. His images are not fragmentary or inadequately related; they are chosen not for their shock value, or for some casual likeness, but for their contribution to the total picture. He is able to explore one well-chosen image in a variety of aspects, concentrating rather than diffusing attention. "Canada: Case History," and "New Brunswick" are excellent examples of this power.

The dating and placing of the poems brings out strikingly the profoundly Canadian quality of his inspiration. Invariably, whatever the theme, he is at his best when his feet are on his native soil, or not far removed from it. This national quality does not lie in rejection or unawareness of the rest of the world. Perhaps on account of his wide acquaintance with various parts of Canada, he has never fallen into the imitative North American isolationism of some of our Eastern writers, an attitude that has never been characteristically Canadian, if only because Canadians could never afford it.

His Canadianism is at once more subtle and more intense. He is not looking for what is unshared, peculiar, and possibly accidental to certain geographical limits, but for what is significant and essential in the life of the people among whom he has lived with an intelligence alert to their thinking and feeling. It is Mr. Birney's good fortune, and ours, that his mind is of a quality to receive accurate impressions, to clarify them, and to render them with poetic force and order.

❦ TIMES LITERARY SUPPLEMENT

There is far more of the gritty detail of Canadian life in Mr. Birney's volume; there is a tone far nearer that of the speaking voice, and there is nothing like the same simplicity or assurance of intention. Mr. Birney nevertheless offers something on a larger scale, more sensitively close to life, and more humanly interesting. He is far more specifically a Canadian poet than Mr. le Pan, and he has the faults of tone common to most Dominions [sic] poets, a tendency to fall now into manly rant, now into manly sentimentality; he has the virtues of such poets, also, freshness, sharpness, shrewdness. These lines from a poem on soldiers coming home show something of his weaknesses and strengths:

> Conforming thighs supply a graft
> to patch the mortared spirit's hand,
> while the accustomed haze restores
> a familiar distance to the promised land.
>
> The soldiers merge and move with all of us
> toward whatever mystery
> bemused that fatal pliant fish
> who first forgot the sea.

The first two lines there, though their general sense is perfectly clear, contain a most awkward jumble of images. Sex, they mean, helps human life to grow healthy coverings again where holes have been blown in it by war experiences, but the juxtaposition of the real thighs and the metaphorical hand has a grotesque effect, as has

"Two Canadian Poets", from the *Times Literary Supplement,* no. 2419 (1948), p. 332. Reproduced by permission.

the notion of the spirit's hand being pierced by a trench-mortar; the next two lines, however, say something quite profound in a simple and moving way, and the next stanza is effective, too. But Mr. Birney's style, pungent and moving at its best, lacks unity. There is no general effect that he is aiming at, and, unlike Mr. le Pan, he obviously composes from line to line. He gets the details he wants and patches them together somehow. He seldom writes a poem that is an impeccable whole, but he is always lively and interesting, and he is worth reading, not only as a poet, but as a man with an affectionate yet critical understanding of his own country, "a high-school land, dead-set in adolescence;" he is the boy who

> wants to be different from everyone else
> and daydreams of winning the global race.
> Parents unmarried and living abroad,
> relatives keen to bag the estate,
> schizophrenia not excluded,
> will he learn to grow up before it's too late?

Not as pure poetry, but as the comments on life of a frank, perceptive, indiscreet Canadian, with a real but uneven poetic gift, Mr. Birney's volume deserves readers.

LIONEL MONTEITH, LETTER TO THE EDITOR OF THE *Times Literary Supplement*

Sir,—Whilst not wishing to enter into any controversial discussion of your reviewer's opinions, I feel that I cannot let pass a most ill-considered generalization contained in his review under the heading "Two Canadian Poets."

Writing of Professor Birney, he stated that ". . . he has the faults of tone common to most Dominion poets, a tendency to fall now into manly rant, now into manly sentimentality." To inquire which Dominion poets have these faults would be of little service since few people in this country are sufficiently acquainted with Dominion poetry to be at all enlightened by the answer—even if one could be given. In my own experience of Dominion poetry over a number of years I can only say that such a statement is signally unjustified. There *are* ranting and sentimental Dominion poets, of course, just as there are ranting and sentimental English poets, but to generalize in either case would be equally misleading.

Although myself English, I cannot but deplore the superior and

From the *Times Literary Supplement,* no. 2142 (1948), page 359.

patronizing attitude of some English critics to Commonwealth work—an attitude of which the comment in question seems rather characteristic. When we have learned that the work of each Commonwealth poet (as with our own) must be judged upon its individual merits, then we may be in a better position to appreciate the outstanding contribution that the Dominion poets are making to our poetic culture.

LIONEL MONTEITH.

Our reviewer writes: My intention was not to patronize, though it was not to be diplomatic either. I stated what seems to me a fact. Writing recently in your columns, for instance, about contemporary Latin American poetry, I said that it has the fault of sometimes rather tasteless verbal exuberance. That was a generalization of the same sort as this. The poetry of young societies, compared with the poetry of old societies, must be expected often to show a kind of crudity—springing mainly, I would say, to risk another generalization, from the fact that in young societies masculine energy is less tempered than in old societies by feminine scepticism. Men in young societies look outward rather than inward, are active rather than contemplative, and their expression of the inner life, therefore, may be vigorous, but is often confused, and rarely refined. The vigour of the poetry of young societies may outweigh its flaws. Mr. Roy Campbell, for instance, stands in the first rank of contemporary poets writing in English, and yet his work shows the flaws I mentioned, as does the work, which I also admire, of Mr. John Manifold and Mr. Paul Potts.

I can attach no useful meaning to Mr. Monteith's phrase about considering the work of every poet on "its individual merits"; I find that I can make useful judgments about a poet's work only in relation to the life he is writing about and the traditions he is developing, and I think the notion of judging poetry out of any context whatsoever is a figment.

❦   GUSTAV DAVIDSON

"The Strait of Anian" (a title derived from Blundeville's account of Sir Francis Drake's first voyage into the Indies) contains the

"Clearing the Brush and Brambles", from *Saturday Review of Literature*, 21 (August 1948); copyright 1948 by Saturday Review Co. Reprinted by permission.

Canadian poet Earle Birney's most recent poems as well as a number culled from his two previously published volumes, "David & Other Poems" and "Now Is Time." The present offering is a representative collection and fulfils the promise of earlier work.

Birney is a particular poet, wholly underivative. Each poem in this book gives evidence of a lyrical instinct in the choice and management of subject matter, of close observation to the Canadian locale, and of a lively awareness of contemporary issues. From "Atlantic Door," the opening poem, where the poet speaks of "the great ships [as] scattered twigs on a green commotion/and the plane [as] a fugitive mote/in the stare of the sun," down to the last poem, "World Conference," wherein the "quiet diesel in the breast/propels a trusting keel," Birney maneuvers skilfully and unerringly through the brush and brambles of poetic pitfalls. He is adept in both the modern and traditional techniques. His settings, while largely regional, continually spill over their banks, for his is a "widely embracing mind," at once practical and imaginative.

He is an excellent balladist, one of the best. His "David," reprinted here in full, is nothing short of a poetic tour de force. It is compact with drama, shimmering with the glacial snows of the Canadian Rockies, arrowed with a wild, pictorial beauty, and "heavy with fate." His "Man on a Tractor" is another "Man with the Hoe." It is to be regretted that he did not include his prose poem "Joe Harris" (from "Time Is Now"), a five-page war elegy of stark power which brought its author overnight fame.

Here and there Birney permits himself a few avant-garde whimsies, as in "Anglosaxon Street." The real Birney, however, is not in such poems, but in "This Page My Pigeon," "Introvert," "Man Is a Snow," "David," etc. Here he soars, though his wings are far from feathery.

He is an unusual phrase-maker, a brilliant word-coiner, a vigorous, arresting, at times sardonic and disquieting voice, but rarely a monotonous or feeble one. His imagination is forever at play with symbols, conceits and auguries. He sees water dripping "cold as hymns," "air by birds hieroglyphed," and man as "a snow that winters/his own heart's cabin/where the frosted nail shrinks in the board/and pistols the air."

In the late war Birney served in the Northwest Theatre where he witnessed sights to which, by their commonplaceness, we have become inured. These things put iron into the poet's song and tempered it to a steely resilience. In a poem called "World War III," he asks:

Will it be much as before?
Shall we learn to wear like fraternity pins the death of our
friends?

❦ A. G. BAILEY

Of the forty-six poems in this book, twenty-seven are republished from Mr. Birney's earlier collections, *David and Other Poems,* and *Now Is Time,* for both of which he was awarded the coveted Governor-General's Medal for poetry, in the first instance in 1942, and in the second in 1945. The present volume is thus one of selected poems and provides the means for assessing the author's character, depth, and range of experience as a poet, as well as the direction his art has taken since he first began to publish over a decade ago. The wide popularity that these poems have enjoyed springs in part from the fresh and immediate sensory appeal of their imagery, and in part from the author's conception of life as a high adventure to be met with courage, and in full knowledge of the odds. They thus represent a departure from much modern poetry in which peculiar states of the individual consciousness are explored and wrought into a neobaroque metaphor that baffles all those who have not succeeded in mastering that difficult language. His temper and his talent, one would guess, have led him through the realm of metaphysical symbol to one of action in space and time. His fusion of the lyric with the dramatic rather than the didactic, and his application of this technique to the great issues of human destiny, both directly in some poems, and allegorically in others, help to account for the new note he has succeeded in striking in recent poetry. His terse utterances grow naturally out of the matter which, in each case, he confronts. Through expressions like "varnished sand" in the poem *Gulf of Georgia* the reader sees what the poet has described without having his credulity strained or being shocked as with pyrotechnics. He often employs words that lack transcendental qualities, and thus in many of his best epithets he achieves a sensory sheerness. For other purposes, as in his treatment of elemental or human forces in conflict, his metaphors have the vigour, clarity and strength of his own mountains, and it is as though the rugged terrain of the western Canadian cordillera had entered into the poet's soul.

From *Dalhousie Review,* 30 (1950), pages 205-8. By permission of Alfred G. Bailey.

One cannot, in fact, speak of his choice of words and the way he forms his images as though these activities were unconnected with his attitudes towards man and nature. In most of his work there is little if any overt sentimentality. When he is most deeply moved, as by the predicament of man in an indifferent universe, or by some tragedy of human provenance, he is a master of his craft and his lines move with the inevitability of true poetry. When he lapses into sentimentality, which happily he rarely does, he seems to lose his customary sureness of touch, and indulges in such banal expressions as appear in line 2 of the final verse of *Invasion Spring*. His poems addressed to women often seem self-conscious, and without authenticity by comparison with poems like *David* and *For Steve,* in which the sentimental note does not obtrude at all and a fine control over the medium is maintained. The poignance of the grief over a lost comrade is heightened by the measure of restraint he achieves by simple statement or understatement, highly charged with emotion. What he cries out against is the senseless destruction of human life, and of the fine qualities of manhood, intelligence, kindness, understanding, vision and skill, but he is not without a desperate faith that the sacrifice, however heroic and, in a sense, however justified it may be in itself, has meaning in the larger human context. Ennoblement through sacrifice would not be meaningless:

> Since you who walked in freedom
> And the ways of reason fought on our front,
> We foresee the plot is solvable, the duel worthy.

This conviction emerges in the second of the two parts into which the book is divided and in which the poet gives literary form to the responses that men have made to the great contemporary sickness in the human family, of which the second World War was a terrible symptom. In the first he speaks for Canada and her waxing nationhood, but the two problems, national and oecumenical, are ultimately the same, because they spring from the more fundamental predicament that confronts humanity as a whole in the face of what appears to be a brutish and indifferent universe. His idea of nature is not the opposite of that of the early Romantic poets, such as Lampman in Canada, for whom the natural order was friendly and spiritually restorative, for what is insensate cannot be hostile. It is this attitude that reveals how the landscape of British Columbia has exerted a powerful impact upon the poet's consciousness, and has heightened that sense of the irrelevance of nature to human purposes which seems most plausible to a generation that has come to accept, in a spirit of disenchantment, the philosophical implications of the Darwinian thesis. In *David,* one of the finest poems yet written in this country, the human drama moves forward to its swift and tragic climax among the "unknowing cascades" and the "incurious clouds". Elsewhere we are urged to think no more than we must

> of the simple unhuman truth of this ocean,
> that down deep below the lowest pulsing of primal cell
> tar-dark and still
> lie the bleak and forever capacious tombs of the sea.

When confronted with the crimes and the stupidities of brutalized men, he may take a grim delight in the thought that "The beautiful bright coyote" will outlast them all, but such reflections seem to release him from the slough of pessimism in which Hardy and Housman were caught. Far more positive than they, he affirms that man's soul is a nursery of qualities of transcendent worth, and neither the blind events of the physical world, nor the ephemeral character of human life can diminish the kingdom to which they belong. Only in terms of these qualities can human life have the meaning that Mr. Birney surely believes it has. To the extent that man transcends the conditions of his brutish origin, he deserves the title of humanity, but there has been an age-old struggle between the finest and best, to which all men may win, and the dark tide of savagery from the presence of which they may never completely free themselves:

> men be swift to be mankind
> or let the grizzly take.

The rise of fascism that issued in "twelve red years of rage" no more invalidates the fundamental tenets of civilization than does the evident reality of the world of beak and claw, but it shows how blurred and uncertain are the boundaries between the kingdom of man and that of the brute, and how hard man must yet strive to conquer the enemy in himself. For Mr. Birney leaves us in no doubt as to where the danger lies:

> No one bound Prometheus. Himself he chained
> and consumed his own bright liver.

In three related poems, *Hands, Dusk on the Bay,* and *Vancouver Lights,* the first written in 1939 and the other two early in the War, he expresses the despair that then possessed him as he pondered the spectacle of a self-destroying humanity. The theory of the freezing universe of contemporary astrophysics may have lurked in the background of his consciousness as he wrote *Vancouver Lights,* but the immediate occasion for the composition of all three poems, appears to have been the prospect, years before Hiroshima, of the extinction of *homo sapiens,* or at best the approach of a new Dark Age. In *Hands* the logic of the organic cycle is asserted to have no counterpart in the death of men. The idea of nature, in this poem, as an inchoate and elemental realm beyond good and evil, is symbolized by the "cold and unskilled cedar whose webbed claws" focus no bombsight, and by the balsam, and the alders that "are not of my flesh". By contrast with these trees man appears as a stranger and a misfit in a universe to which his moral sense seems altogether alien. Man's tragedy seems to lie in the fact that as he has evolved he has found a moral order, essential to his humanity, which appears to be contradicted by the facts of the physical world in which, in his own peculiar and partly selfmade way, he is fated to live. The emergence of his moral sense has been accompanied by a skill in the fashioning of contrivances that have come to endanger all those things that, in his moments of sanity, he holds most dear. *Dusk on the Bay* and *Vancouver Lights* are both developed in terms of the symbols of light and darkness, but with opposite connotations. In the former, to be more accurate, the sun is not so much a symbol as an accompaniment of evil. The sun that "rushes down through Asian skies, garish with burst of shell and unarrested rocket" will eventually come to shatter the precious night that he describes in terms of the sights and sounds of a happy and ordered existence, typified by the bathers on the shore. The words that are used in the early lines to describe the activities of the peaceful Canadian night are later skilfully woven into the contrasted context of war. The legs of the bathers "unsexed by distance" and the "waving arms severed with twilight" become the "limbs unsexed and severed" by the bombs at "stricken dawn in England". The night air that "lets fall a rain of quiet coolness on the flesh" becomes "the rain of iron cooling the flesh" to the temperature of death. The use of this technique of ambiguity is stark and moving in its effect on the reader, but it would prepare him imperfectly for the "epitaphic" forecast of cosmic tragedy in *Vancouver Lights.* This poem has not received the praise it deserves since its first publication, in an unrevised version, in the *Canadian Review of Music and Art* in 1942, perhaps because it has appeared to be less architectonic and not so closely woven in texture as *Hands* and *Dusk on the Bay.* Yet it contains some of the most powerful lines to be found in the whole range of contemporary poetry. Although Mr. Birney can work effectively with the minutiae of nature, as in *Slug in Woods,* his sensibility responds as fully to the challenge of a vast canvas as does that of Mr. E. J. Pratt, although he does not share the puckish and buoyant humour of the latter. In part the impact of this poem is due to the "terror of space" and the awe of "the changeless night" and "the stark ranges of nothing" which his images evoke, but it is also among other devices, due to the use, in an interstellar context, of words that commonly denote small objects. Infinity of space and time, personified by the Nubian, "wears for an evening's whim a necklace of nebulae". In the encompassing night men are "the unique glowworms" or the "spark beleaguered by darkness". The eye that looked out on the miracle of light, breaking for the first time the tyranny of the timeless dark, would come to guide the fashioning hand and reveal the promise of the knowledge of good and evil. If man were a cosmic accident, his light might be extinguished by the same means, but the hazard of which the poet is here speaking springs from the glory and the fatal flaw in man himself:

> These rays were ours,
> We made and unmade them. Not the shudder of continents
> doused us, the moon's passion, nor the crash of comets.
> In the fathomless heat of our dwarfdom, our dream's combustion,
> we contrived the power, the blast that snuffed us.

The author's deep compassion is concealed in this proud and wistful boast which he made as the world prepared to plunge further into the abyss of war. In these poems he does not explicitly affirm any grounds for hope, but in the poems written during the next few years one becomes conscious of a growing conviction that the holocaust may have meaning after all. It is in this hope that we must live, or know life lost.

2. LINES FOR A PEACE: *FICTION, 1949-1955*

A REVIEW OF *TURVEY: A MILITARY PICARESQUE* (1949)

MALCOLM LOWRY

With Turvey, unexpectedly, silently, and from a strange source, a classic has burst into our midst. For this to happen in the case of a brand new work must mean that it fills a gap. Its excellences seem to have been long acknowledged, and yet the book was simply not there, at least not in Canadian literature. The nearest approach would seem, obviously to be the Good Soldier Schweik. Turvey himself is a sort of Good Soldier Schweik in the battle dress of the Kootenay Highlanders. It is true that Turvey never precisely reaches the Kootenay Highlanders—but that is part of the story for you to read. Turvey is Canadian. But he is also as universal as Grandma's Boy, the protagonist of Chaplin's Shoulder Arms, or He Who Gets Slapped. And he pursues his objective of finding the war and joining his friend Lieutenant McGillicuddy in the Kootenay Highlanders with as much fervor and unction as Christian brings to his pilgrimage toward the Eternal City. Turvey too has his Slough of Despond, his Evangelist, his Giant Despair and even his Mr. Linger-After-Lust. Less lucky than Christian, however, his battles, too often for him, take place in psychologists' offices, upon hospital beds, or on operating tables with a sterophagoscope.

Unlike Hasek with Schweik, Birney is dealing not with a corrupt and ramshackle, but with a relatively enlightened army, and without in any way belittling that army, whose peculiar reputation is to be one of the most heroic in the world, he manages to achieve a masterly satire. It is masterly for one thing because he universalises that army to the extent of making it seem all armies, and the struggle for adjustment to it like any individual's struggle to adjust himself to a group, while at the same time never letting you forget that it is the Canadian army, which had, in point of fact, during this last war, its own particular private struggle for collective integrity.

So that finally it is a Canadian Army, a Canadian book, and its

From *Thunderbird,* December 1949, pages 24-26. By permission of Mrs. Margerie Lowry.

speech Canadian speech. Whatever that may be, you hear a great deal of it, and an unexampled amalgam of raw humour it is. Indeed perhaps the essential point about the novel is that it is superlatively and scandalously, uproariously and all but continuously funny.

We come up against the word obscene. Is this book obscene? Some will say it is, that, as some critic remarked of the Restoration dramatists, Birney takes every opportunity he can get away with of being as obscene as he possibly can. I am a dissenter from this possible view. I believe that in the case of an intention such as his the word itself calls for redefinition. Though in war men may perform noble actions, I have yet to discover that that prevents war itself from being obscene, in all the strict meanings of the word found in the dictionary, and in any close enlightened satire of the whole business, including especially the minor horrors of it, I would say that the difficulties to-day for any genuine artist to avoid some aspect of this charge were next to insuperable. We will not go into the unquestioned fact that in the past good and even great books have been written about war that were not obscene per se. Nor that it may be possible to write about obscene things in a "pure" way, as do the composers of editorials in a given country during a given war, but it is at least arguable that this technique, by seeming to invite one so chastely into an obscene thing, is, be the cause wrong or right, more obscene than obscenity itself. The problem here would seem to be, to write of obscene things in an obscene way, and still remain, so to speak, "pure", without any of the equally obscene connotations of this word in such a juxtaposition. Though it depends on the quality, the nexus is laughter. And this ribald and paradoxical miracle Birney is the first writer within my experience to bring about.

A worse charge would be sentimentality. Yet when Birney is sentimental it is deliberately and almost formally so, and he does not for the most part let that get into the caustic of his humour. All this adds up to a poetic attitude, not dissimilar to that toward war stated by Yeats in his preface to the Oxford Book of Modern Verse. As a consequence it is not, on second thoughts, so surprising not merely to discover that its author is a poet, but that his book has an underlying seriousness. Though his facade, with certain striking exceptions, remains carefully naive, this does not prevent Birney from achieving the most ghastly effects, as if one had added several dimensions to the gruesomeness of Grand Guignol and applied to it, as in one scene on a hospital train at the end, surely the ultimate in *Schadenfreude,* the humour of a diabolical Punch, making in one stroke a shattering indictment.

It should be said here that, taken as a whole, Turvey does not seem intended as an indictment, unless it is an indictment of the air we breathe. Nor does it fall, at least to the author's eyes, quite into the category of satire. Birney prefers to call it a picaresque novel. So be it: though his long-suffering hero might well, on top of everything else, take exception to being called a rogue and an adventurer.

To sum up. Turvey is tops. Yet Turvey, as may be expected, has faults. It is too long, for one thing. But most classics, including Don Quixote, suffer in this regard. Nor is Turvey himself, splendidly drawn though he is, and though he may well, especially among Canadians, become an immortal, a particularly "good" character. Birney's method, by and large, is somewhat that of heteroplasty. All the Canadian characters, bad or good as they happen to be, all seem to add up to Turvey. Which is another way of saying that they add up to Canada, adolescent, energetic, large, loutish, noisy, good hearted, anxious to please, eternally hopeful, and eternally put upon. It is to be noted, however, that at the end, Turvey himself loses his temper. It is high time. People will doubtless lose their tempers over Turvey too. May any trouble it may well bring down upon the august beard of its unlikely author, Major Earle Birney, authority upon Chaucer, Professor of English Literature at the University of British Columbia, and perhaps our richest poet, serve to emancipate us all.

THE SATIRIC NOVEL IN CANADA TODAY: *TURVEY*

D. J. DOOLEY

When Earle Birney's *Turvey* appeared in 1949, it was predicted that it might become one of the most popular Canadian books of recent years. Such has not proved to be the case. It is not for lack of interest in military affairs; the volumes of the official history of the Second World War sell out their first printings almost on the day they appear. It seems to me that *Turvey* is too undisciplined to be a first-rate novel, and too bookish to be a popular account of military experiences.

Birney describes it as a military picaresque. The picaresque takes a character through a number of situations which usually offer opportunities for comic or satiric exposure, and in so doing builds up a picture of the society the character lives in. Birney restricts himself to one half of the military world—the base details. His novel deals with holding units and army hospitals; the combatant part of the army does not come in, since Turvey never really reaches it. In a sense, *Turvey* is an exposure of this behind-the-lines part of the military system. Turvey wants to get to the Sharp End of the salient held by the Canadian Army; the reinforcement system is so self-defeating that it keeps him at the Blunt End. But this satiric pattern is not followed consistently throughout the book. For one thing, Turvey is greatly to blame for his own misfortunes. Also, he is not always the little man buffetted about by the system; at times, he is the lucky fellow who lands on his feet, the man who finds a friend just when he needs help most. The book does not hold together as a satire of the military system or as a dramatic conflict between the little man and the impersonal system; instead it remains a collection of broad army stories, or, as Claude T. Bissell called it in "Letters in Canada, 1949", a succession of *fabliaux*.

Every reader of the book probably has his favourite episodes—the Army's first attempt to assess Turvey's intelligence, the court-martial scene, the night in a mine-field, the stereophagoscopy. But many readers must feel that numerous episodes are not particularly memorable. The book goes on too long, and the comic invention flags. The humour is derived from a rather small number of types

From "The Satiric Novel in Canada Today: A Failure Too Frequent?" by D. J. Dooley, *Queen's Quarterly*, 64 (1958), pages 580-584. By permission of D. J. Dooley.

of situation—most of them involve sex, drink, medical treatment, army discipline, or personnel selection methods—so that the later pages bring Turvey into variants of situations he has already been in.

In all these episodes, however, the author seems to put comic effect ahead of satire. In many of them, no one is being attacked; the interest lies in the comic involvements of Private Turvey. Of course, there is a great deal of satire, directed, as in the *fabliau,* chiefly at those in authority. Lieut. Smith, an English instructor before the Army made him a Personnel Selection Officer, writes what he considers a model assessment, in which he describes Turvey as "eccentric and inchoate" and refers him to a psychiatrist; the psychiatrist's diagnosis is caustic: "No neurosis. Intelligence higher than that of some officers I have met." Later on, the psychiatrists get their turn for rough treatment. Turvey, having mistaken his greatcoat for an enemy paratrooper and shot it full of holes, is referred to one of them for a "Roar Shack" test:

> "Umhmn, think carefully now, in answering this. Did your father wear an overcoat much?"
> Turvey thought. "Every winter. Course everybody did. It was cold."

Though he is too cautious to diagnose "Oedipus Complex" on such evidence, the psychiatrist decides that it is a case of "Possible latent father-rivalry." Here the uneducated private soldier comes off better than the highly-trained specialist; he has more common sense.

But it is impossible to see the whole book in these terms; Turvey is not a Schweik, consistently outwitting those in high position. The Canadian Army has no more idea of how to handle Turvey than the Austrian Army did of how to handle Schweik, but Turvey does not enjoy Schweik's success: all his attempts to get to the Kootenay Highlanders end in frustration. Also, the portrait of Turvey is not kept consistent; he varies in intelligence and sensitivity from chapter to chapter. Sometimes his reactions are more refined than they ought to be:

> A van banged past her, drawn by a great speckled horse. Turvey saw that its tail was docked cruelly short, and winced in sympathy.

This is Birney, not Turvey. Also, the Turvey who spent two remarkable weeks in Buffalo is not the person who talks in these terms of going to London:

"I don't really feel aggressive though, Pottsy; it's just, well, you hear all the oldtimers boastin about the swell forty-eights they had in London. And—and golly, I don't even feel I'm in a war yet. About my only fun is horseshoe pitchin. Everythin's so sort of humdrum—not like in the Canadian papers."

A similar inconsistency is to be found in the style. The book opens with Turvey taking an intelligence test and being watched closely by the sergeant in charge:

It was a stare of suspicion; it leapt in a straight beam from the Sergeant's highstool, over the hunched and shirted backs of the other recruits, unmistakably and directly to him.

Since the book contains a prefatory apology for its down-to-earth language, the reader does not expect imagistic description like this, and he begins to watch for variations in style. He finds that they are considerable; in fact, an occasional passage sounds as if it had come from another book:

Over the barren saltmarshes sped the truck, under the floating Disney elephants of a balloon barrage and into the winding hubbub of Antwerp. Past multitudes of giraffish old houses they clattered, past enormous churches, past barbaric ruins, some old and weedy, others (like the Rex Cinema, where a whole Saturday matinee of soldiers still lay hidden) bright with newly-shattered brick. Then north into a flat straight highway again. Now over a groaning pontoon bridge subbing for a blasted canal lock; along the ice-choked ditch was a sprinkling of mounds, and one by the roadside held a faded stake on which a hoar-bright billytin clunked mournfully in the Flanders wind.

Obviously Birney is describing his own impression of a certain scene; in the next paragraph, he switches to the present tense for an effect of greater immediacy:

A detour now through the side-lanes of a village. The main street, either by bad luck or some diabolical aiming, was hit a few minutes ago by a V-Two.

The description is graphic and convincing; it comes directly out of Birney's experience; but it has nothing to do with Turvey.

On the other hand, there is probably as much in the book derived from the author's reading as from his own experience. His Mac talks very much like Dickens' Jingle:

"Delectable child. Blonde. Unheard-of combination: lovely gams, adequate income, able to read and write. Be home any time now. Have a ball. Celebrate. Pub-crawl. Take in a show, something. Got a steady up here yet?

Some other parts of the book follow less worthy models:

> The theatre was the most glittering, the tunes the catchiest, the actors the funniest and the leggy ladies the most beautiful in the world. But more beautiful than even the leading lady were the long lashes and the tip-tilted nose of Peggy whose palm he was now fitfully squeezing as they sat chair by chair in the kingly splendour of a second-storey box.

This is Victorian sentimental fiction, and it is even more out of place than the description of Antwerp. Evidently the author has not decided what kind of book he is writing, and he changes his mind from page to page. *Turvey,* therefore, is not a thorough-going satire, it suffers from the Canadian novelist's usual difficulties with plot, and it shows the usual interference of things read with things imagined or seen.

CREATIVITY THROUGH FICTION

EARLE BIRNEY

When I came to write my first novel, *Turvey*, ... there wasn't the slightest question that it would be a novel—though what kind, and how I would do it, were questions that did not answer themselves easily. The experience of writing it may be worth recalling, as a comment on what the particular activity of novel-writing seems to me to be about.

First, even as with a poem, there was the experience nagging to be worded. I was back from four years in the Canadian army, a complex unit of my life completed, forever finished with—except in my mind, which demanded that it be assessed, and emotionally contained. Here was not one spectre to be exorcized with a single poem, but companies and battalions of ghosts waving their khaki arms; and I myself was *one* of them, and *all* of them. I had been a browbeaten private, a harried cadet, a browned-off lieutenant, an under-confident captain, and over-worked major. But far more important than that, for a would-be novelist, my particular army jobs had brought me in close personal contact with literally thousands of Canadian soldiers from Nootka to Newfoundland. I had psychologically tested them, personally interviewed them, listened to their tales of childhood, their army grievances, their post-war hopes, their marital and extra-marital troubles, their traumatic memories of battles with the enemy, with their fathers, with the regimental police or with VD. I'd talked with them in wintry army jails in Niagara, in dreary holding units in Aldershot, in officer training centres on the Yorkshire moors, in Belgian hospitals and psychiatric wards, and even crouched with some of them in the basement of a Dutch schoolhouse while shells exploded in the playground.

How to weld this into a single book, how to focus, and on what? At first, the problem was one that went on only in the back of my head. The first post-war years were busy ones and I'd no time to write a novel, even though I couldn't help thinking of one. But then in the summer of '47 I had a single clear month to do with as I wished, and a place in the deep woods of a Pacific island in which to do it. Settling down to write I realized at once that my subcon-

From *The Creative Writer* by Earle Birney (Toronto: Canadian Broadcasting Corporation, 1966), pp. 39-44. By permission of Earle Birney.

scious processes had been working for me, over the two years since the war's end, and had made certain decisions, even though I was aware of them as only playful ideas or test-patterns. These unrealized decisions were to determine the nature of the novel. For example, I knew without knowing how I had come to know, that my central character was going to be a dumb backwoods private, an innocent born for trouble, a youth with the cheerfulness and reckless morale of a hero but with the intellectual and soldierly capacities of a farmyard duck. He'd crystallized in my mind out of a number of people: a lovable batman I once had; scraps of memories of those hundreds of youths I had interviewed or with whom I'd shared the wards of army hospitals. And Turvey had emerged also out of myself, out of all my own well-intentioned stupid boners as a soldier, and my own comedies and near-tragedies and loves and hates and fears in the king's uniform. So I sat down in the wilderness quiet of Bowen Island to create him on paper.

But it was impossible to write anything. All sorts of *conscious* choices had still to be made, or they had to be teased or willed up from the subconscious. To arrive at these, long walks were necessary, and a lot of mere sitting, broken by periods of furious physical activity, woodcutting, rock-climbing, and solitary swimming. Out of this came the name of my innocent rogue hero, Thomas, or Topsy Turvey, and, by logical progression, the form of the novel, a picaresque, a succession of incidents half-farcical, half-serious proceeding from his enlistment to his discharge. And revolving the form in my head led me now into more or less deliberate seeking of literary influences. Thinking of Don Quixote, for example, made me realize that *my* hero was a Sancho Panza, and so I must invert Cervantes' form, create a Quixote only as a secondary character, as a romantic, crazy officer Mac, whom Turvey is always trying to find.

Now I could go back to my typewriter and start setting things down. But not sentences yet, only notes about the dozens of minor characters who must be created to make the various scenes of the novel come alive; data about the time and place progression from scene to scene. Sometimes this would come easily out of my memory; sometimes I had to stop and rummage in letters my wife had saved, or in old scraps of diaries I had made overseas, to set the visual recall or the imagination stirring.

Then I wrote the first chapter, and rewrote it, and rewrote it six times, fighting to establish the style I wanted, the balance of overstatement and understatement, to shape the voice and air of

Turvey, and my own voice as his intermediary. Fighting also to discover clearly, all over again, why I was writing at all, what was at the nub of the novel, what were the essential statements I wanted to make, under the foolery, about the army, about war, about any, about all human life.

So the free month vanished as if it had been a day. It was time to go back to teaching, only one chapter written. Everything else had to be postponed till the next year. Perhaps I never would have gone back to the novel, there being so many other things a professor has to do in his life (even with the encouragement I got from a publisher's editor, to whom I sent that first painfully achieved chapter), if I hadn't continued to be prodded and bedevilled by this whole troop of ghosts, and if I hadn't been able to return to my friend's retreat late the following May, this time with the prospect of nearly four clear months for writing. Meantime I had found myself especially driven by the now more substantial shade of Turvey, demanding that I give him not only a decent birth but a sort of ancestry. Brooding about him made me recall further literature in which people a little like him had already appeared, characters more celebrated and human than Turvey might ever be, but in consequence all the more valuable to me now. So I re-read Voltaire's *Candide* and Hasek's *The Good Soldier Schweik*. These, however, though they gave me some ideas for techniques, cast me also into depression, from a realization that I could never write as well as either of those authors.

When I got down to my own book again, the depression vanished in the combined agony and fun of the writing. I did what Sinclair Lewis advised, I applied the seat of my pants regularly to the seat of my chair, five days a week, four hours every morning. Also, on days when the writing went well, I wrote through the afternoon, too, and sometimes far into the evening. At first, if I set down a thousand words it was a good day; but as the work progressed and the characters began to live in my head, I found I could not walk away from the typewriter, even after two or three thousand words, without the next scene starting to write itself, and I had to rush back to put it on paper, however roughly and in whatever state of physical fatigue. By the summer's end I was madly stabbing out the last chapter on my typewriter at the rate of five thousand words a day.

But then, back once more on the U.B.C. campus, came the cooling, the second look at the sprawling overlong confused first draft, in whatever spare time I could snatch from teaching duties on winter evenings—the fully conscious and painful process of forcing myself to find and admit to character inconsistencies, plot ball-ups, clichés, boring writing, wordiness, repetition. All this had to be cleared away in a complete second writing. Some chapters needed a third writing to tighten scenes, deepen themes, polish style. And still it wasn't within miles of what I originally conceived and hoped I could do. But by now there was a publisher breathing down my neck, a contract pending.

The battle with words indeed now changed into a battle to preserve my words, especially the four-letter ones used by some of my Canadian soldiers, against the cautions and pruderies of publishing houses. Fortunately, there was a courageous editor on my side, a liberal-minded Ontario spinster who stood up for the right of my characters to swear in my war novel as they swore in war, and as no one had yet sworn at that time in a Canadian book.

With a few compromises we won, though I sometimes think that an uncensored publication of the letters that passed between the editor and the publisher and me would have sold better than the novel did. Then the battle-ground shifted to the contract, to the share of still highly unlikely royalties from paperback editions, movie rights, etc. No sooner was this engagement settled, this time more to the advantage of the publisher, than the galley proofs were upon me, and with them another typical author's agony. All the hundred little errors or awkwardnesses I'd missed now shone in my eyes from the cold cruel type. How to dig them out and not run up a printer's bill for author's corrections? And while I'm wrestling with them the distant publisher fires off a salvo of telegrams at me because a real-life Mr. Turvey has turned up in Vancouver, name and all, with some of my Turvey's background. He had come as a helper to paint my house, and I had told the publisher, thinking it an amusing coincidence. And the publisher now wants me to persuade him to sign legal waivers.

There was a short deceitful lull while the galley proofs went back, till the page proofs came, and more errors turned up. Then still another bombardment, this time of long distance telephone calls from Toronto. The publisher's lawyer fears we'll be sued by General McNaughton, of all people, because of a joke, basically flattering to him, covering half a page in one chapter. Will I take it out, and invent a new half-page, to fit exactly. I refuse. I have every reason to think the General has a better sense of humour than my publisher's lawyer. So it stands. At last the book comes out. But the heaven of beholding the shiny object, the child, the creation, is quickly followed by the curious purgatory of launching parties, and autograph bees at department stores, and by the plain hell of waiting for the reviewers to pardon or hang me.

After that there was a year of comparative success, by Canadian standards—all of seven thousand copies sold, plus a radio adaptation. And talk of a movie, and a play, and of publication abroad. Then a prolonged anticlimax. Unanimous refusal of the book by London publishers, as being too American in its humour, and by New York ones, as being too English. Not till ten years later does the book have a minor revival, paperback sales, a Toronto stage adaptation, and simultaneous publication in London and New York. But by then it's too late for big sales or movie contracts. *Goodbye for Sergeants* has appeared and scooped me, though it was written later. In any case, it is all beyond my caring. My loyalty has switched to a second novel, a longer and more serious and (I still think) much better one, which took three times as long to write, and was generally damned, and eventually remaindered at seventy cents a copy. And now this too is of little interest for me; I'm being nudged by a third novel—I think it's a novel,—bugged by it as I speak these words and know that I'll be compelled to write it too, if I should live so long, though it may turn out much worse even than the first two.

Meantime, a footnote on *Turvey* apropos of the Canadian tendency to hold the poet and the novelist at arms' length. The novel was selected for reprint in a series of so-called Canadian classics, with a special introduction by a Canadian critic. The view of the introduction was that *Turvey* wasn't of course a regular novel, since it was written by a poet, but that it was interesting as the sort of thing that poets write when they try to write a novel.

INTRODUCTION TO *TURVEY*

GEORGE WOODCOCK

Novels are the holidays of poets, gallant excursions into the workaday lands of other men from which they either return in triumph with strange, outlandish cargoes, or, just as often, come back dashed and dejected by the rains of an alien shore. It is the successful holidays I am evoking, and here one could almost set aside a whole literary category for the fiction of poets—not those youthfully clever tinkerers with verse who find their eventual literary feet as good solid novelists, but rather the dedicated lifetime poets who perhaps once or twice in a career produce a novel as unlike the usual fictional fauna of their age as a unicorn is unlike either a Clydesdale or an Arab racer. Such writers do not feel the novelist's compulsion to explore a world populated by recognizable personalities related to the universe through varying degrees of believable perception; they do not have those worries over plausible psychology or about the consistency of timetables or the authenticity of medical symptoms that pursued even such powerful and free spirits as Dostoevski and Balzac among the novelists by profession. They can choose their own degrees of probability, their own relationships with actuality; the fact that they are poets seems to license any break into fantasy or into controlled or uncontrolled implausibility they may choose to make. And if they write well and with the kind of exhilaration that often comes from the desire to turn to one's own purposes an unfamiliar form, the poets sometimes produce, out of their complex sensitivity to language and their adeptness in the use of evocative images, the kind of glittering *jeux d'esprit,* the fountains of rare wit and fancy, which few habitual prose writers can rival. These are often the kind of works that can be done only once in a lifetime. Yet they are never among the massive and major novels; it is still left to the Tolstoys and Hardys and Stendhals to produce the real Niagaras of fiction.

From such poets' holidays we get offstream, offbeat novels like Alain Fournier's *Le Grand Meaulnes,* Herbert Read's *The Green Child,* Walter de la Mare's *Memoirs of a Midget,* Lermontov's *A Hero of Our Time,* and that most appealing of all Utopian narra-

From the Introduction to Earle Birney's *Turvey* (Toronto: McClelland & Stewart, The Canadian Publishers, 1963). By permission of McClelland & Stewart.

tives, William Morris's *News from Nowhere*. And to this class, yet as unlike any of them as they are for the most part unlike each other, belongs Earle Birney's satirical fantasia on military life, *Turvey*.

In a country whose English-speaking inhabitants, uneasily conscious that they rarely possess the urbane quality of wit, pride themselves on their humour, *Turvey* passes for a humorous novel; I believe it has even won a medal on these grounds. But it is very far from the weak imitations of what was original when Leacock wrote it that customarily pass for humour in Canadian books and journals. Birney has always been ready to wear the mask and motley of the clown, in prose and in verse, but he has generally avoided the easy and empty facetiousness of the professional literary funny man; his comedy, whether one encounters it in the sardonic setting of *Trial of a City,* or in a brief hilarious poem like "Mammorial Stunzas for Aimee Simple McFarcin," or in *Turvey* itself, is rather of the type—full of verbal quippery and social implication—that we once associated with the Marx Brothers. It is stringent, intelligent, irreverent, and a little irascible.

Turvey in fact carries us in many ways far outside the province of "Canadian humour" and equally far outside the Canadian literary situation in its more narrowly local sense. It is a novel about Canada and Canadians, written in a variety of Canadian dictions and exposing with a telling modicum of exaggeration what happens when a still youthful democracy finds itself rather bewilderingly caught in the *mêlée* of total war, which at times approximates to total chaos. But it expands into a world both geographically wider and historically deeper than the Canada of the Second World War.

The adventures of Turvey, that most simple-hearted man from the western valleys of the Kootenays, take him to England and eventually to the traditional Flemish battlefields of Europe; he experiences at first hand the ancient and at times incomprehensible societies of which his own provincial world in the mountains is the distant yet still united offshoot. But Birney does not merely relate Canadian life to the European stock from which it is never wholly cut free. He creates a further link by frankly appropriating and adapting to his own purposes—rather like the Chaucer he admires so much—the central idea of one of the most famous and perhaps the best of the satirical novels written around the previous European war—Jaroslav Hasek's *The Good Soldier Schweik*.

The resemblances between the two books are obvious, and no attempt is made to conceal them. Turvey, like Schweik, is an innocent, with a perpetual grin, who wants to do his best for his country but is constantly frustrated and persecuted by the military machine, so that all his good will is in the end wasted. Both characters are wise fools in the classic style; their simplicity is balanced by child-like logic and innate good sense. They are not anti-heroes in the real sense because their power of enduring and surviving produces its own kind of heroism; nothing ever really downs them.

But Turvey is not an *ersatz* Schweik. He lives wholly in his own right, a character freshly conceived within his own context of time and place, for Birney has used the shape of Hasek's story in the same way as in his poetry he has used the forms of Anglo-Saxon verse and Joycean speech; the result is not a pastiche, but an original work strengthened by allusions that suggest the power of a literary tradition and set in a familiar frame that suggests the universality of the predicaments of men at war. Moreover, where Hasek—as a Czech—exhibits his hero contending with the cruelty and corruption of an alien despotism, Birney shifts the sights completely to take in the frustrations of an individual faced by the anti-human contradictions which a well-meaning democracy develops when it attempts to become a machine of total war.

Turvey is described on its title page as "a military picaresque," and this label does help to define its difference from the customary non-poet's novel of the 1940's, when it was written. The form is the simple linear one of episodes strung along a unifying thread of movement through time and space that Cervantes, the first significant novelist, developed from the early Spanish rogue (*picarón*) stories. But it is a Quixotic tale without a Don, for Turvey, like Schweik, is of the clan of Sancho Panza. He first appears to us as a Depression-age wanderer, bewildering army clerks by the variety of humble casual occupations with outlandish names he has followed in his bum's Odyssey over the breadth of Canada; he has been— among other things—a scurfer and a pouncer, a bucker and a sticker. As the novel goes on, military necessity replaces economic necessity; in his attempt to enlist in the almost-mythical Kootenay Highlanders, Turvey is engulfed in a cumbersome machine that slowly processes him through training camps, goon squads, holding units, and military hospitals, gradually pushing him eastward until he finally reaches England, proceeds to Belgium and Holland, and gets one frustrating and inactive sniff of the front line, which immediately recedes as he is funnelled back through a series of hospitals and hospital ships, to England and Canada and defiant demobilization. He ends by scurrying with delight out of the army which he had joined with such heroic hopes.

The episodes are what really make the novel, as they do all

picaresques. Turvey becomes the innocent accomplice of black-marketeering officers, the victim of plausibly delinquent companions, the despair of commanding officers, the hero of military obstacle courses in which he steps on where braver men fear to tread, and the central figure of ludicrous courts martial. But he is not merely the dupe and the tool. He works with the single-mindedness of a simple man towards his goal of going into action with the Kootenay Highlanders. He succumbs to the tenderness of love. There are times when his irrepressible spirit is temporarily damped down, not only by boredom, but also by compassion.

. . . .

And here one may perhaps speculate—in advance of the inevitable thesis writers—on the extent to which Turvey in some of his aspects is the projection of irreverent and also compassionate impulses within his creator. Clearly here is no realistic portrait of the artist in uniform; on the other hand, some of Turvey's experiences certainly parallel very closely some of Birney's, while Turvey's growing awareness of the sheer absurdity of the military machine undoubtedly resembles the process of disillusionment that went on in Birney's own mind. Turvey and Birney, after all, are mutually assonant names, a consideration we cannot ignore in a poet so conscious of verbal echoes.

Turvey is not intended as a novel of psychological development; the environment changes, the episodes pile up, but Turvey and his companions pass through them fundamentally unchanged. Turvey may, indeed, have learnt a little from experience. At the end of the novel he is somewhat more adept at finangling, and he finally gains phenomenally high O scores in the intelligence tests to which he is continually being subjected by conscientious but unimaginative Personnel Officers. But his paper progress from a moron to a genius is illusory; he has not gained in real intelligence nor has he altered a scrap in character. In fact the whole point of the novel is that it ends showing Turvey as the natural man triumphant, having survived all the numbering and testing and regimenting and bullying and discipline and short-arm inspecting to emerge in the end as irrepressibly his own self as Sancho Panza at the end of the trials of governorship.

One cannot end an introduction to *Turvey* without mentioning two other aspects which deepen its comedy and add to its value as a curious, oblique, and irreverent document of Canadian life.

Birney shows a most sensitive ear to accents and forms of diction; there are long sections of dialogue in which the provinces of Canada are mapped out in the speech patterns of their natives. Personalities and callings are likewise defined by dialogue. There is, for example, Herb, the Personnel Sergeant, formerly a Magician.

....

A character—the professional charlatan who has come to believe his own patter—is delineated in a few sentences of his speech. But, like all the minor figures in *Turvey,* Herb is a character in the seventeenth century sense, trapped in his foibles, his own personal pattern of speaking and acting. There is in fact no attempt at depth psychology in Birney's portrayals of the people he exhibits in *Turvey*. They are all on the surface; they act predictably and according to type; they spring on us no disconcerting surprises that surge up out of Dostoevskian depths of the unconscious. Yet, given this limitation, they are—except for the consistently drab females—usually amusing and often impressive in a rather gaudy way. In their motley colourfulness, they form the chorus to this comedy of Canada Armed in which the fighting war rumbles away offstage while the combat that goes on before the footlights is the burlesque single combat between human individuality, acted by Turvey, and inhuman collectivity. As in all good comedies, the right side wins; Turvey triumphant is Man victorious. In terms of orthodox novel-writing, the whole idea is dense with didactic perils; if one treats it as that literary maverick, a poet's novel, it comes off—a gay but angry tract for the times.

TURVEY AND THE CRITICS

EARLE BIRNEY

This summer I did some moonlighting as a nursing aide in the complicated midwifery occasioned by the rebirth of Private Thomas Turvey as hero of a musicale in Charlottetown's Confederation Theatre. In the course of these duties, sometimes baffling but always exhilarating, I mulled over a scrapbook of reviews of the original *Turvey, a military picaresque* (or "picturesque" as the *Monetary Times* had it). Although some of this material is now seventeen years old, it contains patterns of criticism which seem to me to have relevance still to the problems of the writer in Canada, and perhaps elsewhere. What follows is offered as delayed author's brooding on the judgments of these critics.

1. *Licence, poetic or critical*

Elsewhere[1] I have suggested that one of the peculiar and continuing bedevilments of the Canadian literary scene is a tendency for the poets and the prose fiction writers to exist, or to be expected to exist, in watertight compartments. Our professors of literature take it in their stride that many "foreign" poets, of significance at least in their day, from Boccaccio, through Sidney, Nashe, Samuel Johnson, Goldsmith, Poe, to Hardy, Kipling, de la Mare, e. e. cummings, Lawrence and Graves, also made genuine contributions to the development of prose fiction; but when a Canadian poet offers a plain prose novel, the Canadian critic is stopped in his tracks. At least it seemed so to me in the months following the appearance of *Turvey* in 1949:

"The kind of book . . . that one would not expect a well-known poet to write . . . lurid language . . . decidedly earthy" muttered a Winnipeg reviewer, who did not exactly approve of earth. A Vancouver columnist, hitherto one of my strongest fans, confessed himself mystified that "a distinguished poet . . . should write a 288-page book about a burlesque soldier . . . especially when it's obvious that barrack-room humour (or perhaps humour of any kind) is not his meat. I read it with vague embarrassment." Others, it's true, were more agreeably surprised, but sometimes their aston-

From *Canadian Literature*, 30 (1966), pages 21 to 25. By permission of Earle Birney.
[1] *The Creative Writer*, Toronto CBC Publications, 1966, ch. IV.

ishment revealed an assumption that poets are by definition humourless, dull, and unrealistic creatures inhabiting the non-significant and depressed areas of writing.

It's an image of the Canadian poet which undoubtedly persists, a product of the categorical naïveté of our critics, and of an emphasis upon outmoded romantic poetry by the educators who first formed our critics, and of a tendency in our poets themselves to accept such an image and remain unventuresome in the exploration of their own gifts as writers. Layton and Purdy live content in the valley that Carman and Pratt settled, MacLennan and Callaghan in the next. The critics, on Black Mountain, watch both ways against cattle raids.

Indeed I think the image persists even into that extremely generous and thoughtful and friendly preface to the most recent edition of *Turvey,* written by the editor of *Canadian Literature* himself.[2] For it's plain that my friend George Woodcock expects novels by "lifetime poets" to be "strange, outlandish" and never "massive or major". Such writers, he says, "don't worry about plausible psychology, . . . the consistency of timetables, . . . the authenticity of medical symptoms. . . . The fact they are poets seems to license any break into fantasy." While Mr. Woodcock cites many convincing examples of his thesis, from the roster of poets' novels, I do feel that, in the case of *Turvey,* he has let his preconceptions about "lifetime poets" license him into a critical fantasy. Within the limitations of a satirical picaresque, I certainly had to worry, like any novelist, about "plausible psychology" when I wrote *Turvey,* and a great deal about accuracy of time both in relation to the acts of the characters and to the parallel events of the war; and I have not yet encountered a doctor, out of the good many who have spoken or written to me about this book, who pointed out a single instance of inaccuracy in the handling of medical symptoms. This is no great boast on my part, since most of Turvey's misadventures in this respect happened first to me, and it did not put any great strain on my traumatic memories to pass them on to him.

I am simply arguing for a point which Canadian criticism of this book (and Canadian criticism only) still compels me to make, obvious as it ought to be: that a poet, particularly a "lifetime" one, should be conceivably able to write in any form current in his literary milieu, and *be expected* to perform in it as well, at least, as the next man. If he tries and seems to fail, the critic should perhaps

[2]George Woodcock: Introduction to *Turvey,* New Canadian Library, Toronto, McClelland & Stewart, 1963.

take a second and harder look at the poetry, but not offer an *argumentum ad poetam* about the prose.

2. *The Professor turned Novelist*

"A strange book to come from a professor of English", said the *London Free Press.* The same Vancouver critic who was embarrassed by a Canadian poet attempting a novel of barrack-room humour also "knew" the attempt was doomed from the start because it didn't "come from the level of the soldier . . . but from a highly literate, intelligent and polished professor of English." Here is another of our very Canadian critical shibboleths. I know, I know—I go about the country arguing that prolonged sojourn in Canadian universities, especially in English departments, sets monastic limits to a writer's experience, as well as turning his style to glue. The fact is, however, that most North American novelists who are now in their forties or fifties have taught English in universities. Consequently in the United States no one is surprised when a professor writes a novel, or prejudges it as untrue to experience, for if the professor has succeeded in treating "real" life with veracity, it may well be because he has lived for considerable periods in other groves than the academe, or indeed that he possesses an imagination particularly resistant to campus atrophy. In my case the world of the Canadian Active Army, in which I spent nearly four years of my life, at least kept me sufficiently on "the level of the soldier" to make what I wrote about it look accurate enough to pass unchallenged by the other old sweats (who have been, from the start, the chief readers and buyers of *Turvey*). On the other hand, the critics who found mine a "professor's book" have been, to my knowledge, precisely those who themselves had no personal experience of army life, and probably knew little of writer-professors either.

3. *If I had a daughter*

The alleged sexual revolution has undoubtedly put a more knowing look on the face of Canadian writing in the two decades since *Turvey* was written. It is unlikely that I would become involved today, as I was in 1948, in prolonged and tangled correspondence with my Toronto publisher in order to preserve one letter out of the four in some of the words my characters needed to use.

Let us not have illusions, however. The sale of books in the smaller centres (where most Canadians live) is still very much determined by the reaction of the lone local newspaper reviewer, or a single wire-service journalist. From the treatment recently handed out to books like Vizinczey's *In Praise of Older Women,* and Cohen's *Beautiful Losers,* I have no reason to think that the *Windsor Daily Star,* for example, would not again damn Turvey, surely a mild enough kitten among sex-cats even in his period, as "a rogue of the dirtiest water". And it might be that Malcolm Ross, if he were reviewing my book for "Critically Speaking" in 1966, would still feel compelled, as in 1949, even while praising the "tang and veracity" of its "spoken language . . . fresh to Canadian writing", to add that it was "too fresh for Canadian radio. I shall not risk quotation. The humour is entirely physical—even intestinal . . . successful so long as he avoids the demands of meaning and morality. Once these demands break in, vulgarity is merely vulgar . . ." etc. Fun is fun, but as another C.B.C. reviewer put it, in that not so far-off year: "I will go so far as to say that it is the funniest book written by a Canadian that I have read . . . yet whether I should want my daughter to read it . . . if I had a daughter . . . is another question." Those hypothetical daughters still languish in the homes of some critics and some broadcasting governors.

Nor should Canadians be under the illusion that the prudish reviewer really helps to increase a book's sales. The "shekels" did not "roll in", as the Toronto *Varsity* predicted, when *Turvey* was banned in 1949 by several Ontario libraries, and described in *Saturday Night* as exhibiting "a Rabelaisian reliance on the bodily functions and the Army's treatment of them". For the point which the critic (in this case Arnold Edinborough) made, was that the "Rabelaisian reliance" made much of the book "an unamusing affair". And when a reviewer tells you a novel is unamusing, he is influencing you not to buy it. It happened that *Turvey,* like many another "Rabelaisian" novel—I only wish it deserved the unintended compliment—eventually achieved a good though by no means spectacular sale in Canada, and continues to have a modest one, but all this has been in despite of the critical Grundies, not because of them. Even in its new form this summer as a musicale, *Turvey,* though it had better than average houses, never achieved the sell-out success of its companion offering, *Anne of Green Gables,* for the word went round in Prince Edward Island even before *Turvey* opened that the play's language was not at all like Anne's, indeed unlike anything suited for the ears of Island females. I've no doubt *Turvey* will survive the Puritan provincials, but I'm damned if this will be any reason for thanking them.

4. *Friend or enema?*

From my mail, and from word of mouth, over seventeen years, I know now who *Turvey*'s friends have been. And they are exactly those whom many early reviewers predicted would reject him. They are the ex-army medicos, psychologists and psychiatrists whom the *Montreal Gazette*'s reviewer predicted would be the most displeased. They are the rank and file who returned, and did not find, as did another critic, that the book was "a dismal synopsis of all the dreary conversations they had to listen to so many times in five years of war." They are the fellow Turveys, of both sexes, and all services and ranks (incuding one General), veterans of any war, hot or cold. They are Turvey's fellow clowns, who never twigged, as did the *Saskatoon Star-Phoenix,* that Turvey was merely "a stooge" through whom I vented untimely undergraduate sneers at a government that had done everything possible for the returned soldier. "Perhaps not so warmly applauded by soldiers as by critics of the Canadian literary scene", wrote a *Letters in Canada* critic in 1950. The reverse was true.

Now it is 1966 and the old veterans are dying off; but the new critics have come around, and *Turvey* is supplementary reading in some Can. Lit. courses. I would be inclined to accept this as Turvey's death-kiss if I hadn't been in Charlottetown this summer and watched a new generation of his friends teaching my old half-track to sing and dance, and confront fresh audiences and new critics. He is metamorphosed, but still my wartime *alter ego,* whom I tried to shape out of a need not only to laugh *at* the mechanical and the life-destroying, but to laugh *with* the incompetently human and the naturally loving and the obstinately life-preserving. Some "critics of the Canadian literary scene" have indeed given me credit for such motivation, and praise for *Turvey* beyond its deserts, but there there were not so many when I needed them most, and the steadiest heartening for me has always come from the other Turveys, scattered across this country, recognizing their kin in my novel and in me.

THE SATIRIC NOVEL IN CANADA TODAY: *DOWN THE LONG TABLE* (1955)

D. J. DOOLEY

In 1955 Birney published *Down the Long Table,* a novel sharing almost nothing with *Turvey* except satiric impulse. The rather inept title refers to the table used by a Congressional investigating committee; the hero is prodded into reviewing his past by an unnamed but identifiable Senator:

> Like a dentist. The new specialist, Extractor of Political Heresies . . . Guaranteed painful, fillings probed, old rot exposed.

The patient, Gordon Saunders, was at one time, "before the deadweight lid of the Thirties lifted at last and revealed the bubbling stew of a war brewing", a member of a Communist organization. Now he is shown as upholding personal integrity against the intellectual and moral conformity which the committee attempts to enforce. His past actions are not so much defended as excused; emphasis is placed on his ludicrous failure as an organizer for a moribund Trotskyist group, and on his naïveté his youthful romanticism, his quixotism. But it is hard to accept Gordon as a Quixote. He tilts at windmills out of perversity rather than idealism. His first Dulcinea is another man's wife, and her death through an attempted abortion a testimony to his irresponsibility. In penance, he becomes still more irresponsible: he has an "anguished conviction that he could atone for his manifold crimes . . . only by . . . whirling, to the end of his strength, in the wildest dance that would have him." His joining of a Communist organization is linked with his pursuit of a second Dulcinea, a fanatical Marxist with a petty bourgeois mind and a childlike attachment to her mother's apron strings; in becoming a "convert to Thelmaism" Gordon is anything but a self-respecting human being. So there is a hollow ring to his assertion that judgment on him can come only from his "inconsistent but inviolate self". We expect apology; we get self-mockery. In fact, we come to suspect that the author is trying to gloss over his hero's moral failures, and that he is depending on his reader's antipathy to McCarthyism to secure sympathy for a character who does not deserve it.

From "The Satiric Novel in Canada Today: A Failure Too Frequent?" by D. J. Dooley, *Queen's Quarterly,* 64 (1958), pages 584-585. By permission of D. J. Dooley.

Nevertheless, the book presents a vivid and accurate picture of some aspect of Canadian life in the Thirties, and for this it deserves more praise than most reviewers have given it. Birney employs newspaper headlines and items in the Dos Passos manner to catch the spirit of the times; often there is an ironic contrast between the view of world conditions expressed in the newspapers and the actuality. "PRICE RISE BRINGING BACK PROSPERITY SAYS RAMSAY MACDONALD"— time mocks this prediction, made in 1932, as it mocks Charles Schwab's statement that "The very slackness of the recent months is piling up an opportunity for work for the coming year." In the course of his experiences, Gordon Saunders is expelled from the Social Problems Club of the University of Toronto as a "capitalist spy" and an "agent of counter-revolutionary Trotskyism", and he witnesses the demise of the Vancouver Branch of the Canadian Section of the Communist League of North America of the International Left Opposition (Bolshevik-Leninists) of the Third International. In between he has got from one city to the other by riding the rods, he has joined the thousands clogging Victory Square in Vancouver—"a dump of human litter, one of the myriad impromptu disposal heaps for a civilization mired in its own waste", and he has taken part in a Red raid on a symbol of society's callous treatment of the unemployed, a relief office. All this is described in realistic terms; but there is a good deal of satire running through it. There is satire of Communist demonstrations on behalf of the jobless, which the jobless have come to recognize as only for the Party's good, not theirs. There is satire of left-wing splinter groups, small handfuls of men firmly convinced that their efforts are bringing revolution near, their numbers dwindling as their leaders find jobs and make peace with the capitalist system. And there is irony in Gordon's story throughout, in his misinterpretations of situations and events, his feeble efforts to help, and his eventual rejection by all his revolutionary friends as a "summer-time" rebel.

A REVIEW OF *DOWN THE LONG TABLE*

ARNOLD EDINBOROUGH

Down the Long Table by Earle Birney . . . has a somewhat creaky framework. Although the novel is concerned with the activities of a young Trotskyite in the depression years, it is brought up to date, as it were, by these activities being under investigation by a Congressional Committee. It is down the long table towards the congressional investigator that the central character, Gordon Saunders, looks.

In a way this topicality is unfortunate, since the atmosphere of persecution in American universities has cleared up a great deal since the vote of censure against Senator McCarthy last year.

Not only the framework, but the technique of the novel is a little old-fashioned, too, despite the publisher's blurb, which claims that Mr. Birney "has delineated the character and career of Gordon Saunders with a series of highly varied structural techniques—techniques which are not only intriguing but a landmark in the art of fiction."

These techniques are nothing of the kind. The first device is that of prefacing the chapters with supposed headlines and news stories from newspapers, a device used by John Dos Passos years ago. The second one is to put occasional chapters into dramatic dialogue, and has been used in any number of novels since James Joyce's *Ulysses* was first published. The third one, also a device from *Ulysses,* is the trick of repeating literary quotations as a sort of *leit motif* of each major character or situation.

Having said this, though, we have by no means demolished Earle Birney's novel but merely the unlettered enthusiasm of his publisher's blurb writer. As anyone who remembers *Turvey* well knows, Mr. Birney's great gift is the invention of peculiarly distinctive dialogue. In fact, his characters are created almost entirely by their speech, and are sufficiently differentiated by their choice of words and by their distinctive pronunciation.

Mr. Birney here collects together a group of individuals which it would be hard to match. There is the ponderous Toronto mother, who injects a note of honest horse sense into the Trotskyite intellectualism of the group which meets with her son and daughter. The

From the Kingston Ontario *Whig-Standard,* 17 December 1955, page 10. By permission of the *Whig-Standard.*

daughter, whose intellectual pretensions are not matched by her intellectual or emotional development, is delineated by two letters which are gems of parody. There is a Welsh labour leader, there is a Swede, there is an Irishman, there is a Scotsman. There are varying degrees of Toronto dialect brought on by environment and education. All these we richly enjoy, and these do, in fact, add a new technique to novel writing in this country.

The picture of conditions during the thirties is clear-cut, but there seems to be too little real connection between the Congressional inquiry into the present status of George Saunders, and his performance as a Trotskyite organizer in his post-graduate days. Mr. Birney does not seem to have decided whether he is writing about the thirties or whether he is writing about the fifties.

Nevertheless, this book needs to be read for its ideas and its dialogue. Despite the tricks of the American realist novel, the general impression is of a book in the tradition of Aldous Huxley. Like Huxley, Mr. Birney is an extremely intelligent man, and his gift for satire is highly developed. It is a pity that he didn't allow this gift more scope.

EARLE BIRNEY: *DOWN THE LONG TABLE*

GEORGE WOODCOCK

Down the Long Table is a novel of memory, projected from the silent Fifties into the troubled Thirties. The basic structure is Proustian; Professor Gordon Saunders, a Canadian teaching in the United States, is brought before a Committee investigating Communist affiliations. Before him at the long table he sees a face from the past, that of an ex-Communist turned informer, and this provokes the chain of memories which forms the substance of the book. Gordon remembers the fatal interconnection between personal relationships and political actions, weaving into a rope that shifts his sentimental idealism into militancy, takes him in and rapidly out of the Communist party, and culminates in a brief, violent and disillusioning period as the would-be organizer of a Trotskyist movement among the unemployed and skidroad derelicts of Vancouver.

The greatest merit of *Down the Long Table* is the vividness with which the spirit and even the physical feel of the Thirties are re-created. It is when one considers the book as more than an evocative document that its defects become evident. There is an unassimilable implausibility about Professor Saunders sitting at the long table and, in that instant of time which is undoubtedly all the inquisiting senators would allow him, plunging into almost three hundred pages of chronologically sequential recollection, interrupted, not by the impinging voices of the present, but by chapter-dividing extracts from contemporary newspapers, which enhance the documentary verisimilitude, but which in fictional terms are out of pitch with the essentially romantic tone of the rest of the novel, with its dark but poetic vision of what happens to ideals when they must find expression through human beings twisted and battered by existence. *Turvey* has a wholly convincing comic unity; *Down the Long Table* is divided by the conflict bebetween the historical impulse to reconstruct authentically time past, and the fictional impulse to establish a self-consistent imaginary world.

From *Contemporary Novelists* edited by James Vinson; New York: St. Martin's Press, 1972, pages 125-126. By permission of St. Martin's Press, Inc., St. James Press.

3. ONE WORLD: *POETRY, 1949–1965*

TWO REVIEWS OF *TRIAL OF A CITY AND OTHER VERSE* (1952)

❦ NORTHROP FRYE

This year both of Canada's two leading poets have a new book to be discussed, and as one of them comes from Newfoundland and the other from British Columbia, there was never a neater opportunity of demonstrating the theory of cultural containment. I am inclined in any case to assert the existence of a Canadianism in Canadian poetry. Poets do not live on Mount Parnassus, but in their own environments, and Canada has made itself an environmental reality.

The United States is a symmetrical country: it presents a straight Atlantic coastline, and its culture was, up to about 1900, a culture of the Atlantic seaboard, with a north-south frontier that moved westward until it reached the Pacific. Canada has almost no Atlantic seaboard, and a ship coming here from Europe moves like a tiny Jonah entering an enormous whale into the Gulf of St Lawrence, where it is surrounded by five Canadian provinces, all out of sight, and then drifts up a vast waterway that reaches back past Edmonton. There would be nothing distinctive in Canadian culture at all if there were not some feeling for the immense searching distance, with the lines of communication extended to the absolute limit, which is a primary geographical fact about Canada and has no real counterpart elsewhere. The best painting of Thomson and the Group of Seven have a horizon-focussed perspective, with a line of water or a break through the hills curving into the remotest background. In Emily Carr, too, the real focus of vision seems to be in the depth of the forest, *behind* the picture as it were. The same feeling for strained distance is in many Canadian poets and novelists—certainly in Grove—and it can hardly be an accident that the two most important Canadian thinkers to date, Edward Sapir and Harold Innis, have both been largely concerned with problems of communication.

....

From "Letters in Canada, 1952," *University of Toronto Quarterly*, 22 (1953), pages 269-270, 273-275. By permission of *University of Toronto Quarterly*.

What else is "distinctively Canadian"? Well, historically, a Canadian is an American who rejects the Revolution. Canada fought its civil war to establish its union first, and its wars of independence, which were fought against the United States and not Europe, came later. We should expect in Canada, therefore, a strong suspicion, not of the United States itself, but of the mercantilist Whiggery which won the Revolution and proceeded to squander the resources of a continent, being now engaged in squandering ours. There is in Canada, too, a traditional opposition to the two defects to which a revolutionary tradition is liable, a contempt for history and an impatience with law. The Canadian point of view is at once more conservative and more radical than Whiggery, closer both to aristocracy and to democracy than to oligarchy.

The title poem of Earle Birney's *Trial of a City and Other Verse* is described in its subtitle as "A Public Hearing into the Proposed Damnation of Vancouver." The time is the future, the setting the kind of pseudo-legal kangaroo court which is the main instrument of McCarthyism, as packed and framed as a shipment of pictures, where everything is conducted on the crazy Alice-in-Wonderland principle of sentence first, verdict afterwards. The blowing up of Vancouver has already been decided upon by a mysterious "office of the future," represented by a lawyer named Gabriel Powers. As his name indicates, the setting has for its larger background the ancient theme of wrath and mercy, of man's perpetual failure to justify his existence in the sight of the gods by his merits, a failure now brought to a crisis by his new techniques of self-destruction. Powers, therefore, who seems to be a messenger of the gods, is actually a projection of man's own death-wish.

The only one to speak for the defence is a Mr Legion, who represents the ordinary Vancouver citizen. He has, understandably, a strong prejudice against being annihilated, but it proves more difficult than he expected to refute the case of the prosecution. The city seems to Captain Vancouver only the pollution of the virginal nature he remembers. To an Indian chief, who speaks for what is essentially an aristocratic point of view, the white man's city is an obscene disease that has devoured his own people. To Gassy Jack, a sailor and saloon-keeper of the early days, it represents a perversion of life far more sinister than his own relatively healthy vulgarity and vice. Finally William Langland, author of *Piers Plowman,* appears: in all English culture no better spokesman could have been found for the conservative-radical opposition to oligarchy mentioned above. He finds in Vancouver more or less what he found in mediæval London: a society based on profiteering, or what he personified as Lady Meed.

The trouble with Legion is that he does not speak for the real Vancouver, but for the mercantilist Whiggery that has taken it over. His values and standards are precisely what is being condemned. He is the present as the inevitable consequence of the past, hence a future of annihilation is the inevitable consequence of *him*. At the crisis of the argument, he is suddenly pushed out of the way by a housewife. She stands for the real life of really free people, where the present is, at every moment, a new creation of meaning, of wonder, and of love. In such a conception of the present there is no casuality, no inevitable future, no dead reckonings, and as she speaks the court begins to dissolve into unreality, even the imperious "Powers" being reduced to saying only "I'll have the skeleton."

I have emphasized the unity and seriousness of the theme because the brilliance of the writing may mislead one into regarding it only as a verbal stunt. It is true that for virtuosity of language there has never been anything like it in Canadian poetry. Gabriel Powers speaks in a *Finnegans Wake* doubletalk which, like *Finnegans Wake,* is both very funny and eerily haunting:

> From the ash of the fir springs the fire-weed;
> From the [ash] of his faring your fear.

A professor of geology speaks in the archaic rhythms of Anglo-Saxon, and Legion in what the Germans call *knittelvers.* Langland's speech is, of course, a reproduction of Langland: such phrases as "an ego to an auto" may be a trifle too sophisticated for him, but

> Yea, then I moved west to my hill's margin
> and saw a soft middleclass swaddled in trees,
> in unfrequented churches and fears not a few.

has exactly the right balance between parody and recreation. The play's wit puts it in the same league as E. E. Cummings and Auden; and as compared with Auden, it seems to me to have attained a crystalline transparency of thought. I imagine that the lines of the housewife:

> By all the past we know our freedom is renewable each moment

or

> How could I know, without the threat of death, I lived?

would in Auden be sagging with the weight of Heidegger's *Augenblick* and Kierkegaard's *Angst*. Birney's seriousness is simple (to the verge, on the last page, of being sentimental); it is only his wit that is erudite.

Wit is also prominent in the other poems in the book: it is in a poem about Christmas which describes how a star appeared as a *"nova* in *Virgo"*; in satires on censorship, on signs reading "restricted," on an ill-fated Mr Chubb of Minnesota, and in an account of a plane trip across Canada where, in spite of some excellent passages, some of the boredom of the trip seems to have leaked into the poem. The other poems are largely concerned with the immense trees and sinister mountains of British Columbia landscape, whose moods the poet knows well how to convey. A few gingerbread conceits ("the pacifist firs," "revolver sun," "the pointless point of the peak") are unfunctional, but do not spoil them. There is also a cryptic but very attractive exercise in myth, "St Valentine Is Past."

❧ SIMON PAYNTER

The Minister of History presides over a public hearing into the Office of the Future's proposal for the damnation of Vancouver. Mr. Legion, counsel for the Metropolis, calls as his first witness Captain Vancouver, who declines to give the desired support of the city:

> "Tis big as my old London, and as dun.
> As planless, not so plaguey, but less fun.
> I rather like the sweep of fir and cedar.
> Your city, sir—I can't think why I'd need her."

The next witness is the Salish headman contemporary with Captain Vancouver; he speaks in solemn verse of the life of his people and their doom:

> "There was something, I do not know,
> a way of life that died for yours to live."

Next, a professor recounts the geological past and probable cosmic future of the district; the object of his testimony is not much more obvious than is the relevance of the Anglo-Saxon verse form in

From *Canadian Forum*, 33 (1953), page 91. By permission of *Canadian Forum*.

which he gives it. Gassy Jack of Gastown is introduced to make the obvious contrast and supply the obvious comedy. Then, oddly but most effectively, comes William Langland to give an impression of the city in the manner of *Piers Plowman:*

> "Squared it lay, squamous with shingle and cement,
> Straitly ruled by steel, by stark wire and stucco.
> South walked a hoary wood-waste of houses
> Massing to the river like lemmings on the march,
> Jerry-new cottages jostling jowl by jowl
> (Except to skirt green fields golfers locked away)
> Down to the fouled and profit-clogged Fraser,
> The pile-impaled river plotting its flood."

Finally, an uninvited witness, Mrs. Anyone, breaks in, exorcises the brash chamber-of-commerce Mr. Legion, and takes over the defence herself; affirming, against the puritan destructiveness of Langland and the Leviathan represented by Mr. Powers, the opposing counsel, the power of beauty, humanity and love:

> "It's my defiant fear keeps green my whirling world."

Dr. Birney's radio play has passages of wit, power, and beauty in plenty, and in its broadcast production, though the performance was imperfect, these were dominant. To the reader, unfortunately, the play betrays defects, inconsistencies, and an uncertainty of direction that weaken its satirical force. What is being satirized is generally clear enough, but through most of the work the positive standard necessary to the effectiveness of satire is represented only by the old British-Columbian standby of landscape and nature. Mrs. Anyone does in the end redress the balance, but she is something of a *dea ex machina;* for 41 of the 47 pages the positive element has been absent and the damage has been done. The effectiveness of the play has suffered still more from the author's weakness for verbal exuberance. For the sake of an immediate verbal effect he will throw a character out of focus, as when the crass Mr. Legion says to the Indian

> "O come you always needed us; we had the know-how
> Without the white, the Indian was a lowbrow"

—"lowbrow" being precisely the wrong word, introduced only to make an amusing assonance. Much worse is the Joyce-cum-Fry doubletalk of Mr. Powers, who never misses a chance to distort a word:

> "Like every think of booty,
> Sir, it's copulated to destriction;
> Its lifeliness decreases and must ever
> pass into nothingmist."

I chose this as one of his more lucid passages. When Christopher Fry does this kind of thing, the effect is usually to clarify, not to puzzle; and he does it comparatively rarely. Dr. Birney bombards us with it throughout the play without apparent regard to meaning or relevance. One is tempted to say that The Crazy's Not For Birney.

The book is filled out by a small number of recent short poems ranging from the slight to the excellent ("North Star West" is very fine indeed). But there is, one fears, nothing in the book that will rank among the major creations of one of our finest poetic minds.

It may seem churlish to cavil at a publisher that has done so much for poetry, so disinterestedly, as has the Ryerson Press, but this reviewer's flesh creeps (and so, surely, must the poet's) at the note on the verso of the title-page in which the publisher assures us that in the Indian headman's claim to have descendants among the leaders of Vancouver who do not know or are ashamed of it, "no reference is intended to any actual person, living or dead." Finally, one is startled to find on the front flap of the jacket the author's first name misspelled, and on the back flap, in bold italic capitals of the title of his best book given incorrectly.

EARLE BIRNEY: POET

W. E. FREDEMAN

The eve of publication of the *Selected Poems* of Earle Birney[1] offers a convenient opportunity for re-evaluating the poetic output of one of British Columbia's—indeed, one of Canada's—best known and most highly praised literary figures. Coming rather late to a literary career—after an apprenticeship of hack work, graduate study, odd jobs, and miscellaneous teaching, at the Universities of California, Utah, Toronto, and British Columbia—Birney, at the age of thirty-eight, was suddenly catapulted to national recognition with the publication of *David and Other Poems* in 1942. The combined forces of a variegated background, a decade of depression, and the gathering storm of World War II proved precisely the alembic to stir the poetic sensitivities of the young academic. With the attainment, for the first time, of something resembling stability and security—his doctorate, a lectureship at the University of Toronto, and, most important, the literary editorship of *Canadian Forum*—Birney began to publish his first serious poems in the late thirties.

The intervening twenty years have been fruitful for Earle Birney, bringing him increased recognition in the form of critical praise and literary awards, and the more tangible benefits of grants-in-aid and scholarships. They have also been productive: four volumes of verse, two novels, one anthology, another editorship (*Canadian Poetry Magazine,* 1946-48) and a welter of miscellaniana. Since 1946, Birney has been a Professor of English at the University of British Columbia.

Now, Birney is preparing to launch an edition of his poems, selected, revised and edited by himself. Although authors' selections are always risky, they do give the critic an advantage that he ordinarily lacks, because, more than individual volumes, they stand as manifestoes of artistic creed, enabling the critic to assume a synthesis not always apparent in single publications. This is particularly true in Birney's case, since his previous four volumes of poetry, with the exception of *Trial of a City,* have been cumulative, each adding new poems to a foundation of previously pub-

---

From the *British Columbia Library Quarterly,* 23 (1960), pages 8-15. By permission of the *British Columbia Library Quarterly.*

[1] To be published later this year by McClelland & Stewart in Toronto, and by Abelard-Schuman in London and New York. [This collection was not published.—Ed.]

lished and tested verse. However, the forthcoming edition, comprising some fifty-five poems and his verse play (roughly one-half of Birney's total poetry) will, in a way, be patterned from his previous publications, since, in addition to the forty-five poems drawn from earlier volumes, it will contain ten poems either previously unpublished or previously uncollected. The selections—and rejections—together with the often severe revisions of earlier "established" verse will prove most vital to Birney's critical reputation. However, the most salient fact about the appearance of the volume is that it heralds a new period of creativity, terminating eight years of silence in what seems to have been, for various reasons, a period of poetic sterility.

As a combination of the depression, the impending war, and his own wide background provided Birney with the necessary impetus for writing, so they, together with the left wing political idealism that made of him during the thirties an ardent Trotskyite, provided him with his basic themes. Birney's poems fall into five categories: descriptions of nature, satires, those dealing with war—either imminent or actual—love poems, and those built on narrative or dramatic situations involving one or more of the other four. Thematically, however, they overlap without clear lines of distinction; always they are autobiographical and extremely personal.[2]

[2]Desmond Pacey, in the most recent critical evaluation of Birney (*Ten Canadian Poets,* Toronto, Ryerson, 1958, pp. 293-326), misses the point. Fond of labels, he tags Birney "chronicler". "As applied to a poet," Pacey explains, "the label of chronicler implies that he is primarily a public rather than a private poet, that he seeks to be objective rather than subjective, that he is concerned with the fate of society rather than with the state of his own soul" (p. 294). This rather casual lumping together of the material, the point of view, and the motivation or intention of the poem forms a specious generalization which fails to bear out the definition it seeks to make. One wonders, initially, what a "public poet" might be: Tennyson in his laureate poems might qualify at one extreme; Eddie Guest at the other. Certainly a "social" poet (which seems to be what Mr. Pacey means) need not be "public". As to objectivity, one need only examine "David", "Man is a Snow", "Introvert", "This Page My Pigeon", and "Canada: Case History", five quite distinct types in the Birney canon, to recognize immediately the extremely private nature of the poems and the highly subjective experiences, both actual and psychological, which they describe. Finally, the sense of involvement in society and the case made in the poems for individual responsibility in the ultimate fate of society and mankind is more personal, if not more introverted, than most "my heart is a singing-bird" poetry. "Chronicler", as Mr. Pacey defines it, seems incorrect as applied to Birney; in its more usual sense (and Mr. Pacey belabours the superficial fact that Birney's poems are often topical and focused on the Canadian scene) it is an oversimplification.

In labelling Birney "chronicler", it may be that the critic was greatly influenced by Birney's two novels, *Turvey* (Toronto, McClelland & Stewart,

The central theme in almost all of Birney's poetry is Love, and the most dominant symbol, as well as the controlling image, War. Reiterated throughout the major portion of his poetry, these dichotomous extremes of human impulse mirror the ironic and ambiguous role of man in a universe over which he is never quite master, even in his greatest moments of triumph, and of which, even in his most miserable failures, he is never quite pawn. Caught up in the Puritanical dilemma of sin and responsibility, mankind has at its disposal only Universal Love to combat the atavism inherent both in nature and in humanity itself. Birney's message, following consistently a recurring pattern of idealized optimism and hope, fear, and idealized disillusionment and pessimism, might be succinctly phrased in Auden's similar admonition: "We must love one another or die." As Birney himself puts it in "Time-Bomb":

>O men be swift to be mankind
>or let the grizzly take.

The simplicity of Birney's dominant and persistent theme is intensified and made doubly poignant by the present forces which threaten mankind. War having become nearly obsolete, self-preservation must give way to the higher course of universal love, for man is faced not only with the destruction of his individual self but with the possible annihilation of his species as well.

Birney's poetry is obviously didactic, but rarely in the pejorative sense, for it seldom preaches. A personal involvement in mankind's dilemma, and in the inevitable seeking for solution, pervents the poet's offering patented panaceas for mankind's (and therefore his own) ills; rather, he extends a prophetic hope that tomorrow—if, remembering yesterday, we, living today, are willing to prepare for the future—*may* be better:[3]

1949) and *Down the Long Table* (Toronto, McClelland & Stewart, 1955), the former a humourous parody of the war experiences of the Canadian counterpart to Private Hargrove, the latter a rather abortive chronicle of Canada in the period of the great depression. The novels depend, both in narrative and in thematic structure, on the contextual details of the Canadian scene during the depression and the war, and thereby tend to be much more documentary than his poetry, in which the environment is often no more than an imagistic springboard for the emotions and ideas conveyed by the poem. In his novels, Birney seems everything that he is *not* in his poetry: chronicler, extremely nationalistic, self-conscious. The meeting ground between the two creative roles seems to exist solely in the intensely autobiographical nature of both.

[3]The element of Time must never be lost sight of in Birney's poetry. Apart from its thematic importance in individual poems, it was used as the structural division in *Now Is Time*. For its application in "Trial of a City", see below.

> Somehow, still, we may blow straight,
> come flowing into the couloir's caves,
> funnelling into the gullies, battering
> the bright rock with the hail of our will.
> O we may yet roar free, unwhirl,
> sweeping great waves into the deepening bores,
> bringing the ocean to boom and fountain and siren,
> tumbling the fearful clouds into a great sky wallowing,
> cracking the mountain apart—
> the great wind of humanity blowing free, blowing
> through, streaming over the future.[4]

It is the breadth of the solution offered by the poet—a broad humanism positing individual involvement and responsibility combined with an insistence on the absolute autonomy of the human will, expressed with masculine forcefulness in both imagery and diction—that protects Birney from the snare of sentimental didacticism:

> The compassed mind must quiver north
> > though every chart defective;
> there is no fog but in the will,
> > the iceberg is elective.[5]

Desmond Pacey is undoubtedly right when he says that Birney's greatest strength as a poet lies in his "capacity movingly and convincingly to express a persistent faith in man's power to make or unmake his own destiny".[6]

In Birney's case the question of evaluation is difficult. Although never a poetaster, he has been unable to sustain a quality throughout any of his four volumes.[7] However, each contains poems of exceptional ability.[8] "David" is regarded by most critics as Bir-

---

[4] ". . . or a Wind", sequel to "Man is a Snow".
[5] "World Conference". Retitled "Conference of Heads" in the forthcoming edition.
[6] *Op. cit.*, p. 309.
[7] Many of the poems discussed below have been either thoroughly revised or omitted in the forthcoming edition.
[8] I do not intend to discuss Birney as a "Canadian" poet. As a qualification expressing anything other than nationality, it seems to me to have no critical validity, although it has become increasingly an apologetic epithet among critics too often saddled with what they consider inferior verse. Many critics tend to confuse "regionalisms" with nationalistic tendencies, belabouring the obvious fact that a poet will incorporate into his verse the environment— natural, political, psychological—with which he is most familiar. But a good poem is a good poem, quite independent of national origin. The impulse and experience of "Tintern Abbey" would have been equally exciting, irrespective of Wordsworth's nationality. It may be that Birney has won more fame in Canadian letters than he might have realized in a more competitive intellectual climate, but certainly he would be regarded as a serious poet in any country.

ney's finest poem, by many as a masterpiece in its own right. In "David" the close caps perfectly a series of near climaxes, and in the final line—"That day, the last of my youth, on the last of our mountains"—there is truly magic, as E. K. Brown saw: "an unpredictable extension of meaning, . . . at one stroke raising the experience of the poem to another level where pain and constraint and self-reproach are no longer matter-of-fact but full of tranquillizing imaginative suggestion."[9] So often in Birney's poetry the greatness of an individual line or lines completely overshadows the poem as a whole. In "David" this is not true; the climactic close reinforces and enriches all that precedes it. In lesser poems, however, it has a weakening effect, especially when it occurs at the beginning, as in "Man is a Snow":

> I tell you the wilderness we fell
> is nothing to the one we breed.

When its position climaxes a generally poor poem, as in "Within These Caverned Days", it becomes merely a facile device that hardly compensates for the lack of quality throughout the poem.[10] Generally speaking, Birney's forte is the succinct, elliptical, highly compressed, tightly woven poem in which unity can be sustained without affectation or artificiality. To this category belong such poems as "Introvert" (in many ways one of his finest poems), "Time-Bomb", "Gulf of Georgia", "Slug in Woods", "From the Hazel Bough", and "Ulysses", a kind of sixteen-line Meredithian sonnet, concluding with the synthesizing couplet:

> but the bow is yours and you must bend it
> or you'll never finish what Homer began.

In the same way, "Hands", somewhat longer than the other poems cited, demonstrates Birney's remarkable facility for tightening and unifying the poem by the use of the epigrammatic couplet:

> We are not of these woods, we are not of these woods,
> our roots are in autumn, and store for no spring.

Birney's weakest poems are those which are purely topical expressions of passing or changing social conditions, such as "For

---

[9]*On Canadian Poetry,* Toronto, Ryerson, 1943, p. 77-78.
[10]Many of these weaknesses are recognized by Birney himself. The above couplet has been deleted in the revision of "Man is a Snow" and the entire poem has been substantially rewritten. The loss of the couplet, one of his best, is unfortunate, but the poem is greatly improved. "Within These Caverned Days" has been excluded from the volume.

Steve", "Joe Harris", and "Man on a Tractor".[11] Many of the war poems, inspired by temporary conditions, seem cold and remote when compared with "Hands" and the paired poems "Dusk on the Bay" and "Vancouver Lights", in which Birney is seeking not to record realistically the conditions of the moment but to get behind the human condition in a world in which man is threatened by forces against which he has no protection save the robes of his own mutual humanity. Birney's satirical poems, most of which are topical, fail for the same reasons. Occasionally successful, as in "Canada: Case History" and "Anglosaxon Street", they are too frequently marred by self-consciousness, flippancy, and artificiality. Poems such as "Ballad of Mr. Chubb", "The Monarch of the Id", "Christmas Comes"—even "Restricted Area", Birney's trenchant satire on anti-Semitism—fail because of their obvious embarrassment to the poet, who, throughout, is making a nervous attempt at objectivity. It is the failure of the satire that makes *Trial of a City and Other Verse* Birney's weakest volume, despite the near-brilliancy of the verse play which gives the book its title.

"Trial of a City" should not be lightly dismissed by anyone interested in understanding Birney's work. In many ways it was the culmination of all that he had written between 1937 and 1952, for obviously on trial is not only Vancouver but civilization itself and all the accomplishments of mankind. In this sense, it is one of the most universal pieces that Birney has written. In the play the present has been doomed by the future, and an inquiry has been called at which only witnesses from the past may offer testimony. The counsel for the present, an insensitive everyman named Legion, is singularly unaware of any of the important issues with which mankind has for centuries been involved; rather he is a devoted Pangloss of the present, hymning, and understanding only, the materialistic side of man's endeavours:

> We're the hub of Tomorrow, the Future's baby,
> We're here to stay, and I dont mean maybe.

and peremptorily dismissing any criticism of his materialistic values. Against his opponent from the future, Gabriel Powers, Legion's arguments "defending civilization" are totally ineffectual, and one recognizes in his condemnation of the Snow-kwee

---

[11]Confirming the severe critical light in which Birney has recently re-examined his poetry, all of the topical poems mentioned in this paragraph have been omitted from the forthcoming edition. Those few examples of topical poetry which have been allowed to remain have been brought up to date by revision.

Salish—that "These fellows never learned defence because they'd nothing to defend"—both his own and society's *damnatur*.

In the end, Powers is outstripped, not by Legion but by a Mrs. Anyone, an unghostly citizen of the world who refuses to stand witness for Legion's picture of civilization. Bearing vociferous testimony to the humanity which she truly symbolizes, she dispels Legion and asserts the positive values of mankind. To Powers' indictment, "But what is peace if all the earth's a gassy Jacktown?" she replies, "It still has its becoming." "How could I know," she asks, "without the threat of death, I lived?" The end of the play restores the time-sequence that Birney has so often insisted upon in his poetry: the present, growing out of the past, determines the future. In that sequence, which Legion's complacent acceptance of the present denied, lies the hope of mankind. "The only future's what I make each hour," Mrs. Anyone tells Powers:

> Without my longer Will, my stubborn boon,
> You'd have no mate to check with but the cornered moon.
> It's my defiant fear keeps green my whirling world.

So completely does this play summarize thematically the whole of Birney's poetry, he has chosen it to conclude his forthcoming volume.

It is never an easy task to arrest the creative process temporarily and evaluate a living, producing poet; to predict the consideration which the future may offer a contemporary is fatuous. This is particularly true in Birney's case, since he is first of all a verse experimentalist who almost always stimulates opposite reactions in different critics. Birney's chief poetic flaw lies in a strong academic tendency which leads, on the one hand, to the experimental transfer of archaic meter and diction to such poems as "Anglosaxon Street" and "Mappemounde" and the introduction of Long Will of Langland to "Trial of a City", and on the other, to a complexity of diction and an elliptical succinctness that makes his poetry, superficially at least, obscure. The principal quality of Birney's poetry is undoubtedly its sharp pictorial imagery, abetted by a sensitive and acute feeling for both the sound and the meaning of words.

E. K. Brown once commented on the "authentic originality" of Birney's poetry:

> ... he owes nothing at all to earlier Canadian writing and scarcely anything—when he is fully himself—to recent verse anywhere else. He has a harsh and intense sensibility which makes his pic-

tures and rhythms fresh and living, and his technical accomplishment is brilliant, at times bewildering.[12]

Another critic, W. P. Percival,[13] has spoken of Birney as "poetically athletic" and noted the sharpness of the impact made by his verse. Desmond Pacey has felt in Birney's poetry a "reserve power",[14] and has seen in it "a useful synthesis of all the major tendencies up to his time."[15] Contradictory as these judgments are —covering a span of years from 1943 to 1958—they testify to the essential fluidity of critical opinion that must always exist in evaluating the work of any contemporary.

[12] *Op. cit.,* p. 78.
[13] "Earle Birney", in *Leading Canadian Poets,* ed. W. P. Percival, Toronto, Ryerson, 1948, pp. 23-29.
[14] *Creative Writing in Canada,* Toronto, Ryerson, 1952, p. 141.
[15] *Ten Canadian Poets,* p. 326.

THE WRITING OF A POEM: COMPULSION AND SUPPRESSION

EARLE BIRNEY

One day I was taking a shower in the University of British Columbia gym after a swim in the pool. In the next cubicle two other professors were showering too. They were shouting because of the noise of the water, and their conversation carried to me. They were talking about whether it would be a good idea to buy cabins up in the Rockies and start stocking them in case of atomic war. That night I kept thinking about these two men. They looked so flabby and white and over-civilized, even naked, they talked with such ignorance about conditions of life in a cut-off mountain cabin, that I couldn't imagine them surviving even for a night. I began thinking what I'd have said to them, if they'd asked my advice, which they hadn't. How to tell them what life alone, high in the mountains, is like, even without a war. After all, I was brought up in the Rockies.

So I began the poem. I thought it was going to be a satire. The first draft started: "O professor, letting the gym shower fall on the white cocoon of your paunch, shouting unspectacled out of the steam . . . " I soon scrapped that. It was flip, too much on the outside. As usual in starting a poem, I was having to learn the hard way how I didn't want to write it, by trial and error, draft and redraft. In my second attempt I put myself back in the scene, listening to these two smug codgers, but building their conversation my own way, changing it—but why? Because there was some far deeper emotion I wanted to get at than satiric amusement with them; memories of the reality of what they were so ignorantly talking about began flooding in on me. So there were three voices now in the poem:

"First Prof: Hell, Bill, this fall-out stuff's been over-played. They only need a small bomb to pick off Vancouver. And they won't waste even stump-powder on the rest of B.C.

Second Prof: Yeah, maybe so, Fred, but how can you *live* way up there, with a family and all? It's damn lonely, I'm telling you. We had a cabin up on Mystic Lake last summer. One month was enough.

Third Prof: (that is, Me—muttering to myself as the other two

From *The Creative Writer* by Earle Birney (Toronto: Canadian Broadcasting Corporation, 1966), pp. 29-33. By permission of Earle Birney.

shout over the shower-partitions to each other): Mystic Lake, where I once camped. The Indians say it holds all broken rainbows.

First Prof: Live? Why you'd build a *big* cabin, stock it with canned goods, guns, fishing gear, cards, radio, books. There'd be lots of fish, eh?

Second Prof: (The noise of the shower is drowning out his friend's voice) Mist? Only in the early morning.

First Prof: Not *mist,* FISH!

Second Prof: Oh, yeah, you can get cutthroat, but you'd have to build a raft. The ospreys get most of them; they been fishing longer.

Me: The mists fell each night like dreams and faded in the dawning. And each day was the blue high humming of my youth.

First Prof: Is there *game* there?

Second Prof: What? DAMES! O, Game. Well it's too high for deer. Lots of porcupines—they say the belly is good roasted. We brought in cans.

Me: Once when I was a kid I stroked my hat over a porky and had quills to trade at school and wear in my Stetson.

First Prof: Nuts! What about sheep and goats?

Second Prof: Yeah, but it's a park, you know—game wardens.

First Prof: Man, they wouldn't be worrying about us once the bombs started dropping. And what about bear?

Second Prof: Hare?

First Prof: *Bear, Bear!*

Me: The wild goats, like statues high on the ridges of that mountain so big it slowed my mind to look at it—and that old cabin where the sorrel creek broke the shore, and the shore like a symmetrical carving of tree and reflection as darkness smoked out of the valleys under the cold alpenglow.

Second Prof: Yeah, we could get a bear or two. But what about winter. They hibernate.

Me: Each morning even in August the dawn came colder, tardier, and sometimes it was only a smoulder of light seen through a sky like a pile of old flannel. Who survives the winter?"

Here I quit a second time, disgusted. The thing was getting nowhere, steadily becoming wordier, sentimentally nostalgic, prosaic, falling part. A week later I had time to cope with the renewed nagging of the poem to be written. The cabin, that was what mysteriously bugged me. Not the unlikely cabin those two profs would have built, but the old one, already deserted, by Mystic Lake thirty-five years ago when I'd passed it by. Why, why, did

I keep remembering that cabin, in which I had never stayed, about which I knew nothing then, or since? And what had all this to do with the vapid talk of two professors in a shower?

I hoped, by writing a third draft, to find out. Over the next month I went through four more drafts before I really knew. Knew that my poem wasn't about the professors at all, or about atombomb survival, but about a cabin I had never seen, and its inhabitant, whom I had last glimpsed when he was a corpse muffled on a pack-saddle. The name Mystic Lake, spoken by one of the men in the shower, had triggered first the memory of an old abandoned log cabin there, and then a far deeper more scary vision from an even earlier day, when I was perhaps twelve. It was a late spring day when, walking home from school, I saw a Mountie riding, leading behind him a packhorse on which the outline of a dead man was bundled. And the next day my father told me it was the bearded trapper, Old Sam, who used to come into town every spring from some cabin far out, beyond the Park boundaries, to stock up supplies for the year with what pelts he had caught and carried on his back over the wild mountains. Suspicious-eyed, crazyhaired Old Sam, silent even in the store, shoving his pencilled list of needs over the counter with big scaly hands. That spring he hadn't come in. The Mounties went out to his cabin. They had to break in, for it was barred on the inside. They found his half-starved corpse frozen on the bed. But there was still a store of food in the cabin. "Bushed", my father said. "The woods got him, the loneliness." *Bushed*! That was my title, my theme.

I suppose the mystery of that old man's death, the awful corridors of the human mind it hinted at, had been too much for my twelve-year-old psyche to face; I had suppressed all memory of the man and his death, I had refused to let my imagination wrestle with it. And again, a few years later, when I camped with other teen-agers by Mystic Lake, the deserted cabin there had prompted a recall of the life and death of Old Sam, and again I had repressed the association. But it was there, bedded deep in me, till a professor in a shower, when I was fifty-two years of age, had said "Mystic Lake", and my unconscious stirred and bedevilled me till at last I had given it the words that left me at peace—nine drafts and two months later.

At peace, though not of course satisfied. It's just that I reached the point beyond which I'm incapable of exploring this Image in words, my words; a better poet would have gone on, or gone more quickly, and written a better poem. This is simply the best I can ever do with it. I am purged. There can't be any more drafts sweated out of my bowels. About this memory I am once more sane, unpixilated. Now it is whatever poem anybody else can make of it for I am busy licking my new cubs into shape. About them, of course, I'm as protective as any she-bear; but *Bushed* has left the den. The critics can attack, ignore, even praise it without stirring me to defence or encouragement. True, it's one of a small group of my poems which I will read aloud when I'm asked to present my work publicly; but I read it to you now chiefly as an illustration of the problem of making a particular poem. It also perhaps reveals something about how my own mind would go, if I were no longer able to shape its schizophrenic moments into an amulet of words. . . .

. . . .

From this poem, and the poem *Aluroid* earlier,[1] and from my stumbling analyses of how they came to be written, you may draw many conclusions. You may decide that I've shown only that a poet can't explain himself, or really understand the effect of his work. And you may well be right. Or you may agree with one at least of the Confucian arguments: the poem has added to your memory-bank a curious use of the word "bushed". I'm sure, however, it has not taught you to honour the Queen, or to resent evil. By my own admission, in fact, the poem was a piece of escape mechanism from a moral-political issue, for it led me away from thinking about atom-bombs. But if my account of its birth has heightened your awareness of the Unconscious lying under each of us, and of the power that world exerts in the shaping of the conscious creative process, I am content. And if the poem itself has, in any way, made you feel more understanding, more tolerant, of my old mad trapper in his cabin—if it has in any way "universalized" him, brought him and you and me into some community of sharing of the mysterious human condition, however briefly—then it serves in still another, and important capacity, for you. For me it had already served when it purged me of yet one more of the fearful ghosts of my separateness.

[1][See below, pp. 199-202.—Ed.]

EARLE BIRNEY AND THE COMPOUND GHOST

PAUL WEST

No pomp or poet's pose: just a tall, self-contained self-analyst dominating the lectern and mixing shrewd points with occasional smiling mutiny, as if to suggest a terrible soul beneath: not professional or vatic, but a gently wild man born in Calgary in 1904. That is how he must have appeared, as lecturer and reciter, during a multitude of performances in North America, Japan, Mexico, India and London. It is typical of him that he should speak of "saying" his poems, display a genial regard for beer-parlours and write, he supposes, to prevent himself from going mad.

The poet in this poet-professor has always delightedly fastened upon the unfamiliar: not to show off with, not because the Pacific Coast bores him or because he finds the ordinary too difficult, but because he has always been something of an animist. For him the temperate Canadian pastoral kept leaping into pageantry, bestiary and something close to the heraldic. We could liken him to his favourite Chaucer: voracious for the detail of contemporary life and yet, while musing on and exposing foible, lunging after ghosts, the miraculous or the shimmering timeless. The Birney of "Anglosaxon Street" is an inspector of human customs:

> Then by twobit magic   to muse in movie,
> unlock picturehoard,   or lope to alehall,
> soaking bleakly   in beer, skittleless.
>
> Home again to hotbox   and humid husbandhood,
> in slumertrough adding   sleepily to Anglekin.

The pastiche disguises nothing: this is the flavour of Chaucer but with more feel for the motion of life than Chaucer has; the method is compactly allusive, as if he wants to transform everything. And the key to Birney's power, as to the disciplines and rigours he has imposed on himself, is his urge towards myth. This is why his Canadian pastorals never quite succeed. Because he is a lover of myth, he tends naturally to the dislocated reality of mountaineering and the lost reality of the Indians: for instance, the title-poem of his first book of poems, *David and Other Poems* (1942) is

From *Canadian Literature*, 13 (1962), pages 5-14. By permission of Paul West and *Canadian Literature*.

peculiarly diffuse yet crammed with exact data. The data is placed exactly nowhere:

> One Sunday on Rampart's arete a rainsquall caught us,
> And passed, and we clung by our blueing fingers and bootnails
> An endless hour in the sun, not daring to move
> Till the ice had steamed from the slate. And David taught me
>
> How time on a knife-edge can pass with the guessing of fragments
> Remembered from poets, the naming of strata beside one . . . .

One might call it the inevitable Canadian metaphor, this siting of particulars in the vast blank. And whatever one calls it—whatever it tells us specially of Canada—it keeps falling short. Supposed to refer universally because it is of no region, it misses the suggestive power of such lines as these of Eliot:

> Summer surprised us, coming over the Starnbergersee
> With a shower of rain; we stopped in the colonnade,
> And went on in the sunlight, into the Hofgarten. . . .

Eliot's two tent-pegging references—the colonnade and the Hofgarten—complicate reality all over again; they restore whole worlds to us, whereas Birney's descriptive sequence followed by that not very firm allusion to the poets merely insulates us. We have to set to work in order to get beyond the phantoms of atavism, the primitive pattern.

Having objected to the delicious particulars of such poems as "David" I have also to confess that I find the philosophical Birney (strong in *David and Other Poems* and repeated in more senses than one in the second volume, *Now Is Time,* 1945) just as far from enlightening me as I find, say, the Speech of the Salish Chief in *Trial of a City* (1952) a bit fusty, not a little fustian. Much of the early Birney is an express of vivid description with philosophical baggage to follow by the next train. There is no synthesis; but in his deliberate habit of reprinting earlier poems in the context of new ones there is an effort meriting great sympathy. It is Birney trying to put a world together: now blurring with general ideas, now thrusting detail (either urban or pastoral) into the middle of philosophising. He cannot keep the pastoral intact, he knows, and the presence in *Now Is Time,* which is mostly war poems and excellent ones at that, of philosophical poems from *David* warns us that he is groping after something: a fusion, an amalgam, a compound. Again, in *The Strait of Anian* (1948) he juxtaposed his poetic past and his present, and in *Trial of a City* turned to satirical fantasy and recaptured the mordant note of some poems in *David.*

This progress is worth pursuing in further detail: it crazy-paved the way for what is Birney's finest and most recent achievement, *Ice Cod Bell or Stone,* the very title of which suggests a miscellany rammed together; a reconcilable quartet. He has approached it by finding various modes of expression variously unsatisfactory. First, the remote and straitened reality of "David" in which the conversations seemed hardly artificial enough: "but he cried, louder, 'No, Bobbie! Don't ever blame yourself; You can last.' He said only, 'Perhaps . . . For what? A wheelchair, Bob?' " Then the war poems, with an imagery that knocks us over before we have time to assume any attitude at all:

> The clusters of children, like flies, at the back of messhuts,
> or groping in gravel for knobs of coal,
> their legs standing like dead stems out of their clogs.

And then the satirical semi-dramatic, the vocal equivalent of myth: the poet is seeking again the movement of conversation, trying to find an idiom and inflexion to partner the jumble he has now acquired of Seal Brother, Hell, salmon, seawolves, the Tide of the Thimbleberries, cetegrande, popcorn, "Narvik's blanching hulks", the "rotograved lie", the slug's "greentipped taut horns of slime", "dying Bering, lost in fog" and lilies growing their pungent bulbs unprompted.

After a silence of ten years he finds his way out in *Ice Cod Bell or Stone,* through a loose combination of voices. There is the deliberate patience of the professional gazer: as in "El Greco: *Espolio*":

> The carpenter is intent on the pressure of his hand
> on the awl, and the trick of pinpointing his strength
> through the awl to the wood, which is tough.

The flat tone and meticulous eye seem to insulate the horror from us without, oddly enough, soothing us one bit. The point is well taken because we are allowed no guesswork. Because we are not the intended victims (not on *that* wood anyway) Birney deprives us of vicarious pain. Contrast this cool recital with such ventriloquism as the following:

> Ah but I saw her ascend up in the assendupping breeze

> There was a cloudfall of Kewpids
> their glostening buttums twankling

That comes from a poem called "Mammorial Stunzas for Aimee Simple McFarcin"; not far from Eliot's Aristophanic melodrama, but closer than Eliot ever is to illustrious vernacular and rendered with a Dickensian relish for caricature. Just *listen* to this:

> Jesus man what did you expect
> Queen Liliuokalani spreadeagled on a tapa mat?
> Sure they got a farm in Diamond Head crater this
> a big place state cap world tour—
> but any guy dont like Waikiki say we got
> more catamarans surfboats fishspearin palmclimbin
> than all them native saw in a thousand
> years waitin around for us okay maybe the hula
> aint

The book displays three principal idioms: cool meditation studded with vivid detail, and pastiche of raw vernacular; these tend to slide into each other when the poet is emphasizing hard or really wanting the contrast of two points of view. The third is represented by a few poems in foundering, chaotic typography the point of which—presumably visual enactment—escapes me almost entirely. All three idioms, however, tell us a great deal about Birney the rebel. He is repudiating the professorial sage, the mug tourist and (I think) the Birney who shrinks from typographical trickery and therefore forces himself to attempt it. There is no need to choose between Birney the eloquent and reflective intelligence and Birney the mimic; in each role he is anxiously trying to relate himself to the world—and with gratifying success, all the more so when he deepens a poem by transcending while evoking the academic mode:

> Lo as I pause in the alien vale of the airport
> fearing ahead the official ambush
> a voice languorous and strange as these winds of Oahu
> calleth my name and I turn to be quoited in orchids....

The mimicry is the fact, more or less, and the comment is the endlessly interpreting mind. Sometimes they are sandwiched in an impacted conversation:

> *But arent there towns in Mexico more av-?* Dear madam,
> Actopan is a town more average than mean.
> You may approach it on a sound macadam....

Always, however, whether or not the mimicry is full-blooded or tame, the conversations—like the personae, the academic-sounding exercises, the brilliant vignettes of Japan, Mexico, Siam, are metaphors for the essential loneliness of any articulate observer. The mimicry is the lunge out of oneself, the effort to transpose oneself without however losing the advantages of intelligence.

Ice Cod Bell or Stone is a conspectus of the poet's honesty while he strives to be more than a tourist in a world of gaudy surfaces and fraying skins. No-one anywhere is treated more impersonally than the tourist, and this book is a record of being a geographical and spiritual tourist. Observe the names, weird and unfriendly, which populate the Mexican reservation in this volume: Najarít, Ajijíc, Irapuato, Pachucan, Tepoztlán, Tehauntepec. This poet responds acutely to the out-of-the-way; apart from the twelve poems about Mexico, which must almost all of them rank among his best, there are many novel themes or points of departure: a bear on the Delhi road, Captain Cook, El Greco, a tavern by the Hellespont, Ellesmereland, Kyoto, a Bangkok boy, two poems by Mao Tse-tung, Wake Island, Honolulu, Yellowstone, and (that telling mutilation) Aimee Simple McFarcin. By contrast the few Canadian poems seem less mature: quiet demonstrations of fidelity tucked in between bouts with seductive haunts where life is more intense.

Yet I do not think Birney yields to the meretricious or pursues novelty for novelty's sake (except typographically). In one poem called "Can. Lit." he explains that

> We French, we English, never lost our civil war,
> endure it still, a bloodless civil bore;
> no wounded lying about, no Whitman wanted.
> It's only by our lack of ghosts we're haunted.

It is precisely that lack of ghosts which emerges in the Canadian poems in this collection and which handicapped the early Birney until he went to war. Even this haunting poem about a tree seems no more, finally, than a punctuation mark added to a vast meaningless process:

> Then the white frosts crept back. I took
> to slipping out when no one looked
> and poured the steaming crescent of my pee
> over the shivering body of my tree.
> That brown offering seemed to satisfy;
> a warm tan mounted to her head.

The tan is a substitute for those ghosts. Significant too is the poem which gives the title:

> Explorers say that harebells rise
> from the cracks of Ellesmereland

> and cod swim fat beneath the ice
> that grinds its meagre sands
> No man is settled on that coast
> The harebells are alone
> Nor is there talk of making man
> from ice cod bell or stone

It is all "say" and "alone"; he evokes a land of little purchase. He is supposed to deal with a country upon which the history of man's failures and triumphs is hardly even recorded. Phantom hypotheses make a poor show alongside those who

> . . . came chattering and dust-red from Asia
> to these wharfstones, a tipsy Xenophon in tow. . . .

or that small Japanese boy with his kite:

> tall in the bare sky and huge as Gulliver
> a carp is rising golden and fighting
> thrusting its paper body up from the fist
> of a small boy on an empty roof higher
> and higher into the winds of the world.

"It is not easy to free", one poem says, "myth from reality"; we might have expected that from Birney. It is no surprise either that he appears with just a few poems on a country whose main reality is the Great Outdoors, and then seeks ballast in more storied countries. And yet, even allowing that he has a distinct point to make about being at home abroad and yet never belonging there, I feel somewhat uneasy about *Ice Cod Bell or Stone*. I feel prompted to ask: Has he done as ingeniously, as vividly, as boldly, by Canada as he might have done? All great northern boredoms and ice vacancies apart, surely this raw material from the only poem about modern North America could have yielded something more arresting:

> wordswords are oozing and ooshing from the mouths of all
> your husbands saying SPACEWAR and FIGGERS DONT and
>   EGG
>   inter
> HEADS and WY and plashing on the   of   national
>   plastic
> buses and dribbling on barbecues the slick floors of
> autocourts saying WALLSTREET saying BIGSTICK and
>   TAXES and REDS

The acerb satires of Cummings and Irving Layton are more carefully calculated than this. Birney is quick to point out that Mexican strawberries resemble "small clotting hearts"; but is there no Canadian version of that, or of this?

> El Capitan Jasón Castilla y Mordita
> shoulders his golden braiding through the shitten air,
> rolls in a fugue of sporting up the Street
> of Games—crossing the already strabismic
> eye of the chess-carver tiptapping in his brick
> cave—and swings at the Lane of Roses. . . .

The English poet, D. J. Enright, has written of modern Japan in the same kind of idiom: raw, discordant, with close-ups that carry a climate and generalizations that go sour even while being made. But Enright has written, in that same idiom, about the English Black Country. Surely when a poet has so brilliant a technique as Birney has, it is a pity that he doesn't focus on the homely palpable, the squalid next-door.

I can't help thinking *Ice Cod Bell or Stone* a bit of a poet's holiday; I might even say an excursion into idyll—not idyll in the absolute sense but, comparatively speaking, idyll in the sense that the exotic (as Byron proved) makes more impact for less work. In other words, Birney has got a start from the exotic and redeemed himself by displaying so magnificent a technique that we know he never *needs* the exotic anyway. The over-familiar will serve him just as well; and it is surely the over-familiar that the poet has to teach us to see as if we have never encountered it before. Here is a man who has gone abroad and shot scores of zebras, impala and elephant because, it seems, his guns cannot touch moose.

All the same, I can see why Birney does as he does. Poets please themselves anyway. And those Mexican ghosts enable him to inherit myth while dealing with daily reality whereas Birney the Canadian realist inherits only a few vague sideshows:

> O mammoma we never forguess you
> and your bag blue sheikel-getting ayes
> loused, lost from all hallow Hollowood O
>
> Aimee Aimee Tekel Upharsin

Birney's Mexico is dry, foetid, fly-blown, cruel, pauper-thick, tequila-eased, lottery-optimistic, tourist-pestered and legend-heavy:

> Wholehearted Aztecs used this isle
> for carving out the cores of virgins.
> Cortés, more histrionic, purified it

> with a fort and modernized the Indians
> in dungeons contrived to flood each time
> the tide was high.

History has bled to death there, but so it has in Rome, and there is much in Rome that is not imperial. It may be an advantage to a poet to have a theme with the grandeur or pain of history about it, but it should not be an essential. Otherwise the poet will become a mere historiographer. In one of his best poems the Italian poet Eugenio Montale makes highly effective use of a popular song, "Adios Muchachos"; Eliot's throbbing taxi is sinisterly eloquent and so are Pound's excerpts from headlines. If modern Canada has no legend, then the opportunities for imagism are considerable. Present the thing, for once, in terms of itself.

I feel supported in these thoughts by Birney's own practice as a novelist. I am thinking not so much of *Turvey* (1949), his military comedy, but of the less applauded *Down the Long Table* (1955), which is primarily concerned with Leftist activities in Toronto and Vancouver. It opens with a public hearing where Professor Saunders, tired Canadian radical and specialist in mediæval English at a Mormon college in Utah, is denying un-American activities. But once a rebel.... The novel plods back over his picaresque career: as a young lecturer, quitting both Mormon college and pregnant mistress; pursuing a Ph.D. in Toronto; muddled politics, muddled love, bumming across Canada on freight trains in order to start a Third International in Vancouver; donnishly quizzing the layabouts of the South Vancouver Workers' Educational Army; eventually returning to Utah, respectability and a safe chair (now having his doctorate). With less documentary purpose and more panache this might have been a disturbing and savage book. Birney separates his chapters with excerpts from newspapers, and this Dos Passos technique surely belongs in his poetry too. It proves he has some feeling for life's miscellaneous and kaleidoscopic quality and therefore too for such techniques as we find in poets as different as Eliot, William Carlos Williams and Pound. (Obviously Birney has enjoyed and learned from his Joyce; Aimee Simple McFarcin comes to us by that route.) *Down the Long Table* also reveals a flair, as I suggested earlier apropos of "Anglosaxon Street", for the motion and feel of life: a wilder Chaucer. And this flair, combined with the by no means idealizing or evasive eye intently turned on Mexico in *Ice Cod Bell or Stone,* is just what most Canadian poets lack. Irving Layton is too self-consciously tough; Jay Macpherson and James Reaney are too academic in flavour; Louis Dudek, if anyone other than Birney, has been close to what I am specifying, and his magazine *Delta* regularly offers samples of the right thing, although these are sometimes carelessly put together.

Birney alone, I feel, at present, has the necessary equipment. His sense of pageantry curbed by a gritty realism, he apprehends the squalid or the dull with visionary zest. Take this, for instance, from *Ice Cod Bell or Stone*:

> those ladies work at selling hexametric chili,
> and all their husbands, where the zocalo is shady,
> routinely spin in silent willynilly
> lariats from cactus muscles; as they braid they
> hear their normal sons in crimson shorts go shrilly
>
> bouncing an oval basketball about the square—

The power of that is not in the exotica but in one phrase, "all their husbands", which suggests in the echo of that popular-song fragment—"where the zocalo is shady" an absolute, almost preposterous vision of labour. All the husbands (as in the poem quoted earlier) are collected up and frozen into a helix of work, rather like those streams of soaring and diving souls in William Blake's drawings. It is a microcosm: mysterious women obedient to occult routine; their husbands, *all* of them, animated by something heavy —all the suet in suetude; and the "normal" sons not yet conscripted but devising their timekiller just the same. It is a most original and graphic piece of summary poetry: tough enough to stand a little experiment I tried by altering a few words:

> Those ladies work at selling Pentagonic jelly,
> and all their husbands, where the conifer is shady,
> routinely spin in silent willynilly
> lariats of smoke from new Havanas; as they fume they
> hear their normal sons in boxer shorts go shrilly
>
> bouncing an oval basketball across the border—

A small homage to Birney the satirist. But a presumption and defensible only because I think poetry ought almost always to be contaminated by the great deal of our living that is ugly, awkward or vapid. Ice, cod, bell and stone belie the book, are more pastoral than the symbols Birney manages best, and more Canadian-sounding than the book's contents. They remind us that the most characteristically Canadian thing is the Canadian landscape; cities, on the other hand, merge together. One would like to see Birney at the automat or the supermarket; if he can tackle a diaper, as he does in the present collection, then the rest is easy. Our civilization is unlikely to restore itself to a life based exclusively on ground-roots and the pasturing of animals.

Let us hope that Birney's proposed trips to the Caribbean and Latin America are intended to give him an objective view of the home image, for a graphic synopsis to come, with the whole of the world jumbled together on the poet's own planet. *Ice Cod Bell or Stone* marks a tremendous access of vision and technique, and proves that the lack of ghosts is, properly speaking, immaterial to a poet as good as this.

A REVIEW OF *ICE COD BELL OR STONE* (1962)

ROBIN SKELTON

Our poetry has circulated within a national wall, and American as well as English readers have not cared to know what was going on inside.
                                                              E. K. BROWN

The critic to whom falls the enviable task of studying Canadian poetry in the sixties will, I trust, be dealing with a fully matured culture, no longer preoccupied with the empty unpoetics of Canadianism, but with the genuine tasks of creative power.
                                                              NORTHROP FRYE

These two statements, the first made in the forties and the second in the fifties, present one aspect of the problem of Canadian poetry, and suggest the question that most critics are inclined to put. Is Canadian Literature, as George Woodcock maintained in his editorial to *Canadian Literature* No. 12 in 1962, only just coming?

On the evidence of the books before me I would suggest that, while much excellent and mature work has been produced, some poets show a consciousness of the 'Canadian problem' which mars their work. This takes many forms. On the dust-cover of Earle Birney's latest book he is described as an 'internationally acclaimed poet', and there is a formidable list of his publications and of the places where he has given readings of his verse. This, in its over-protestation (for, frankly, Birney is almost completely unknown in England, and the amount of acclamation his work receives in the United States is negligible), reflects something of the aggressiveness of the poetry itself. Birney is a clever writer, but little more. He goes in for superficially exciting verbal tricks, playing with Joycean devices in 'Mammorial Stunzas for Aimee Simple McFarcin', producing rather silly typographical eccentricities in 'Njarit', and frequently creating lines which have a glossy avant-garde surface but little else. His work is veneer and marquetry, and almost never whole wood. This is apparent when we read in 'Irapuato' the lines:

> Toltex by Mixtex Mixtez by Aztex
> Aztex by Spanishtex Spanishtex by
> Mexitex by Mexitex by Mexitex by Texaco

From "Canadian Poetry," *The Tamarack Review,* 29 (1963), pages 71-73. By permission of Robin Skelton.

If we contrast this with the opening of Wallace Stevens's 'Bantams in Pine-woods', the difference between the real and the meretricious is made clear. Stevens wrote:

> Chieftain Iffucan of Azcan in caftan
> Of tan with henna hackles, halt!

Birney is crude, obvious, and rhythmically dull: Stevens is subtler in his alliterations, and more deft in his use of cadence and stress. This kind of criticism applies throughout Birney's book. Setting aside mere sillinesses (of which there are a number), and pretending not to notice the exhibitionist use of allusion, however, there is a real vigour in many poems, and a sensual vitality that occasionally emerges as sheer poetry rather than as mere aggressive gesticulation. Some of the poems about Mexico are as pleasing as others are foolish. Contrast some lines from 'State of Sonora' with some from 'Sinaloa'.

> By puma-coloured crossroads
> with names dry and implacable
> as locusts—
> Chirriones, Bacarac,
> Los Muertos—
> men pad weeklong after lean
> sheep and flinteyed goats through crack
> of thin dust between
> the joints of cactus-
> armoured land.

This is good evocative stuff.

> Si, senor, is halligators here, your guidebook say it,
> Si, jaguar in the montanas, maybe helephants, quien sabe?
> You like, those palm trees in the sunset? Certamente
> Very nice . . .

This is amusing as television comedies are amusing, making its point by avoiding any serious exploration. In a different book it would be acceptable; in this one its superficiality is too typical to be anything but depressing.

I wonder very much if it is the awareness of Canadian Isolation that makes Birney so aggressively avant-garde and globe-trotting?

EARLE BIRNEY, LETTER TO THE EDITOR
OF *Tamarack Review*

Dear Sir,

Mr Robin Skelton, in a re-hash of a review he wrote for a Vancouver daily nearly two years ago, lambastes me in your Autumn issue. If he were merely expressing an honest opinion there would be no need for me to reply. Mr Skelton, however, is being dishonest. He himself is the author of books, and knows quite well that writers do not formulate or control the statements made about them on 'dust-covers'. I never described myself as an 'internationally acclaimed poet' and I know that I am not one. It is both disingenuous and slightly malicious to argue therefore that such a statement 'reflects something of the aggressiveness of the poetry itself.' As it happens, my publisher specifically refused me permission to see either jacket, cover or inside designs for the book Mr Skelton has been reviewing. It is obvious that if I *had* seen them, the stupid error in the illustration of the title would not have have been made.

Nor has Mr Skelton, who has no knowledge of me or of my life, any justification for describing me as 'aggressively globe-trotting' and suggesting this to be a result of my 'awareness of Canadian Isolation'. I have visited or lived in other countries for much the same reasons perhaps that have impelled Mr Skelton to come to my country: the acceptance of travelling fellowships and of teaching or lecturing engagements in furtherance of my professional life.

Mr Skelton may still be right, of course, that my poetry is mostly meretricious, silly, crude, obvious, foolish, dull, exhibitionist, aggressive, and depressing—if clever. But nothing I have yet read of Mr Skelton's prose or poetry convinces me that he could tell.

Yours sincerely,
EARLE BIRNEY

From *The Tamarack Review*, 30 (1963), page 96. By permission of Earle Birney.

THREE REVIEWS OF
NEAR FALSE CREEK MOUTH (1964)

❦ A. W. PURDY

Earle Birney thru the years has been a poet whom I've admired with rather a schoolboyish veneration. Some of his early poems ('Vancouver Lights', 'Mappemounde', 'Bushed') have a fateful quality which you can lift like a grid and place over any almost hopeless situation.

Greek tragedy? I don't really think so, except perhaps in 'Bushed'. But this 'fateful' inevitability is a thing most of us experience at one time or another. We feel harried, hemmed in, tapped, beleaguered & hopeless, perhaps bored as hell among the narrowing conditions permitting us to be alive.

Those older poems dealt with the particular, universalizing it, allowing us to glimpse the desperation behind much of human existence. Only now and again could one see the poet himself, moving behind and among his poems.

Earle Birney believes there was more rhetoric in those early pieces than in later poems. If so, it was a rock-hard rhetoric. Little of the personal; concepts particularized; an unsentimental bite to words; many times a deployment of language to permit unstinting attack.

The poems of *Near False Creek Mouth* are very different. The situation and feeling have become personal. What Birney calls 'rhetoric' in early books has disappeared. He is 'inside' these poems, tho the abstract and conceptual mind retains its full and active force.

I've always felt Birney could write a poem about a doorknob if he felt like it. But earlier it might have been a doorknob signifying the door between adolescence and maturity, say; or between one age and another, perhaps in the person of Isaac Newton opening a heavy portal. Now, however, it is Birney's own hand on the doorknob, and it signifies transition between the two Birneys.

I know quite well that the batter or reviewer should keep his eye on the ball, i.e., current poems. But I can't, and must keep looking at *all* the poems, a little fascinated by change itself. And I resist strongly the temptation to say earlier or later poems were/ are better.

However, in reviewers' jargon, Birney's 'technical' powers are

---

"A pair of 10-Foot Concrete Shoes", from *Fiddlehead*, 65 (1965), pages 75-76. By permission of Al Purdy.

increased. He is more fluid and sharply observant than ever. Okay. The doorknob parallel holds; these are poems of Birney's maturity. And I don't mean senescence.

Most of the earlier tragic qualities are gone. Immediate impact is somewhat lessened. For instance, a leisurely philosophic walk around False Creek suffers dramatically by comparison with the same man waiting for the forces of war to overwhelm his 'winking outpost' on the edge of night. Yet both are real. And let's not get into inane semantics of real, realer and realest—or is it realist?

The impression I want to leave in this review is that here's another chapter in the continuing wonder of being Earle Birney. It would be a good thing to read the other chapters too, for only part of the man is visible now unless you also look at the past. A more personal, human chapter: by reason of the process of addition and subtraction (change) which we all undergo.

Well, some things in this new book are a delight. I don't like them all. To do so would seem to me a very bad judgment about any book. Besides, there's a good possibility I may like tomorrow what I don't care for today.

But keeping to the here and now, I especially like 'Cartegena de Indias', which centres around 'los zapatos' of the Colombian poet, Luis Lopez. And who but Latins would dream that a monument to a dead poet must inevitably be a pair of 10-foot-long concrete shoes? The monument springs from a line in a Lopez poem (which Birney translated) in which he remarks concerning his native city:

> ... Still, full of your own [familiar] rancid disarray
> you manage to win, even from me, that love
> a man finds he has for his shoes when they are old.

After the poet died, his fellow townsmen took him up on that remark, erecting a monument of 10-foot-long concrete shoes.

Birney has woven his many-coloured self into that tapestry of Lopez, 'los zapatos', searching thru Cartegena bookshops for a copy of the book containing that poem. I'll remember a long time, the picture of Birney: sitting on the curb in Cartagena de Indias, lanky legs folded against the traffic, reading a book of poems and thinking about Luis Lopez' old shoes.

MILTON WILSON

Near False Creek Mouth is Earle Birney's sixth book, his second in two years. The sixties have been a prolific time for Birney, and, although he likes to depict himself as bald, pasty-faced and something less than agile ("there is nowhere I need go that quickly"), I can see nothing poetically senile about his latest collection. Certainly if I wanted to convince a reader of contemporary poetry that Birney was worth his attention, this is the book I would give him. Not that there's any futile attempt to compete with a new poetic generation on its own terms. But age *has* opened his sensibilities, extended his range, deepened his patterns, strengthened the authenticity of his voice. Birney is the exception to the Canadian rule that poets don't mature (they just repeat themselves or give up). He remains recognizably the same poet, but both his role as a human being and his functioning as a writer seem more secure than ever before.

When I say that he's the same poet, I'm remembering his Canadian landscape and manscape of twenty years ago, a precarious shelf, thrust up at the sun between the Atlantic and Pacific doors of a prehistoric sea, layered with the discontinuous steps of geological and cultural time, haunted by the ghosts of unavailable primitive myth and the visions of unachieved humanity. The long introductory poem ("November Walks near False Creek Mouth") that introduces this latest volume exists on that same shelf. But so do many of the travel poems that follow, like the Peruvian "Machu Picchu." Birney has always liked to be both a very local and a very global poet. The two-part division of *The Strait of Anian* (1948) made that clear long ago. In *Near False Creek Mouth* the identity of home and world is unmistakably built into the patterns of each, and Frank Newfeld's cover drives the point home.

But I'm also remembering Birney's war poetry of the forties with its sense of involvement from the western edge of things, its Canadian scapegoats for a war they never made and yet were somehow responsible for: in short, its equivocal relations between (and even identity of) guilt and innocence. In *Near False Creek Mouth* Birney plays the role of innocent surrogate for the sins of the wide world with charm and comic timing, no less than high seriousness. "Meeting of Strangers," in which, with a ballet leap and a taxi *ex machina,* he escapes being skewered by "somebody big / redshirted young dark unsmiling" in the Port of Spain dockyard at dead of night, is a masterpiece of tone and staging. The book ends with "Arrivals," a powerful poem about a level-crossing death on the Wolfville-Halifax run in a blinding snowstorm. The dead man's legal papers scattered in the snow (he was driving to the Wolfville assizes), the bland, innocent diesel-face of the train, the passengers' defensive comments and obscure sense of implication, the irrationality of the death and of the sudden blizzard itself, and finally the corpse's long-fingered, legalistic hand, which the blanket is unable to cover, add up to one of Birney's best treatments of an obsessive theme.

But whether it's the cosmic chain of being or the social chain of society that this poet is talking about, his job is to provide the missing link.

> Somewhere there must be another bridge
> from my stupid wish
> to their human acceptance.

I'm quoting from "Cartagena de Indias," one of the longest and best pieces in the book, in which Birney's combination of social eagerness and tourist's alienation is dramatized with admirable verve and lots of comic detail. The bridge here turns out to be the concrete, ten-foot-long pair of shoes which serves as a monument to the Colombian poet Luis Lopez. Around it Birney manages to imagine a society sufficient to include even him. In "Turbonave Magnolia" he presents himself as a kind of centre of cohesion in the subdivided world of a passenger ship, shuttling from deck to deck, bar to bar, and sitting to sitting, although there turns out to be a final division that even he can't bridge.

> I am deck-strolling now with an Oxford graduate
>   who sold a good business in Tobago
>   to be a social worker in Liverpool
>   We discuss the trapping of cockroaches in cabins
>   and how to contrive to eat together
>   For he sleeps in Cabin   being flush
>   and I in Other   being other
>   but he eats in Other   being gravy-brown-skinned
>   And I in Cabin Early Sitting   being potato-white
>   We call on the Chief Steward and get a final brush-off
> Eat together?! This is the one improbability.

I have of course been talking about the poems I like. There are a few in the book that I have no inclination to read again. "Buenos Aires: 1962" is an ambitious failure. The poems that rely too heavily on Birney's (not always very fresh) ear for North American cliché and vulgarity are unimaginative and tiresome, although "Billboards Build Freedom of Choice" is a good deal more interesting than "Most of a Dialogue in Cuzco" and "Toronto Board of Trade Goes Abroad." "Testimony of a Canadian Educational Leader" is pretty heavyhanded satire. But the duds have to be searched out; and in the longest section ("Caribbean Turnout") it's hard to find any.

❦ A. KINGSLEY WEATHERHEAD

About twenty-five years ago, just before the last war, Louis MacNeice wrote:

> The sunlight on the garden
> Hardens and grows cold,
> You cannot cage the minute
> Within its nets of gold . . . .
> Our freedom as free lances
> Advances toward its end . . .
> And soon, my friend
> We shall have no time for dances. . . .

MacNeice is not a widely read poet, but for the English at least, the poem now perfectly recreates the general mood of the time of Munich, at the end of the "chromium-plate" era and its dizzy mayfly blisses—Lagondas, roadhouses, cocktails, and tennis in white flannels.

In "November Walk Near False Creek Mouth," the long, opening poem of his new volume, Earle Birney has found, one generation later, that the sunlight has again grown cold, and he anticipates a cataclysm equivalent to the cosmic changes which have taken aeons to complete. His way of going about things is longer and profounder and, in a word, entirely different from MacNeice's, and it would hardly be worth quoting the earlier poem were it not that "November Walk" is similar in that it speaks and will later speak with some precision to the mood generated by this moment in history: they will say (please God, even *we* may say), This is how it was. Birney embodies some of the pleasures of the sunlight that MacNeice refers to, which rattle like small change in the face of the five-figure losses to come. There is the trivial conversation:

> . . . she said   I *am*!
> I'm one of the Lockeys!
> *Not* the Lockeys of *Out*garden surely
> I said. *Yes* she said but I live
> in Winnipeg now.

"Back to Canada", from *Northwest Review*, 7, No. 1 (1965), pages 86-89. By permission of A. Kingsley Weatherhead and *Northwest Review*.

or there are the childish fragments that tourists have shored against their ruin—

> ... plastic totems   a kewpie
> a Hong Kong puzzle for somebody's child
> who waits to be worshipped
> back on the prairie farm.

And then above all there is the pervasive sense of destruction and doom to come.

The poem proceeds by way of a "periplum"—the word Ezra Pound gave to a poetic journey which, not overtly looking for images for a theme, furnishes what may add up to one. In Birney's poems the forthcoming images bear, more or less freely, upon the theme of the lost geological past and the lost human future. Obviously the season, time, and place of the walk, a late November afternoon at the western edge of the western world, are not artlessly chosen; and the images they provide are naturally those of decline and death. But the more freely they work the more powerful is their effect: the remark that the kids swimming are the "last maybe of whatever summer's swimmers" is not so terrifying as the natural image of the last flash of sunset, for example, the "unimaginable brightness," or that of the dead maple leaves, which

> ... glistening with salt
> have turned the ragged lawns
> to a battlefield bright with their bodies.

In addition, the shadows cast by the future are made more ominous and, paradoxically, are enlarged by the sense we gain that this ending of an era is only a moment in the aeons of geologic time. The imagery evokes past ages when the sea threw up monsters upon its littoral as it now throws up driftwood.

Rhyme is almost entirely dispensed with in the poem, but much use is made of alliteration and assonance. There is no punctuation; pauses between words are indicated by double spaces. Here and there between the irregular stanzas are passages in italics in which the poet comments on the poetic techniques, usually the beat, as they develop: *"the beat is the slap slip nudging / as the ledges are made unmade"*; or

> *Slowly   scarcely sensed   the beat*
> *has been quickening now as the air*
> *from the whitened peaks is falling*
> *faraway sliding* . . . .

Just prior to this last italicized passage, the rhythm *has* in fact been speeding up:

> the stinking ledge disputed by barnacles
> waiting for tiderise to kick in their food
> contested by jittery sandfleas
> and hovering gulls;

and, as the acceleration is "scarcely sensed," it seems useful to have attention drawn to it. But the total effect, a familiar one in modern poetry, is not simply to show up the products of the technique but to add another dimension, so that we become the audience not only of the poem but of the poet at work in it.

"November Walk" is the longest non-dramatic poem Earle Birney has ever written. I don't thing he has ever written better. There are the good words with the exactly right connotations and exactly right sounds, not now and then by happy accident, but again and again in long successions. Here, for example, he contrasts the modern shore with what it used to be:

> ... under the leafless maples
> between the lost salt home
> and the asphalt ledge where carhorns call
> call in the clotting air by a shore
> where shamans never again will sound
> with moon-snail conch the ritual plea
> to brother salmon or vanished seal
> and none ever heard
> the horn of Triton or merman.

Literary; romantic; musical; rich; superbly anachronistic? I suppose it could be damned by any one of these terms. But then, who knows: the current taste for naked sandwiches on paper plates, even if one or the other can be chewed to the rhythms of jazz, may not always be in vogue. Poetry may transpire once more, when the wheel has come full circle, to be the best words in the best order.

The poems in the rest of the book are not so new in genre to those familiar with this poet's earlier work. They are poems of faraway places in the Caribbean, Peru, Chile, and elsewhere, with descriptions of scenes, customs, and incidents, discovered by the poet on his own journey or in recent or ancient history. Sometimes the point of a poem is tied pretty closely to an objective scene and incident: in "Barranquilla Bridge" boys standing on the bridge fish up floating fruit, discarding what is too rotten to eat. Smaller boys on the downstream side of the bridge fish up what their elders discard, hoping for edibles the latter have missed, but surreptitiously feeding the rotten fruit back into the stream higher up. The thing is lightly and economically sketched, with some good vivid touches; it ends:

> It's the only rough justice
> the weak can perform on the strong
> And in Barranquilla hunger
> fortifies Gresham's Law.

But often the point of the poem is further removed than here from the objective scene or incident which occasions it. In the short "Guadelupe," for instance, Birney draws the irony out of the clash of human paradox in senoritas who park their Alfa Romeos and crawl on their knees to confession; in "Caribbean Kingdoms," a fine poem which entirely resists paraphrase or summary, the meditation of the poet upstages the description altogether:

> When all the life of sound has milled
> to silence I think these vines will find
> a way to trumpet green and purple still
> and jacarandas ring their bells down ruined streets—
> Our kingdom comes and goes with mind.

Among the poems of foreign parts are two or three portrayals of tourists, which better than anything else in the volume display the gay, irreverent side of this poet. In themselves mere fun, the placement of these poems is purposeful: Birney attends with more evident care than most poets to the ordering of poems within a volume and derives contrasts and counterpoints from it. Thus, for one example, the monologue of the compulsive talker with the paranoia about communism immediately precedes a narrative poem of shepherds who, incited by the local priest, led a little demonstration and were shot. Nor, in fairness, does the poet forget that he is a tourist himself. He makes some capital out of the incongruity of a "baldheaded professor (Canada)" surveying Machu Picchu, which otherwise

> Picked clean of writhing vine or man
> . . . eyes the swords of the Andes.

It is refreshing after the solemn meditations to have the irreverence of the tourist poems. But which controls which, in this poet-novelist-Chaucerian scholar, the *solempnitee,* the zest or the zest, the other? One doesn't know—only that both must be registered to get the measure of the man.

The poems are ordered superficially on the arc of the wide circular tour the poet made, and in the end he comes back to Canada. He does not come back to False Creek Mouth; the last poem is of a railway accident near Wolfville. Birney picks up vivid details of scenes and conversation as passengers straggle out of the cars to see the wrecked chevvy at the crossing. One hand of the victim emerges from the blanket with which he has been covered; it is "stretched in some arresting habit of eloquence / to the last irrational judgement." It is not in the geographic locale but in the fact that the theme of guilt in this last poem refers back to the "November Walk" that the poet's end is his beginning.

4. SELECTED POEMS 1940-1966

A UNIFIED PERSONALITY: BIRNEY'S POEMS

A. J. M. SMITH

With the publication this spring of Earle Birney's *Selected Poems,* a generous and representative gathering of a hundred poems, many of them long and ambitious and all of them interesting, we have an opportunity to sum up a long, fruitful, and varied poetic career —a career which this volume indicates has grown steadily in significance. The poems from Birney's two most recent books, *Ice, Cod, Bell or Stone* and *Near False Creek Mouth,* have a power and mastery that was foreshadowed but only occasionally attained in *David* or *Trial of a City,* the works on which Birney's reputation has been founded and established. Though Birney has written two novels, edited an anthology, and published a good many scholarly articles, including an immensely valuable analysis of the poetic reputation of E. J. Pratt, it is as a poet, a teacher of poetry, and a publicist for poetry that he is chiefly and rightly known; and it is his poetry only that I propose to examine here.

I don't remember when I first read a poem by Earle Birney. I know that when Frank Scott and I were preparing the manuscript for *New Provinces* in 1935 we had not heard of him, though we soon began to read the pieces that appeared in *The Canadian Forum,* of which Birney was literary editor from 1936 to 1940. It was not, however, until the publication of *David & Other Poems* in 1942 that it became apparent that a new poet had arrived, a poet who gave promise of being a worthy continuer of the tradition of heroic narrative established by Pratt and perhaps the precursor of a new school of modern poetry in Canada. Now a quarter of a century later and with the present volume before us we can see that these hopeful anticipations have been amply fulfilled. Birney's career— even more certainly than F. R. Scott's, which I hope to examine

From *Canadian Literature,* 30 (1966), pages 4-13. Reprinted in *Towards a View of Canadian Letters: Selected Critical Essays, 1928-1971,* University of British Columbia Press, 1973. By permission of A. J. M. Smith and *Canadian Literature.*

in these pages in a subsequent essay—has been analagous to the development of modern Canadian poetry as a whole. Both poets have been leaders in some respects and followers in others. From the beginning both have been adventurous and experimental, and if occasionally they have seemed to be groping or merely wandering, the occasions were remarkably few. Scott, in spite of his liberal and leftist point of view, has been mainly traditional, while his experiments have been in the direction of new and avant-garde techniques. Birney, who is also politically and socially of the left, takes more naturally to the experimental, though in his case, paradoxically enough, his most successful experiment is the experiment of being traditional. Some of the best of his earlier poems—"Slug in Woods", "Anglo-Saxon Street", "Mappemounde", and parts of "Damnation of Vancouver" as well—while not mere pastiche or parody, certainly owe their success to the skill with which the poet has utilized his scholarly knowledge of *Beowulf,* Chaucer, *Piers Plowman,* and Hopkins. To the advantages of a western mountain childhood and hard work as a manual labourer and logger in his youth, Birney added those of a thorough academic training in English literature, culminating in a Ph.D. from the University of Toronto in 1936. With the exception of some years spent in study and travel abroad on various fellowships and grants, all his life since the end of the second world war has been spent as a university teacher of literature and creative writing. The rather touchy remarks about academic critics and anthologists in the "Preface" to *Selected Poems* should not be taken too seriously. They are partly confessional, for Birney has been both. A few of the poems (I shall cite instances later) do suffer because the literary sophistication of the technique calls attention to itself in a way that is distracting rather than expressive. But this does not happen very often, and in any case it is the price that has to be paid for the successes.

There are some things about *Selected Poems* I do not like, and my praise of the poet would be less convincing if I did not say what they were. Let me do so at once. Some of them, of course, are not the poet's responsibility. The make-up of the book, like so many of McClelland & Stewart's recent volumes of verse, seems to be pretentious and flamboyant, while the illustrations, though good in themselves, seem to be competing with the poems. Poetry ought to be left to speak for itself.

For me the same criticism applies—and here the poet himself must bear the responsibility—to the typographical gimmicks and punctuational nudity imposed on many fine straightforward clear poems that when originally published made their point convincingly and movingly without the promptings of visual aids. In his "Preface" Birney is facetiously indignant at the expense of provincial journalists and conservative critics who have registered a similar objection. Actually it is beside the point to cite the practice of E. E. Cummings. Cummings is a unique, highly special, and absolutely consistent poetic individual. If his influence is to be felt in more than a superficial way it has to be felt in the blood. It will probably be expressed by nothing more showy than the slightly unusual placing of an adverb or the curious elongation of a cadence. To put on another man's hat doesn't make you that man. Birney is so good a poet when he is himself that he has no need to seek a fashionable "modernism" in typographical eccentricity. Poems like "Appeal to a Lady with a Diaper" and "Mammorial Stunzas for Aimee Simple McFarcin", light and satirical as they are, have been made distractingly difficult to read. The visual-aids have become handicaps. The eye has to run an obstacle race.

These are practical and specific objections. I realize perfectly well that there are many typographically expressive passages that are not confusing or difficult at all. Here is a passage from "Letter to a Conceivable Great-Grandson":

> Now we've got automation   Our
>   letters
> are set to de
>   liver them
>   selves
>   fast
>   er than
> meteors   Soon we'll be
> sending wholemanuscriptsprepaidtothe
> planets
> But what's crazy for real is
> we're so damned busy no
> body has time to de   what
>   cipher
> language it is we're   iting
>   r
>   w

This is clear enough, though a little inconvenient to read; and its purpose is clear enough—to make the reader experience, physically and mentally, just what the poem is saying at this particular point, i.e. that we write and transmit so fast that what we write is inconvenient to read. This of course is the modern dogma that Wyndham Lewis and Yvor Winters have attacked—that to express confusion we must write confusedly. My objection to this kind of thing is not that it lacks clarity but that it lacks point: the device is so childishly obvious. However, if as Birney says in his "Preface" these devices are spells to appease an intermittent madman within him let us be grateful and turn to the true poet and the true poems.

Selected Poems is divided into six sections. The first, made up mainly of later poems, is entitled after one of the best pieces in it, "The Bear on the Delhi Road", and is a record of Birney's travels westward from British Columbia to the South Seas, Japan, India, Thailand and back through Greece, Spain, England, and the Arctic home again. These poems, with one or two not very important exceptions, date from the late fifties and the early sixties, and include half a dozen pieces that are among the best things Birney ever wrote—"A Walk in Kyoto", "Bangkok Boy", "The Bear on the Delhi Road", and best of all, the magnificent "El Greco: *Espolio*." Here too is one of the not-so-many light, satirical, gently comic poems that is completely successful—successful I think because the satire here directed against the world of tourism and public relations is directed, even if ever so gently, against the poet himself too. This is the delightful "Twenty-Third Flight" that begins—

> Lo as I pause in the alien vale of the airport
> fearing ahead the official ambush
> a voice languorous and strange as these winds of Oahu
> calleth my name and I turn to be quoited in orchids
> and amazed with a kiss perfumed and soft as the *lei*.
> Straight from a travel poster thou steppest
> thy arms like mangoes for smoothness
> O implausible shepherdess for this one aging sheep—

and continues to the tragi-comic conclusion of the poet so welcomed being nevertheless soon ruthlessly abandoned: "Nay, but thou stayest not?"—

> O nubile goddess of the Kaiser Training Programme
> is it possible that tonight my cup runneth not over
> and that I shall sit in the still pastures of the lobby
> while thou leadest another old ram in garlands past me . . .
> And that I shall lie by the waters of Waikiki and want?

This is my favourite among the comic poems, but there are many others almost equally seductive, some satirical, some whimsical, and some with a wry seriousness, as in the brilliant series of Mexican poems. I don't know where you'll find anything better in modern North American poetry than the combination of wit and sentiment, pertinent observation and auricular, almost ventriloquistic precision than "Sinaloa", "Ajijíc", or "Six-Sided Square: Actopan".

These last poems are in the second section of the book, which is headed "Trans-Americana." The section begins with a series of satirical pieces on certain unlovely aspects of "civilization" north of the Rio Grande. Most of these, when compared with the charm and sureness of "Twenty-Third Flight," seem weak or forced—a defect which may be partly due to the arbitrary typographical eccentricity that has been imposed upon them since they first appeared in earlier volumes.

When we come, however, to the poems on Mexico, Peru, and the Caribbean islands all such cavilling falls away. These are not only among the finest of Birney's poems; they are just simply and plainly, *man, the finest*. The new style that some of our West Coast poets learned from Olson, Creeley, and the Black Mountain writers (and from Birney himself, I suspect) has here been put to uses that transcend the personal and the purely emotional. Poems like "Cartagena de Indias", "Machu Picchu", "Letter to a Cuzco Priest", "Barranquilla Bridge", and others sum up a whole ancient and alien civilization and bring it—and our own—under the scrutiny of a sharp, sensitive, and discursive mind.

When these poems are compared with even the best of the poems of the early forties that make up the next part of the book ("War Winters") we see how great and how sure has been Birney's development as a craftsman in poetry, a development which depends upon and expresses a development in intellectual and emotional maturity. Perhaps this growth in maturity is the achievement of originality, the setting free of a unique poetic personality that after years of work has at last found itself and its true voice. This is not to be taken to mean that such well-known early poems as "Hands", "Vancouver Lights", and "Dusk on the Bay" are not sincere and accurate expressions of what a Canadian felt in the dark days of 1939 and 1940. But it is easier to see now than it was then that they speak with the voices of Auden, Rex Warner, or Stephen Spender, as we feel they might have recalled Rupert Brooke had they been written in 1915. They are true to their time rather than to a unique person, and they are not, therefore, without their own kind of historical significance. They do certainly present an attractive contrast to the war poems of some of the aged survivors of an older generation. Even today only a few poems written later in the war—Douglas LePan's poems of the Italian campaign and Pratt's *Behind the Log*—stand higher than these as interpretations of Canada's war.

In the next section, "Canada: Case History", Birney has grouped those poems, some of them satirical but most of them serious and, indeed, "devout", in which he has come to grips with the problem of what it means to be Canadian and what it is to be a Canadian poet. Viewed as a problem this theme has become something of a nervous obsession, and Birney, like Scott and some others, is at his best when he approaches it obliquely and allows his hawk's eye and his adder's tongue to do the work for him. Everything that is really important is conveyed in the imagery and the diction. Cadences like

> the moon carved unknown totems
> out of the lakeshore
> owls in the beardusky woods derided him
> moosehorned cedars circled his swamps and tossed
> their antlers up to the stars . . .
>   *
> a marten moving like quicksilver scouted us . . .
>   *
> the veins of bald glaciers blackened
> white pulses of waterfalls
> beat in the bare rockflesh

—to give but three brief samples, are simple, sensuous, and passionate. Such indigenous music and imagery give to poems like "David", "Bushed", and the poems of transcontinental air travel, "North Star West", and "Way to the West", a richness that Birney and a few other poets rooted in the native tradition seem to have derived from the earth and air of Canada itself. This is a northern style, and an excellent one. Our sense of its validity is increased when we realize that it is not peculiar to Birney but is a common heritage. Here are some examples chosen almost at random from *The Oxford Book of Canadian Verse*:

> No more the slow stream spreading clear in
>   sunlight
> Lacing the swamp with intricate shining
>   channels . . .
>   the mica glint in the sliding water

>   The bright winged flies and the muskrat gone
>   like a shadow . . .
>   (Floris McLaren)
>   *
> The sachem voices cloven out of the hills
> spat teeth in the sea like nails . . .
>   (Alfred Bailey)
>   *
> On the North Shore a reptile lay asleep . . .
>   (E. J. Pratt)
>   *
> Sinuous, red as copper snakes,
> Sharp-headed serpents, made of light,
> Glided, and hid themselves in night. . . .
>   (Isabella Crawford)

This last passage, and the poem from which I have taken it, shows better than all the explanations in the "Preface" why Birney is impatient with commas and rhyme.

Of course not every one of the northern poems has the linguistic rightness of "Bushed" or "David". Sometimes his Eng. Lit. sophistication betrays Birney into an overstrained conceit, as for example in these lines from "Page of Gaspé"—

> Between over-generous margins
> between the unprinted river and the rubbed-out peaks
> run the human typelines . . .
> farms split to sentences by editor death
> fattening subtitles of rockfence . . .
> In this repetitive prose a sawmill
> sets quotemarks after the stone windmill's period . . .

or leads him to indulge in a sort of metrical plagiarism. "North of Superior" is filled with more or less erudite allusions to Scyldings, Excalibur, the Green Knight, the Den of Error, Azazel, and Roland, and the metre which recalls Pound's "Seafarer" in the first stanza reminds us of "Evangeline" in the second.

But these are occasional failures. To risk making them is the price every alive and eager artist must pay for his successes. One such success is surely the fine reflective poem "November Walk Near False Creek Mouth", the major work in Birney's last collection of new poems. It is dated "Vancouver 1961—Ametlla, Spain 1963". "November Walk" is a rich meditative ode-like poem that gathers up the themes of the long series of descriptive, narrative, and reflective poems set in or near Vancouver from "Dusky on the

Bay" and "Hands" to the present, and finally and on a much larger scale achieves what the poet had been groping for from the start of his career—an orientation of himself and his place and his time in terms that are both emotionally and rationally satisfying. This poem stands with the poems on Mexico and Peru as the high water mark of Birney's achievement up to now. Most encouraging of all, it gives promise of fine things still to come, for it shows the poet has found a style commensurate with the theme he has approached in many different ways in many different poems— man's effort as microcosm to come to terms with society, nature, and the macrocosm in the brief moment of allotted time. It is a promise that makes Birney's remark in the "Preface"—"In my next work I am thinking of pasting my poems on mobiles"—seem like the frivolous joke it's intended as.

The fifth section of *Selected Poems,* headed rather journalistically "Letter to a Conceivable Great-Grandson", is the least successful part of the book. It is a somewhat haphazard collection of pieces on the threat of atomic extinction and the ironies and confusions inherent in the world of cold-war distrust and science-fiction posturing. The point of view is liberal and humane, and the sentiments are those which all decent men must share. The trouble with this sort of poetry is not something that can be laid at the door of an individual poet. The responsibility is elsewhere. These excellent sentiments are shared (and expressed) by politicians, statesmen, editorial writers, publicists and generals who find them no bar whatsoever to actions and votes that lead in the practical world to the aggravation and perpetuation of the crisis that they (hypocritically) and the liberal poet (ineffectively) lament. The result is a widening of the gap between the poem's practical intention and the possible achievement of that end. Perhaps its most successful accomplishment is to demonstrate the futility of poetry as propaganda and drive home the corollary that action alone is adequate. This built-in demonstration of its own uselessness is what vitiates nearly all poetry that takes a bold stand against sin, and makes the social poetry of Birney, and of Frank Scott too, the weakest part of their work. Two of the finest poems, however, in this part of the book are translations from Mao Tse-tung made with the assistance of Professor Ping-ti Ho, of The University of British Columbia and Peking University. Here the cleverness and strain of some of the poems and the echoes of Spender and Rex Warner in others give way to a simple direct style that is very moving indeed.

There is not much that needs to be said here about "Damnation of Vancouver," which forms the final section of this book. Originally published as *Trial of a City* in 1952, it was recognized as one of the most original and technically accomplished of Birney's poems, a *tour de force* of linguistic virtuosity and a satire as biting as anything in Canadian literature. It marked a distinct advance on the simple and unified narrative "David", mingling as it did the colloquial and the grand styles and the satirical and the affirmative modes. It thus anticipates the South and Central American poems of the sixties and fuses perfectly for the first time in Birney's work the two themes that Northrop Frye has named as central to Canadian poetry, "one a primarily comic theme of satire and exuberance, the other a primarily tragic theme of loneliness and terror."

For the new book Birney has revised what was originally a poem or masque and turned it into a play, complete with elaborate stage directions, descriptions of actions (business), and statements about the emotional implications and tones of voice to be got into some of the speeches. This is fine for the amateur actor and the inexperienced director, but the reader of poetry, I should think, would prefer to take his poetry neat. The development of the theme —which is the rape of the land of the Indians by the forces of commercial exploitation and "progress"—comes through more vividly in the original version.

What remains to be said in conclusion? Not very much surely. It is quite clear that Earle Birney is one of our major poets, perhaps since the death of E. J. Pratt our leading poet. Certainly he is the only rival of Pratt as the creator of heroic narrative on a bold scale and, unlike Pratt, he has been consistently experimental. He has not always been successful, and he has sometimes aped styles and fashions that are unworthy of his real talents; but without a somewhat boyish spirit of adventure his successes would have been impossible too. The real triumph of *Selected Poems* is that it demonstrates so clearly and forcibly—as does indeed the whole of Birney's career—a unified personality of great charm, wit, strength, and generosity. I recall Louis MacNeice's description of the modern poet. I have quoted it before, but it fits the poet I have been discussing so well that I can think of no better words to end with. "I would have a poet able-bodied, fond of talking, a reader of the newspapers, capable of pity and laughter, informed in economics, appreciative of women, involved in personal relationships, actively interested in politics, susceptible to physical impressions . . ." This is the man I know, and the poet who rises out of this book.

POET WITHOUT A MUSE

MILTON WILSON

You might suppose that Earle Birney was too busy creating new poems to worry about collecting old ones. But for a writer whose old poems never stop pestering him to be transformed into new ones, the first task is hard to separate from the second. These *Selected Poems 1940-1966* aren't really a retrospective show; they challenge us to see Birney not so much plain as anew. I've read his work far too often in the past to make a fresh look very easy. What follows is at best a series of notes towards an unwritten revised portrait.

1

The more Birney you read, the less he looks like anybody else. His asymmetrical, bulky, unpredictable accumulation of poems gathers individuality as it grows. In context even the least distinguished members start to seem unlikely and even independent. For a poet so unmistakably of his own time and place, he is a surprisingly free agent. Certainly no influential contemporary has ever taught him how to iron out any local idiosyncrasies and unfashionable commonplaces that he preferred to keep. He has learned only what he wanted and at his own speed. Any inescapable influence of his generation that he found irrelevant (T. S. Eliot, for example), he has managed to escape completely. What gives his work distinctiveness, I suppose, is not so much its originality as its mixture of openness and stubbornness, of cleverness and provinciality, even the way it sometimes stumbles over its own reality, like that half-teachable bear the title of whose poem Birney sets at the entrance to this selection.

2

If the problem of Birney's education as a poet is worth a second glance, it ought to be a very careful and sceptical one, particularly now that we have these *Selected Poems*, which throw doubt on many of the old Birney legends. Take the matter of chronology.

From *Canadian Literature*, 30 (1966), pages 14-20. By permission of Milton Wilson and *Canadian Literature*.

The legend of Birney the late starter may have to give way to Birney the late publisher, depending on how seriously you take the vital statistics of date and place with which he has labelled his offspring, some of them—like "North of Superior" (labelled "1926-1945") and "Mammorial Stunzas for Aimee Simple Mc-Farcin" (labelled "Toronto 1932-San Francisco 1934," but first printed in a *Prism* of 1959)—apparently twice-born or at least held in suspension for a long time. Did Birney draft a full-scale version of "North of Superior" in 1926 or did the 1945 version just incorporate a jotted image or two from the distant past? Was "Mammorial Stunzas", which seems so characteristic of Birney's linguistic high spirits in the fifties, entirely conceived in the early thirties or did the young Birney merely give Aimee her graffiti from Belshazzar's feast and a pun or two on her name and then wait twenty-five years for the right poem to go with them and justify publication? The dating, in this case, seems to insist on a finished product in 1934 (or as finished as a Birney poem ever allows itself to be—the format has been completely reshaped for 1966). At least I will now stop being puzzled as to why anyone would choose to write Aimee's definitive poem long after everyone else had forgotten her.

Then there's the legend of a poetic hiatus in the mid-fifties, of a Birney unproductive because he had maybe lost faith in poetry or humanity or even himself. But, from the new vantage point, any hiatus, if it existed, starts to look pretty small, the sort of thing that needed little more than a trip to Mexico for its cure. And anyway, if Birney can write and only publish twenty or twenty-five years later, who knows what piles of unpublished poems lie in his bottom drawer waiting for their public moment?

3

Simple questions of chronology may be tricky, but the difficulties are multiplied for anyone who ventures to talk about Birney's poetic development and its relation to his poetic contemporaries. Most of the obvious half-truths that used to occur to me, I now find myself wanting to qualify almost as soon as I have uttered them. The staple product of conventional up-to-date British and American poetry can (very broadly indeed) be described as having moved from a metaphoric and allusive phase in the thirties and forties to a more linguistic—idiomatic and syntactic—one in the fifties and sixties, from the rhetoric of the image to the rhetoric of the voice. It's tempting to see Birney's own development following a similar course, with *Trial of a City* (1952) as the Janus-faced turning point. Nobody could be surprised at the date of an elaborate editorial conceit like "Page of Gaspé" (1943-1950) or an even more elaborate tidal one like "The Ebb Begins from Dream" (1945-1947)—despite Birney's difficulty persuading editors to print the latter. Still, although they date, they aren't just dated. The slightly later "North Star West" (1951) seems more of a mere period piece, the sort of inventive and readable exercise in imagery that with luck you might be able to bring off in those days. Indeed, if I interpret a remark in Birney's Preface correctly, that may be part of the point of the poem. But, while some of Birney's poems could (and in fact did) fit quite snugly into the post-war world of *Penguin New Writing,* the philologist and verbal mimic didn't need to wait until *Trial of a City* to be released. Among the early poems for which obviously no retrospective indulgence at all is needed are "Anglo-Saxon Street", "Mappemounde" and "War Winters". Birney is amused by those critics who though that to write the verse of these poems he had to be an imitator of Hopkins, instead of just a mere student and teacher of mediaeval literature. Although he is properly aware of the dangers in any academic-poetic alliance, his own academic niche could hardly have been a luckier choice.

4

Birney's vocal virtuosity hasn't seemed out of place in the more recent worlds of "articulate energy" and "projective verse", or on the p.a. circuit. But he can't be confused with the new virtuosos of breath and syntax, and his academic context certainly predates structural linguistics. There's also something a bit old-fashioned about his taste for "phonetic" spelling; it doesn't help much for Birney to write "damnear" or "billyuns," when nobody says "damn near" or "billions" anyway. I suppose that it all justifies itself, in that without it the "Billboards" and "Diaper" poems couldn't have been written at all, but they remind me a bit of the easy old days when all a writer had to do to present his readers with a recognizable substandard dialect was to spell their own standard dialect as they really pronounced it. Birney's phonetic technique works best with an exotic like the speaker in that delightful monologue "Sinaloa". The people who strike my ear most successfully, however, receive no such phonetic help, like the two-tongued Colombian bookseller in "Cartagena de Indias", which (if I had to make a choice) I would call his finest poem.

5

Birney's other notational idiosyncrasies interest me far more than his spelling. Except for a few poems (notably "David", "The Damnation of Vancouver" and the translations) and a few special places within poems (mainly conversations), instead of using the conventional comma, semicolon, colon and period as rhetorical and syntactic signposts, he now relies mainly on spacing and lineation, and has revised his old poems accordingly.

He is not (so the Preface tells us) trying to facilitate immediate and accurate reading or comprehension by these changes; on the contrary, his aim is "the art of indefinitely delayed communication —Infinite Ambiguity." I don't know how seriously to take these last phrases; I do know that the new ambiguity is real enough, and in a few cases results in a new awkwardness. The chief problem is at the end of a line, where the distinction between endstopped and run-on lines is no longer visible, even when still relevant. One space starts to look like any other space, whether it breaks or ends a line. In "Captain Cook" when

> flashed him a South Sea shilling; like a javelin
> it split the old shop's air.

is revised to

> flashed him a South Sea shilling   like a javelin
> it split the old shop's air

the phrase at the end of the first line can now look backwards and forwards instead of just forwards. It wouldn't be hard to defend the ambiguity of *that* revised version. But in the same poem when

> First voyage, mouths burning
> from the weevils in the biscuits,
> charted New Zealand.

is revised to

> First voyage   mouths burning
> from the weevils in the biscuits
> charted New Zealand

the new syntactic ambiguity of the second line is a doubtful blessing indeed. It may be amusing, but the joke is at the expense of the poem.

The advantages and disadvantages of the new notation are worth weighing not just from passage to passage but from poem to poem. One fine poem that I much prefer to see in its old format is "Wake Island": the format in the *Selected Poems* seems more confusing than ambiguous. On the other hand, while not a word of "Late Afternoon in Manzanilla" has been altered, the poem looks twice as good and comes off twice as well in its new format. I had no idea until now what an excellent poem it is.

Of course, the reaction against the clutter of punctuation in favour of the austerity of space Birney shares with a good many of his newer contemporaries. But he isn't always that austere (dashes, apostrophes, question marks, etc. are used), or, for that matter, consistent. In the new space-filled pages, even a few concluding periods still survive (I'm glad that he kept the one at the end of the "Diaper" poem), although, so far as I've noticed, only one anomalous comma (near the end of "Tavern by the Hellespont") :

                                    Between
        the individual tables   couples   uncoupled
      by the radio's decision, turn to their true oneness—

and here, although I like to think that it's an unexpected attempt to limit Infinite Ambiguity, it may be just an editorial or proofreading oversight, like the mislineation that disfigures "The Damnation of Vancouver" on page 176.

6

Not that Birney minds anomalies anyway. Some of his best poems are sports. No one could possibly anticipate them, he has shown no desire to repeat them, but once written they are an inevitable choice for his *Selected Poems*, no matter how stringent the selection. "St. Valentine Is Past" is an obvious example. One of the few Birney poems that reads like a pure gift from his muse (he is not the sort of poet whom one usually credits with a muse), it has remained virtually unchanged since appearing in 1952's *Trial of a City and Other Verse*. In these ballad quatrains, while Theseus is off on his boar-hunt, and death seems mercifully at a distance, love finds late fulfilment under a shadowless sky. The lovers, like the age-old elements of earth and water, renew their long-past youthful fertility, and, for a day at least, seem to have Time on their side.

> While he is rooted rock she strikes
> to foam a loud cascade
> that drowns the jeering gullish wings
> far crashings in the glade
>
> No more while lizard minutes sleep
> around a cactus land
> they'll blow their longings out like spores
> that never grass the sand.
>
> No longer Time's a cloud of cliffs
> unechoed by her Nile . . .

But these elemental lovers or late-coupling birds or aging Venus and Adonis (or whatever you wish to call them) are no match for dusty Time. And, as their elegiac, unkept sounds fade away, the pastness of St. Valentine's Day is sealed by the return of hunter, boar and pack.

> And yet and yet a failing rod
> strikes only dust from rock
> while all the tune and time they breathe
> is never kept in talk
>
> Now water sky and rock are gone
> the huddled woodbirds back
> and hot upon the throbbing boar
> comes Theseus and his pack

Although Birney, in his primitive or mediaeval or modern vein (sometimes all at once), is often a poet of myths, as such different poems as "Mappemounde", "Pachuchan Miners", "Takkakaw Falls", "Bushed", "Ballad of Mr Chubb" and, of course, "November Walk near False Creek Mouth" (with its updated characters from the sagas) make evident, nevertheless the sort of Renaissance myth-making that "St. Valentine Is Past" does superbly seems to me totally uncharacteristic of him. If I had to choose a historical niche for him other than his own, the Age of Spenser would be my last choice.

And yet, in other respects, this is a typical Birney love poem, typical at least of his published range. In a recent article on Irving Layton, George Woodcock has praised our older love poets at the expense of their younger rivals. But Birney's love poems have been elegiac and autumnal from the start, or, when not elegiac, at least about love at a distance (e.g., "This Page My Pigeon" and, in a sense, "The Road to Nijmegen"). The very lovely "Under the Hazel Bough" (stylistically another anomaly, but quite different from "St. Valentine is Past".) is destined to this end:

> but no man sees
> where the trout lie now
> or what leans out
> from the hazel bough

In some recent poems the autumnal erotic note takes on a January-and-May form. I'm thinking not just of "Haiku for a Young Waitress", "Curacao" and "Twenty-third Flight", but also of "On the Beach" (which I miss from these *Selected Poems*), where the no longer agile speaker cries:

> I will follow in a small trot only
> not whirling
> O girl from the seafoam
> have pity

and even of "A Walk in Kyoto", where sex somehow triumphs over "the ancient discretions of Zen".

7

Perhaps all that I have just been doing is applying to his love poems the cliché that Birney is in some respects a very Chaucerian kind of poet. That cliché deserves its wider application too. To begin with, there is his basic impersonality. You can learn practically nothing about him as a private person from his published poems. Self-revelation or self-analysis is not his business. And yet, like Chaucer, and increasingly with age, he enjoys offering us a kind of persona in the foreground: the innocent scapegoat of "Meeting of Strangers", the aging and garlanded ram of "Twenty-third Flight", the absurdly grateful initiate of "Cartagena de Indias". If one of these days somebody writes a Ph.D. thesis called *Birney's Irony,* one person on whom the irony will not be lost is Birney himself.

UP, OVER, AND OUT:
THE POETRY OF DISTRACTION

HAYDEN CARRUTH

Normally when a reviewer is confronted by a book he does not like, but whose author is nevertheless a distinguished elder of the tribe, he is inclined to say nothing about it—in one thousand nice, ripe nothing-words. After all, what is the point of belabouring work that is done: it offers so little likelihood of significant alteration and improvement. Let it rest; like everything, it will seek and in due course find its own level; probably sooner than later. Let its author take what comfort he can from the knowledge that he has worked hard and honestly, has done the best he could 'in the circumstances' (that marvelous *ur*-phrase); and from the gratifying daily disclosures that his effort has acquired for him a fair degree of public approbation, etc., etc., etc.

The case of Mr Earle Birney forces us, however, to take a harder view of our obligation. In a small-minded, testy little preface to his *Selected Poems,* he makes two points (somewhat improbably conjoined): first, that he despises virtually all reviewers; and second, that he is indifferent to virtually all reviews. This being so, what shall we do but plough ahead, in an answering spirit of disregard? As Mr Jackie Gleason has remarked so cogently: 'Away we go!'

But first I must point out, in hasty if inadequate amends, that Mr Birney says his preface was written at all only at the urgent behest of his publisher. If this is true, then certainly no publisher ever gave his author worse advice. Let it be stated categorically: in the selected and collected editions of the works of established writers *any hermeneutic or apologetic material of any kind whatever* is a distraction. Further, in ninety per cent of such cases it is an unseemly distraction. Of course Mr Birney should have been pig-headed enough to resist his publisher; but we know that such cases often require a finesse of temper exceeding the syntagma of 'ordinary reality'; we know we must not ask too much, especially from poets. I had read few of Mr Birney's poems prior to receiving his selected edition in the mail, for none of his books has been published in the U.S., but I had heard him read some of them on the CBC, and had heard him also expound his poetic convictions,

From *The Tamarack Review,* 42 (1967), pp. 61-69. By permission of Hayden Carruth.

and he had struck me then as an intelligent, urbane, amiable, forthright, and interesting person; I have no reason to believe otherwise now.

In the context of these first three paragraphs, then, I shall, with my readers' indulgence, set down my observations of Mr Birney's poems in a somewhat random manner, since any attempt to organize an all-out attack on the issues raised by his book, and by its relationship to the general cultural mess, would extend far beyond the limits of a book review.

1. Descriptive and catalogue material first. Mr Birney's *Selected Poems* contains, by his own count, one hundred pieces. I have no idea what proportion of his entire *œuvre* this represents; but presumably, since he has chosen them himself and since the book is offered to us with all the flourishes usually accompanying a 'definitive edition' and a 'major literary event' (Index of Titles, Index of First Lines, copious auxiliary press intelligence, etc.), it is at least adequate. Almost all the poems bear datelines: Elphinstone 1946; Peru 1962; Hong Kong 1958; etc. Some bear doubledatelines, *e.g.,* Nueve Ixtapan 1956-1962, or Colombia 1962-Greece 1963, indicating not only an enviable amount of moving around but also some protracted, serious, and doubtless self-critical labour. As I thumb through the pages of his book, the earliest date I see is 1921, the latest is 1965—a considerable span. Mr Birney says in his preface that all the poems but one have been published previously, and he leaves it up to the 'numerologists', as he calls them, to discover which is the added poem; a task that may not be easy since all but eight of the poems, as Mr Birney also informs us, have been altered from their original forms, in some cases substantially. Although my own attitude toward hard-working bibliographers is much more respectful than Mr Birney's, I have no access to his previous texts, and hence must follow his example in leaving this work of identification to others. One of the most offensive aspects of Mr Birney's preface, incidentally, is his extreme condescension to the entire academic corps, in the face of what we are told on the flap of his dust jacket and in the ancillary press releases, viz., that he has been supported for years and years by the universities. Granted, most teachers are jugheads; but considering the extraordinary reliance we place upon the minority who are not, I doubt that anyone may wisely commit himself to this kind of hurtful, generalizing scorn, least of all someone who has been working the same end of the street. Finally, Mr Birney's book is decorated with six pen-and-brush drawings by Mr Leonard

Brooks. To my taste, whatever merit these drawings may have *in se*, they are so abominably reproduced in the pages of this book that they can only be assigned to the same distractive rôle as the preface.

2. Turning to the substance of the *Selected Poems,* we find that the main alteration Mr Birney has made in his work is perfectly evident to us without any reference to the earlier texts. He has removed all the punctuation. Or rather, he has substituted one method of punctuation for another; or, more precisely still, he has substituted a method of punctuation which he very deficiently understands for a method which he probably understood rather well. The result is equally plain in almost any of the poems. Here are the opening lines of 'Dusk on the Bay', dated 1941:

>   The lighting rooms perfect a checkerboard
>   across apartment boxes   Through the popcorn
>   reek   hotdogs and chips   the air lets fall
>   a rain of quiet coolness on the flesh   The calling
>   bathers trot the footpocked sand on legs
>   unsexed by distance   waving arms severed
>   with twilight   from the whitening ribs of the raft divers
>   flash cream arcs across the expiring
>   sunset   and are quenched   Beyond the bay the files

No one can justly object to any poet using any convention of punctuation he chooses, provided he understands it and uses it well. Here we are faced with something entirely different. Obviously Mr Birney has tried to modernize an old-fashioned poem by making a change in its appearance, *i.e.*, by inserting spaces where formerly he had commas, semi-colons, and periods. But no amount of superficial tinkering could disguise this poem. Even if he had not attached a date to it, we could not fail to recognize the characteristic heavy and pointless rhetoric, the absurd hyperbole, of the Forties and Fifties; this is third-rate Eberhart, fifth-rate Tate. It is pretty awful. But what is more important, it shows that Mr Birney is insensitive to the actual value of space in the typographical re-presentation of a poem. For what do his spaces accomplish? Exactly what his commas, semi-colons, and period accomplished, except that the spaces are harder to read and distractive (like his preface). Mr Birney says that he has learned his method of space-punctuation "willingly" from younger poets, but I wonder who they are. If there are young Canadian poets who use spaces the way Mr Birney does, they must be remarkably obscure. George Bowering, André Major, and Paul Chamberland, among others, have used spaces within lines, but sparingly and never, I think, in lieu of other punctuation; while in the U.S. various poets, notably Gary Snyder and Robert Duncan, have used space to indicate a pause within the line which cannot be indicated by conventional punctuation. But Mr Birney did not need to turn to his juniors. William Carlos Williams began experimenting with the uses of space in the late Thirties, I believe, and Ezra Pound even before that. The point is that space can be used to do something which cannot be done otherwise, and this is its appropriate use; Mr. Birney seems unaware of it.

. . . .

What Mr. Birney has done, on the other hand, has no reasonable explanation whatever. It is prosodic fiddle-faddle.

3. Even so, we could take it if the poems were good enough: the authority of a good poem drives everything before it, putting us, while we search out the goodness, to glad offence and joyful exasperation; as we have seen in our time often enough. Unfortunately Mr Birney's poems lack this authority. I judge from his datelines that he has travelled a good deal, and his poems have the traveller's superficiality. Most of them spring from a particular occasion; something arrests Mr Birney's eye—women in a marketplace, dandelions beside a brook, old ladies on a summer verandah —it can be almost anything. He describes it for us, usually in a forced, artful diction, and then at the end tacks on his own feeling about what he has described, usually sociological in nature. Of the hundred poems in his book, I would guess that eighty conform to this pattern. In short, they are sermons-from-stones poems. The pattern is an exceedingly common one, of course, that has plagued poets for hundreds of years, so that it is almost second nature for people who wish to contrive a poem to let their thoughts fall into three parts. In the first the poet shows us the stone as he has first seen it; in the middle part he walks around the stone and gives us the varying views; and at the end he gives us the sermon. Now no one would be foolish enough to deny that a few splendid poems have been written in this pattern, especially by the English Romantics. But how few! Think of the beginnings of great poems:

> And yet this great wink of eternity,
> Of rimless floods, unfettered leewardings

> Bright star, would I were steadfast as thou art!

April is the cruellest month

Afoot and lighthearted I take to the open road

They flee from me that one time did me seek

Of asphodel, that greeny flower,
    like a buttercup
        upon its branching stem—
save that it's green and wooden—
    I come, my sweet,
        to sing to you.
We lived long together

Descriptions in every case, but in the functionally revaluative language of coterminous mythopoeic commitment, to speak in a ghastly jargon. Isn't the feeling—the sermon, the meaning—instinct in these poems from the first syllable? And isn't this virtually the definition of a good poem? When Eliot invented the 'objective correlative', he placed as much emphasis on the second term as on the first; an object less than completely correlated with the poet's feeling would be no object at all, poetically speaking. But the correlation of object and feeling, of language and intention, in most of Mr Birney's poems is uncertain, to say the least. Many of his poems have the air of having been 'worked up' from meagre beginnings: worked up, worked over, and—too often—worked out.

    4. Mr Birney's best poem—and I think this is significant—is the long poem called 'David', which is an uncharacteristic poem for him because it is a narrative, the only out-and-out narrative in his book. Here the correlation I speak of is unavoidable; the 'story' demands it. The language is mostly apt and restrained, the rhythmic pattern works well, the substance is simple and original. Mr Birney seems positively put out because this poem, which he does not think his best, has been so popular, and he cites ruefully (but he cites!) the 'twenty-three anthologies' in which it has appeared. One need not be in love with anthologists to realize that they are, nevertheless, more often right than wrong. At any rate, they are right in this instance. It is notable also that 'David' is the one poem in his book, not counting a radio play and several translations, which Mr Birney has failed to repunctuate with spaces: I say 'notable', but why was 'David' spared? One can think of . . . oh, well, let it pass. Two or three of Mr Birney's conventional lyrics, which no amount of space-punctuation can

de-conventionalize, are charming and workable; such poems as 'From the Hazel Bough' and 'Wind Chimes in a Temple Ruin'. Among his satires I find two especially that are taut and sharp and bright, 'Billboards Build Freedom of Choice' and 'Canada: Case History', but others, like 'Ballad of Mr Chubb', are simply banal. The long poem called 'November Walk near False Creek Mouth' is too long and a good deal too imitative to be ultimately interesting, though it contains some engaging passages.

5. In the press releases Mr Birney is called 'the dean of Canadian poets', and I am told by people who probably know that the epithet is just; that is, among literate Canadians who know anything about contemporary poetry, a large number regard Mr Birney as the leading Canadian poet. I do not know how Mr Birney feels about this; sometimes he seems to wish to be modern and radical, sometimes he seems to wish to be Top Dog in the Establishment. His position is ambiguous; or perhaps he really doesn't care one way or the other. What is significant is that he has become dean by common consent, so to speak. This shows something—I am not prepared to say exactly what—about Canadian civilization at large; or perhaps I should say about English-Canadian civilization. It is always invidious to compare the actual poetic accomplishments of leading poets, and I will not do so with Mr Birney, at least not any more than I have already; but it is not invidious to compare attitudes. Whatever one may say about Eliot, for example—and I have written many things both good and bad about him—he was without doubt the dean of English-speaking poets before he died, and he was also without doubt a serious poet. He failed in some important respects, but in all his work he met his own criterion of genuineness. There was no playing around by Eliot, no working up of meagre poems on set themes. He was, that is to say, the serious leader 'elected' by a serious society. In Mr Birney's case, my criticism under Paragraph 3 above comes down to this: a lack of poetic seriousness, a lack of poetic faith. Is it Mr Birney's fault? Judging from his work and what little more I know about him, I expect he is very profoundly a product of English-Canadian culture. What about the younger poets? Not long ago in this magazine (Autumn, 1965) George Bowering had a poem called 'Windigo' that seemed at first, to us in the United States, just what we are looking for from Canada: fresh, clean, and natural in its formal elements, distinctively Canadian in its thematic elements. But as we read on, we began to be disappointed, for we saw it falling into the same pattern: the

sermon in the stone. The three parts; discrete and, as Eliot would have said, dissociated; betraying lack of feeling, lack of faith. Many sound historical objections have been raised to Eliot's concept of the 'dissociation of sensibility', chiefly because Eliot himself made it more pretentious than it should have been; it is simply a catch-concept, and as such very handy, for determining genuineness or lack of genuineness in the poetic faith of a society at large or of a poem like Bowering's. Not that there isn't plenty of such poetry, and worse, produced in the U.S.: tons and tons of it every week; I do not mean to be inimical or rancorous, merely questioning. There is a considerable step forward, I think, from Birney to Bowering—and to Newlove, perhaps to Purdy, Everson, and Davey. Is a breakthrough coming? Is the pattern eradicable? I don't know, and in order to find out I should need to read much more Canadian poetry than I shall have time to read if I am to meet my other obligations, though I have read far more already than most people on this side of the frontier. But it isn't necessary, is it? There must be Canadians sensitive enough to these delicate aspects of cultural sociology to tell us that the breakthrough *is* coming, and when, and where. What we are awaiting now is for them to stand up and say it loud enough for everyone to hear.

A. W. PURDY, LETTER TO THE EDITOR OF *Tamarack Review*

I'd like to commend *Tamarack* for its review of Earle Birney's *Selected Poems* in issue No. 42. I think it was an excellent idea to have a non-poet do the review.

The important business of using spaces instead of punctuation in poems was treated with admirable brevity in a page and a half. The reader is also furnished with a definitive list of first lines from great poems as an illustration of the 'objective correlative' and the 'functionally revaluative language of coterminous mythopoeic commitment' which Birney has not got.

I am grateful to Hayden Carruth for pointing out the delicate shades of difference between Birney being called the dean of Canadian poetry by 'common consent' and T. S. Eliot as 'the serious leader "elected" by a serious society'. I'm sure that in the great and serious democracy of America an elective office is more significant than common consent.

From *The Tamarack Review*, 43 (1967), page 100. By permission of Al Purdy.

But the review's most valuable contribution comes in mentioning a poem called "Wendigo' (first published in *Tamarack*): 'that seemed at first, to us in the United States, just what we are looking for from Canada: fresh, clear, and natural in its formal elements, distinctively Canadian in its thematic elements'.

Hitherto Canadian poets and other Canadians of a dissident nature have been rather in the dark as to what was required of them by the United States. There has even been some degree of cynicism in the matter, which Hayden Carruth has most happily dispelled. In a prose message at once logical and inspiring he tells us that what is required is good poems, 'fresh, clear, and natural' that are 'distinctively Canadian'. Thanks to Hayden Carruth there is no longer any evading this ringing clarion call for the Canadian beaver, Canadian maple leaves and sugar, Winnipeg gold-eye, fiddleheads, wendigos (northern spirits), ookpiks, baked apples, Arctic char, and Quebec separatists. The formal and thematic elements of these, allied of course to the objective correlative and the functionally revaluative coterminous commitment, should ensure that great poetry is available for export in sufficient quantity. Of course this might affect stock market quotations on other exports, such as oil, iron, newsprint, and napalm; but it is a risk true Canadian poets will have to take.

Alfred Purdy

JOE ROSENBLATT, LETTER TO THE EDITOR OF *Tamarack Review*

With the occasional aid of a seeing-eye Webster I managed to trudge through the viscous prose of Hayden Carruth in his review of Earle Birney's *Selected Poems*.

I have never read such a sniping review of a poet's work! It seems to have been written by a small-minded Yankee pedant and grammarian. At least a thousand words of the 'criticism' consisted of Carruth taking Birney to task for 'inserting spaces where formerly he had commas, semicolons, and periods . . . Mr. Birney is insensitive to the actual value of space in the typographical representation of a poem'. If E. E. Cummings heard that, he'd roll over in a comma. Perhaps Hayden Carruth, whose poems I can't find in any of the Toronto libraries, will instruct Dr. Birney in the importance of space navigation?

From *The Tamarack Review,* 43 (1967), pages 100-101. By permission of Joe Rosenblatt.

Another cardinal Birney crime (requiring an additional thousand words of recrimination) is that his preface slams back at his critics. Why in the old days a critic would be challenged to a duel by a poet who had been given heat treatment. At least Birney prefers words to bullets. But it seems Birney has attacked the entire academic herd (in which Carruth is at least a faithful steer). How terrible! Birney betraying his class? 'Granted', says Carruth, 'most teachers are jugheads. . . .'

The gist of Carruth's complaint seems to be that Birney writes 'sermons-from-stones poems'. Really, I can't imagine Cromwellian Birney, who has stepped on the heads of the critics, writing a 'sermon' about a luscious Spanish female his eyes have snared in a Mexican market place. If his poetry reveals anything, it's not sermonizing but healthy observation on the part of a poet in his sixties. But try to explain that to the kind of pedant who uses jargon like 'conterminous myothopoetic commitment' [*sic*—Ed. (*Tamarack Review*)]!

I really don't know what possessed the editor of *Tamarack*, 'elected by serious society', to publish such a garbage review of a major Canadian poet. Birney's serious commitment to the poetry-reading public and the long record of aid and encouragement he has given to hundreds of young poets entitle him to be assessed by someone better known as a poet and more competent as a critic.

Joe Rosenblatt

TURNING NEW LEAVES

GEORGE WOODCOCK

Earle Birney is not the kind of poet who is willingly definitive about himself. Many younger men than he have come forward with their Collected Poems, and some of them, like Spender and Roy Fuller, are among the best poets of our time, but Birney will have none of this closing off; though he talks wryly about his "poetic cinders" in the introduction to his new volume, in fact he is not willing to admit that his past is without a future. And so he presents, as the nearest thing to a definite retrospective gathering of his best works, a thick and attractive looking volume of *Selected Poems*. Its great visual handsomeness, let me say before going any farther, is due mainly to Birney's old friend, Leonard Brooks, who has illustrated the poems with a series of ink and collage drawings which are among the best of his works I have so far seen.

Though past titles have somewhat masked the fact, this is the last of a whole series of Birney "selected poems," but we must be on our guard against assuming that these are quite the same poems as we have read before. As Birney tells us, all but eight of the ninety-nine pieces now collected "are altered from their first printing"; altered, indeed, several times in some cases, as anyone who looks through the past volumes and sees some of these poems appearing time and again, will have realised. This sense that the future is always open, that nothing written is ever quite finished while its author is still alive, is one of Birney's special characteristics as a writer, and it is this, more than the accident of their having lived in Vancouver at the same time, more even than friendship, which explains the peculiar affinity he felt with Malcolm Lowry, that arch-reviser who found it more difficult, the longer he lived, to bring an end to the process of constant rewriting that would make a work ready for final publication. Birney edited the only volume of Lowry's poems that has so far appeared, and this also, significantly, was a *Selected Poems*.

This attitude towards his work can tell us a great deal about Birney as a poet, and particularly it helps to explain the feel as much as the content of his writing—and he is too sharply intellectual a poet for us ever to be lulled into under-estimating the latter. It helps also to explain the image of Birney that has arisen in the

From *Canadian Forum*, 46 (1966), pages 115-6. By permission of George Woodcock and *Canadian Forum*.

minds of so many of his readers, the image of the late but speedy starter, perhaps best expressed in a sentence by John Robert Colombo. "He seems to have discovered the fountain of youth late in life; he drank from it but broke all the rules by retaining the wisdom of his previous years." But, as anyone who studies the dates which are honestly appended to the pieces in *Selected Poems* will realise, Birney was not in fact a late starter. Some of the poems, though revised later, were first written forty-five years ago, and quite a number, including—one is surprised to be reminded—"Mammorial Stunzas for Aimée Simple McFarcin," during the 1930's. Indeed, what does impress me about Birney's career is not a sense of late blossoming, of chrysanthemums precariously daring the first frosts, but rather an almost unique combination of tenacity and freshness. When I first visited Birney in his office in the Old Arts Building at the University of British Columbia, more years ago than I care to count, I was surprised to see that he kept his rejection slips and had plastered a wall with them; he seemed to treasure the wounds his poems had suffered as much as their victories. Even now it is with pride that he tells us in the introduction to his *Selected Poems* that one of the pieces included was turned down twenty-seven times before acceptance, and another thirty-six times. So doggedly to have seen his poetic children through multiple editorial failures to ultimate success, and at the same time to have generated and built up the vigour that marks his best poems, shows not only an unusual obstinacy of character, but also a talent so set on its autonomous course that nothing would keep it from its chosen road even if no destination can yet be announced. For this book, which is Birney's best to date, sets him in Janus stance, looking back over the career which has already made him one of the best poets actually writing today, but also forward to the productive years before the Selection closes into the Collection; given Birney's present reality, there may be many of them.

I mentioned, a moment ago, "Mammorial Stunzas" and this poem—incidentally one of Birney's own favourites—seems to me the kind of piece that immediately sets up a verbal mirror to the poet: not the poet as seen in his subject, though there is something of the adept spellbinder about Birney himself, but rather the poet as seen in his way of presenting the subject, the voice and the manner rather than what is said. Parody—the utilisation of Joycean wordplay for poetic ends—is obvious, and parody is the occupation of a deliberate poet rather than of the man who waits like a microphone for the voice from the cellar. Parody is also criticism and Birney—despite his avowed contempt for literary critics—is not merely a writer who keeps up a kind of running stylistic criticism of poetic modes in his own way of writing, but also very much of a moral critic of the world he sees, at least in the sense of presenting it in satirical manner. His poems on the United States and pieces like "Canada: Case History" are criticisms of the society in which, unavoidably but not entirely willingly, he lives; his poems on South America and Asia are, though less directly, criticisms of other ways of life. One is aware, all the time, of a man observing and reflecting on his own and other worlds; yet what we see is not merely the observed but also the observer. For Birney projects, through a voice, a personality, and a very idiosyncratic one. The voice often takes on—and especially in poems like "Mammorial Stunzas"—an emphatic jerkiness—almost spasmodic—which affects the visual shape of the poem as much as its read sound. In other poems—and particularly those of the last decade—the voice slows, broadening its flow, taking the narrative pace necessary for the content, as in the Mexican and Asian poems and in the best (for me at least) of his Vancouver poems, "November Walk Near False Creek Mouth". Here the verse walks in lanky paces, though the steps still break, and the tone is at times almost whimsically laconic. One is aware all the time of an irritable vitality, at times joyful but more often impatient, and impelling that search for brotherhood, for the lost links between persons and peoples that becomes, with the need for wandering which is its other aspect, the great theme of Birney's later poems (and perhaps not only his later, if we remember "Mappemounde" of 1945—"Adread in that mere we drift to map's end").

He finds himself in the decaying Colombian city of Cartagena, an obvious tourist among the obscenely poor:

>Somewhere there must be another bridge
>from my stupid wish
>to their human acceptance
>but what can I offer—
>my tongue half-locked in the cell
>of its language—other than pesos
>>to these old crones of thirty
>>whose young sink in pellagra
>>as I clump unmaimed
>>in the bright shoes
>>that keep me from hookworm
>>lockjaw and snakebite.

He stands among other passengers of a train that has just killed a car-driver at a level crossing in New Brunswick:

> We too anonymous one to the other
> but our breaths write on the air
> the kinship of being alive
> surrounding the perfect stranger

And as the poem ends, and he remembers the outstretched hand of the dead man, still uncovered by the blanket thrown over him, the ambiguous thought occurs:

> Or is it only in me that the hand hooked
> And I who must manage it now like a third?

Experience always, but seen in its moral dimensions, yet presented with a hand as workmanly as that of the carpenter who builds the cross in Birney's own poem, "El Greco: *Espolio*", itself suggestive of the ambiguity that the artist's task must sometimes assume.

Birney has always been a humanising landscapist, and for me, an incurable moralising traveller, the most congenial of his poems are those in which he combines his topographical flair with his sense of history and his power of conveying the immediacy of present experience. This he does magnificently in "Machu Picchu", where the precipitous heights of the Peruvian mountains and the vaulting darknesses of the past form the incongruous setting for a meeting of four assorted tourists who

> stand
> higher than the highest watchtower
> like Brocken spectres magnified
> on the black peak   and see the Sun
> rise still on what was built
> to worship Him.

This is, on the whole, a good, very representative selection of Birney in his various moods, not neglecting the traditional. A few poems, one feels, have been included mainly because of the effort that produced them; for all their virtuosity, I cannot in the end experience much more than amusement at such American vernacular poems as "Billboards Build Freedom of Choice." I also note with relief that "David" is not one of Birney's favourite poems; I find its appeal, for all its narrative vigour, lessening on each re-reading. And I am not sure that the dramatic poem, "Damnation of Vancouver", is really in place in this collection. But in the end, all poems considered, "Selected Poems" finally established Birney in my mind as one of the most individual and one of the four most maturely vital poets writing in Canada today.

5. WEED BED: *NEW DIRECTIONS*

INTRODUCTION TO *PNOMES JUKOLLAGES & OTHER STUNZAS* (1969)

BP NICHOL

someone once said (maybe northrop frye) that there was no such thing as experimental poetry, that there were only poems that worked & poems that didn't. you gotta admit there's some truth in that. only trouble is there's so much hassle about what a poem is. like i once wrote to frank davey about opening himself up to the wider possibilities that visual & sound poetry offered & he dismissed me in a few well chosen words (they really were well chosen). now to me experimental poetry is poetry which falls outside what have classically been called poems & hence i found myself writing THE POEM IS DEAD LONG LIVE POETRY over every available wall. poems (to my mind) are the finished artifacts and poetry the alive process, the organic flow within the poetic body (which is called "poems". but let's forget all that.

this is an introduction to a section of earle's work which has been termed "experimental" by every review & critical article i've read. to my way of thinking it is the body of work which best reflects the flow of his mind. the truths of most eastern religions concern the beauty to be found in simple things. "concrete" or "experimental" poetry concerns itself with a return to the simpler elements of language. for birney this has meant a return to the ear, and a search for some way to orchestrate for it. (when dave aylward and i worked at the u of t library one of our jobs was putting theses away in the theses cage (faeces cage we affectionately called it) and i used to thumb thru earle's phd on chaucer. now who can love chaucer and not love sound. chaucer had one hell of an ear for voice rhythms).

okay so how does he go about it. early things like "shetland grandaunt" show an awareness of dialectic, of accent. and accent is the key here. enhancement. he wants to show the rise and fall of the human voice so he lets the line rise and fall. regrettably (as

From *Pnomes Jukollages & Other Stunzas,* grOnk, series 4, no. 3 (Toronto: Ganglia Press, 1969). By permission of bp nichol.

always) his critics go confused. (i remember reading a review once in which the reviewer chastised him for wasting his time with "foolish typewriter experiments"). but it moves on from there. "alaska passage" gives us the actual flow of his mind, words working their way thru the riots of impression left by the trip, sprayed on the page, their million voices talking to you at once leaving you gasping for cool air "to slide its bones in a green tide". a double-layered poem. linear to describe a linear voyage. simultaneous to describe the mind's working, to put you in the poet's mind, into the living process of poetry. and there it is. the visual used to accent the linear massage, the senses brought into use by the poet's fingers providing alternative routes into and out of the act of poetry. visual & semantic content.

these are acts of giving. the poet allowing you into the flow of his mind, into the creation of poetry. accept them in the spirit they are given and so much could be learned. birney is one hell of an artist and he's trying to describe some roots your mind could try, directions to explore. for your own sake listen!!

FIVE REVIEWS OF
RAG & BONE SHOP (1971)

❧ CARL BALLSTADT

In Earle Birney's latest volume of poetry, *Rag & Bone Shop,* there is, as the title suggests, something to suit the taste of most readers of poetry. It includes a considerable variety of forms and tones: the limerick, pastiche, allegory, narrative and reflective poems, found poems, concrete or "shapomes". The latter category has majority status in this volume and a first glance through the book serves to inform the reader that the emphasis is on visual effects and ideas which the poet attributes to the influence of bp nichol and his generation who turned him on, presumably to the importance of experimentation with the combination of linguistic and graphic art. Perhaps Birney would have been fairer to himself to note that what bp nichol and his generation have done is to stimulate certain tendencies which are deeply rooted in Birney's career. Poems such as "Anglosaxon Street", "Mappemounde", and the verse play, *Trial of a City* (1952), give ample testimony to his interest in verbal juggling, and *Ice Cod Bell and Stone* (1962) provide examples of extensive experimentation with visual effects.

Certainly, *Rag & Bone Shop* is visually attractive and intriguing on many of its pages, and the interplay of linguistics and design in "up her can nada", "Newfoundland", and "canada council" is both provocative and humorous. But such poems are likely to be the more ephemeral and less memorable of this book and of Birney's total output. They seem to emphasize the fun of experimenting with words and shapes and of breaking through semantic barriers, but they do not represent the best of this volume, nor do they reflect the strengths of Earle Birney as a poet. His strengths are still reflected in the narrative and meditative modes in which his ability as keen observer and listener and his lively sense of the ironic and ridiculous in human behaviour are well revealed. Such strengths are manifested in several poems in this volume, particularly in "the mammoth corridors", "in purdy's ameliasburg", "four feet between" and "kiwis".

While the concrete poems in this collection represent an elaboration of Birney's long-standing interest in visual effects and word

---

From *Canadian Forum,* 51 (July-August 1971), pages 36-37. By permission of Carl Ballstadt.

play, the meditative and narrative poems serve to reinforce other facets of his work, both in terms of technique and theme.

In *Ten Canadian Poets* (1958), Desmond Pacey termed Birney a chronicler of Canada, basing his observation on the sociological significance of such poems as "Man on a Tractor", "North Star West", "On the Road to Nijmegen", "Anglosaxon Street" and numerous other poems related to wartime and to Birney's travels in Canada. Since the publication of Pacey's book, Birney's travels have been extensive and, accordingly, the poems based on his ex- experiences as traveller have multiplied. His *Selected Poems* (1966), with its sections "The Bear on the Delhi Road" and "Trans-Americana", indicates the range and importance of Birney's travels as stimuli to his poetic activity. Many impressive poems have emerged out of his travel experience: "A Walk in Kyoto", "Bear on the Delhi Road", "Cartagena De Indias", and "Bangkok Boy", to mention a few. *Rag & Bone Shop* adds significantly to the number with poems focusing on both Canadian and exotic places.

Poems which reflect the temper and times of Canada are represented in *Rag & Bone Shop* by pieces chiefly in satirical tones varying in intensity and technique, from the limerick "p e i", to the extended "beast" metaphor of "halifax", and the spatial arrangement of reflective and factual passages in "the mammoth corridors". With the personal perspective and memories of the poet placed in ironic juxtaposition to the confident and detached tone of the travel pamphlet, the latter poem embraces some of Birney's familiar themes: the aborigine's integral relationship with the land, the white man's alien status and his abuse of the land, a heightened awareness that man's endeavours here are permitted by a single swing of the geologic pendulum.

"the mammoth corridors" brings to mind earlier Birney poems in which parts of Canada are surveyed. One thinks of "North Star West", "Way to the West", and "North of Superior". With few exceptions, such poems present the poet as a vehicular traveller, or in some other manner detached from men. As a result, he is in meditation, and the poems reflect general characteristics of people or focus on geographical features and towns seen from a distance.

In contrast, poems based on travel in such exotic places as Mexico, Fiji or New Zealand reveal the poet in face to face encounters with people. Conscious of his differences as a Canadian and a member of a highly industrialized society, he has abandoned his vehicles and become a pedestrian. Indeed, "the walk" and "feet" seem to be increasingly important images in Birney's poetry.

In *Rag & Bone Shop* the use of the image "feet" in expression of the paradox of commonality and difference in people is best revealed in "four feet between", wherein the Canadian poet is humbled by the appearance and power of the Melanesian elder:

> But most of all he couldnt understand what hurt my feet
> And so he stood   a black-red statue of Melanic Power
> round storm of hair   maroon cheeks & torso cicatriced
> with the darker scars of tribal rites a half-century old
> his only covering a chamba skirt of sorrel colored reeds
> & all mounted on two pedestals of ancient meat
> two huge flat sun-barbecued tough plank-steaks of feet
> like those his cousins use   across the bay on Benga
> to walk on white-hot stones   for magic or for tourists
> *What wrong my feet*   i said *is I not born here too*. . . .

It is in such poems as this and earlier work such as "Cartagena De Indias" and "A Walk in Kyoto" that we discover Birney's foreign travels to be opportunities for walks into brotherhood.

One hopes for more such poems from Birney. They excel in ironic and humorous tone and detail, and skillful rendition of setting and colloquial flavour. Birney's flare for encountering the ridiculous and the redeeming in human nature makes such work always fresh and enlightening. He is a shrewd and alert observer in all his travels, and, though it may be heretical to say so, I hope this poet will write his autobiography.

🌷 FRED COGSWELL

One of the poems in *rag & boneshop* is entitled "for maister geoffrey". After doing Chaucer the honour of skilfully imitating him, Birney ends this poem with a statement ("In Chauceres haselwood I walke alwaye / And never thynke out of hise shawes to streye") which would certainly have caused Plato, had he read it, to boot Birney out of his republic for the usual reason. No one poet's "shawe" can ever content Earle Birney. In this book, he poaches on the preserves of writers as various in time and style as the author of Beowulf and bp nichol, adding little new in the way of thought or form, but redeeming every borrowed mode by a combination of technical proficiency, particularly of experience, and the flavour of a downright attractive personality.

"Nearer the Bone", from *Canadian Literature,* 49 (1971), pages 96-98. By permission of Fred Cogswell and *Canadian Literature.*

Earle Birney, more than any other poet I know, is typical in thought and outlook of the average liberal-minded Canadian. His responses to life in Canada and his tourist impressions abroad are predictable and our own. But if he is the "average man" in this respect, he is rare among our writers in his ability to use forms derived from the whole tradition of poetry to express brilliantly and freshly whatever insight he does have. Moreover, he has an intelligent dedication to his craft that only a professional can possess. He can always be trusted to put old wine (which looks like new wine because it is made today) into old bottles (which look like new bottles because no one has seen them in a long time and because he has subtly adapted them to the styles of our time) in such a way that every draft we take in is to us a new and heady experience.

Having said this much about Birney's work in general as continued in this volume, I should like now to comment somewhat haphazardly about particular poems or groups of poems that to me appear, for good or bad, worthy of particular mention.

First, with respect to the concrete poems, I shall only comment on a few, but what I say of these is typical of Birney's use of the concrete poem in general. It is always interesting, but the failures, I feel, tend to outnumber the successes.

"campus theatre steps" attracted me by its striking format, but after turning the book around and reading it, I was disappointed. It is a kind of "in-joke", which one is not apt to understand unless he comes from Eugene, Oregon. I come from Fredericton, New Brunswick. Once its typography has been unscrambled "Alaska Passage" is, one discovers, a typical Birney "wilderness" poem, made more difficult, not more understandable, by its author's attempt to make it look like a typographical wilderness. There is more organic justification for the formats of "Buildings" and "Outdoor Zoo", which fail, it seems to me, not because of their form but because they are "cute" only, and a poem ought certainly to be more than "cute".

"in the mammoth corridor" Birney pits his poetic prose against that of a tourist "blurb"; not surprisingly he wins, but his strength might have been more impressive had he merely flexed his muscles by himself. "in the night jet" is a brilliantly apt imagistic poem, and the printing of inverted black and white is annoying in that it is too crude and unimaginative a device to be worthy of the brilliance of the poem's actual language.

"up her can nada" is Birney's masterpiece in the concrete mode

—clever, intriguing, economical, yet imaginative, it presents a map of limitation and prejudice in an ugly, inimitable way. The clever "canada council" only suffers by comparison—one wonders, though, why Birney does not incorporate "oui" into the Council's vocabulary. It has not always said "non" to him.

Of the more orthodox poems, "once high on the hill" is the longest and most ambitious. This poem, Birney's reminiscences of San Francisco forty years ago, is a successful and moving work, giving a sense that, however men disagree over the meaning and value of life, the excitement and flavour of its flow is of itself value enough to justify existence.

"kiwis," "christchurch, n.z.", "strine authors meet" are the usual swipes that a creative giant delivers against non-creative academic pygmies. Birney, like Pope, has not discovered that these skilfully delivered blows are all that keep such beings alive. If poets left them alone, they would die of their own insignificance.

Birney, the liberal, is at his best in "four feet between", a poem that reminds me of Wordsworth's encounter with a leech gatherer in "Resolution and Independence" and more than challenges comparison with the latter poem.

"Oil refinery", Anglo-Saxon in form and imaginatively mythopoeic in the best sense, is a masterpiece, and for it I forgive Birney the kind of practical joking that "poet-tree 1" is, and his printing of "found prose from the Leacock centenniel", which he certainly ought to have left where he found it, in Orillia, Ontario. For me, "song for sunsets" and "if you were here", redeem their schmalziness by the aptness of their particulars and the beauty of their rhythms and make totally irrelevant all I have said by way of criticism and praise: "Beauty is its own excuse for being." I am grateful to Earle Birney for this book, and I hope that, for many more years, he will be spared to ask his interminable questions, that he will continue to mix up and write down his answers in what, despite all his gifts of imitation and parody, ultimately becomes his own inimitable way.

❦ ANDY WAINWRIGHT

In his *The Politics of Experience* R. D. Laing has said: "Words in a poem, sounds in movement, rhythm in space, attempt to recapture

"Two Hoary Old Poets", from *Saturday Night,* 86 (May 1971), pages 25-26, 27. By permission of Andy Wainwright.

personal meaning in personal time and space from out of the sights and sounds of a depersonalized, dehumanized world. They are acts of insurrection . . . through all the contention of intentions and motives a miracle has occurred." This is perhaps criteria of the highest order but, if the words "poem" and "poet" are to have any significant meaning, and if we'd like to think there are "major literary figures" in this country, then we should examine Birney and Layton with Laing's statement in mind.

In 1929, when all the young and serious writers went to Paris, Earle Birney was in San Francisco teaching at the relatively quiet Berkeley campus; in 1965, two years before Haight-Ashbury, he was out on Al Purdy's farm in Ameliasburg, Ont., trying to help myth defeat modernity; and in 1969, when all the young and serious writers were everywhere, he was in the South Pacific with Fijian chieftains and "New Zild" (New Zealand) academics. Now, these journeys and their accompanying experiences wouldn't necessarily mean much if Birney weren't able to re-create their particular atmospheres with such skill and obvious delight as he does in his latest book, *Rag & Bone Shop*. So we have the sights, smells, and sounds of vintage-Beat Telegraph Hill with "no streets . . . no English . . . no rich . . . no cobbles" and "what's more no telegraph," of a disappearing rural Ontario where the village hardware man stocks can-openers but "I'd have to look / drop in next week mebbe," and of New Zealand poetry where you'll "be lucky tev affenahr fer wotyayver yew intindin tew do."

In these longer poems that describe places he has been, Birney is an acute observer and, subsequently, a relator of what he sees. But moments of experience *happen to* Birney—he is a passive observer walking through his chosen landscapes: he becomes active only as an interpreter of these points in time and space. And if the territory is not entirely alien, at least it is refreshing. He treats his world as animistic—San Francisco, Ameliasburg, the New Zealand dialect all come alive because they *are* alive, and it is to his credit that he sees them as such. It is when he stops describing and tries to manipulate the animism, to compact his experience into a less verbose poetry, that he misses his chance at the "miracle."

In poems about buildings written in the shape of buildings, poems written in circles to suggest eddies, and those like "up her can nada" (a map of Ontario with simple political comments attached) there is very little depth for the reader to draw on—these concrete poems contain the assumption that the linear aspect of poetry is not alive and to make it so one must make pictures with words. But they defeat their own purpose for, in giving his close attention to the word antics, the reader remains firmly rooted to the printed page. He remembers, perhaps, what he saw (shapes, etc.) but because there is more effort than imagination involved, the memory has little meaning. Concrete poetry, in Birney's case, is a placing of style before content, and the content suffers as a result. To wrench a word out of the usual straight line format might well be an "act of insurrection," but unless there is a deeper meaning than change of style it parallels the static act of revolution for revolution's sake.

....

It might be harsh to say that, outside of the recent events in Quebec, nothing has really happened *within* this country. It also might be true. The big events have nearly always been external— the World Wars, the threat of U.S. takeover etc.—and there have been very few moments in our internal history from which a "great literature" might have arisen. This has put the creative onus squarely on the shoulders of the individual artist. In this day of trans-global communication and instant *karma* there have been few artists (and fewer Canadians) who have turned their own personal experience into what enough of us would accept as truly universal terms.

So we have Earle Birney and Irving Layton who are still writing, still being published, still receiving the reviews after thirty years. With so many books and years of survival behind them they offer, perhaps, our only Canadian guidelines for what we expect from the poet and the poem. *Rag & Bone Shop* and *Nail Polish* indicate where they stand. In the alien territory, so necessary to enter, Birney still walks the borders while Layton moves constantly towards the capital.

❦ LIONEL KEARNS

The publication of Earle Birney's latest collection of poetry, RAG AND BONE SHOP, is an event of considerable importance, despite the frivolous put-down the book has just received by Michael Finlay on the pages of the Vancouver Sun's Leisure supplement. Finlay, that aspiring corporal of the new Vancouver literary establishment, may be remembered as the author of a maliciously in-

From *Georgia Straight,* March 1971, page 21. By permission of Lionel Kearns.

accurate picture of the Vancouver poetry scene presented several months ago on those same pages, to which Gladys Hindmarch made an extensive rejoinder in a recent issue of the Straight.

In any case, the appearance of a collection of new poems by the country's best known poet deserves some small amount of responsible scrutiny and commentary by the press of his own city. And that is why I'm going to talk a little about the book right here.

Birney takes his title, RAG AND BONE SHOP, from a line of Yeats, a poet whose career is, in a certain respect, similar to his own. Birney has been creatively productive over a long span of time, and, like Yeats, he continues in his later work to write with energy and freshness, experimenting with poetic and linguistic form in the on-going development of his style and art. In fact, it is this constant push to cover new ground, to try different methods and novel approaches, that lands Birney in wrong with conservative critics and scholars, who think he should continue to turn out poems like those he wrote twenty-five or thirty years ago. Luckily, however, Birney has little interest in parodying himself.

One of Birney's current interests is spacialism, or as he calls these poems, "visuals"—works which exploit the various possibilities of the page. Sometimes his visuals take their formal contours arbitrarily from the object of focus: a building, trees along a shoreline, a flight of stairs, or the map of Upper Canada, the initial effect being to disrupt the usual linear sequence of linguistic units. That is, the habitual patterns of the letters, syllables, morphemes and words are broken up, allowing the freed elements to participate in newly constelled relationships that form in the eye of the reader, with references and images building up simultaneously or cyclically to generate the cumulative experience of the poem. It is impossible to reproduce any of the visuals here, for not only are they set in a mixture of typefaces, but they also rely for their full effect on a contrast of coloured ink.

For those whose poetic taste does not extend to visual iconography there is a variety of other material in this collection. In respect to much of this material, Birney's title seems particularly well chosen, especially if one keeps in mind the original Yeats context, which went something like this—"Now that my ladder's gone/ I must lie down where all the ladders start/In the foul Rag and Bone Shop of my heart". Yeats was referring to the primal deposit of sensation and memory that was the lyric core of his creative being. And so, in keeping with this image, Birney's collection is predominantly lyrical, with many of the poems treating the subject of love or personal relationships. This one I particularly appreciate:

THERE ARE DELICACIES IN YOU

>there are delicacies in you
>like the hearts of watches
>there are wheels that turn
>on the tips of rubies
>& tiny intricate locks
>
>i need your help
>to contrive keys
>there is so little time
>even for the finest
>of watches

The power and validity of Birney's statements stem from the fact that he is tuned into the fine vibrations and thundering rhythms of his own memory. A person is what he has experienced, and as a poet he comes to terms with his own identity by keeping in touch with its sources, bringing again to the light of consciousness in the form of language the essential patterns of what has gone before in his own life. One of the strongest poems in the book, for example, is a long narrative rendering of a romantic episode out of the long gone past (1930) when Birney was living on San Francisco's Telegraph Hill, trying unsuccessfully to integrate with his wine-making, goat-breeding, Sardinian and Neapolitan neighbours, and commuting across the bay to the Berkeley campus to make his small wage as an English TA. The whole experience is illuminated by the wonder of the poet speaking from the point of view of the present, removed by how much time and change in both himself and the world, but able, nevertheless, to call up the complexity of sound and sight and sensation which made up that experience.

>... Funeral & shrill as crows
>each morning over their tubs between the backyard ledges ...
>while they swabbed & slapped & tore & patched the shirts
>of all us dirty atheist *inglesi* who imagined
>they could seduce their clean Catholic daughters
>God knows we tried
>Rejected, fucked only academically   selfunbelieving writers
>whose aging mothers back home needed cash & careers from us

The last section of the book contains a set of travel poems which have their immediate source in a reading tour Birney made of Australia and New Zealand, and a recent visit to Samoa and Fiji.

These poems are mostly presentations of particular incidents, with the poet describing and responding to new environments, both physical and human. Frequently the drama of situation is heightened by a skillful rendering of the respective native dialect. I will not attempt to quote passages out of their contexts, it is worth nothing that the pidgen-speaking Fijians are presented as more sympathetic and human figures than the strine-speaking members of the Australian Author's Society or the tight-jawed and smugly nasal patrons and matrons of the New Zealand literary set. Birney's success in presenting their tortured accents in readable form combines with his knack of focussing on essential detail to give impact to his satire. Fortunately, the poet retains the ability to laugh at himself as well, a feat which contributes to the overall good humour of the collection. Here, for example, is a short poem set in Christchurch, N.Z.

> I have just flown 1100 miles from Australia
> & landed in a Victorian bedroom
> They sent up cindered muttonchops for lunch
> There is an elderly reporter in my room with pince-nez
> He wants to know why I have sideburns
> & if I dont think being patronized by the Canada Council
> isn't dangerous for my art or don't I feel I need to suffer?
> In stone outside my window Capt. Scott
> is nobly freezing to death near the South Pole
> Suddenly I know the reporter is right
> Sideburns have been sapping my strength.

There is much more in this book as well, but I do not intend to be exhaustive. It is enough to say that this is an interesting collection of poems, and a worthy addition to the continually expanding corpus of Birney's work.

❦ JUDITH COPITHORNE

Earle Birney, able to switch mediums, styles, generational gaps, very consciously, yet easily enough to catch the poem's life, has produced another book and in reading this book one gets what one ultimately gets from all books, a glimpse into the life of a man who trusts himself enough to tell us who he is, what he is feeling, where he is at.

A writer adds to the general pool of utterance in the most creative

From *Georgia Straight,* No. 151 (October 1971), page 21. By permission of Judith Copithorne.

way possible and the play continues whether one is looking or not. Birney represents a living tradition. One that I'm part of. Most of the traditions dying around us seem in their imperious assumptions of superiority to be better off gone. But throughout the general slush of self preservative double talk there's an alternative tradition of question and change. It is a difficult position at any age.

Birney started the creative writing department at U.B.C., no longer interested in it he maintains a voluminous series of communications on a personal level with people of many ages, times and spaces. He keeps himself open to the young people emerging, helps them and learns from them in turn.

An example of this is how he specifically acknowledges the presence of Bill Bissett when reading the poem Alaska Passage. There has been a good interchange between the two and Bissett's and Birney's chanting are also strongly related. Alaska Passage, like his poem of the Himalayan Bear, has that unstated subliminal expression of essential aloneness which is the badge of individuation.

As he states, much of his work is open ended, unfinished, his concrete poems are sketches often, outlines and in this refusal to close his work off grows the intimacy of his work.

His poemscapes, sculptural objects created by piling together the letters of the object's name could be carved from granite, instead they are rudely drawn on page after overlapping page. And the humor of these situations is rarely missed.

There's something very sad in much canadian poetry. It comes from the experiencing of a non-sanctified universe without the joys of an accepted animal existence. Now's the time to touch gently. Dreams we all have, are we realizing them?

The poem, "There are delicacies," expresses this and by its delightful precision grows beyond our normal sludge. It goes:

>   there are delicacies in you
>   like the hearts of watches
>   there are wheels that turn
>   on the tips of rubies
>   & tiny intricate locks
>
>   i need your help
>   to contrive keys
>   there is so little time
>   even for the finest
>   of watches

And how little time indeed. One might wish Birney had written more, a lot of his time has been spent working with other writers, editing Lowry's manuscripts and teaching. He is a multi-faceted man. Our lives are everything we do, our work's a reflection of it.

The Rag & Bone Shop reflects Earle Birney's life and it also reflects a common life we canadians lead, shattered almost to schizophrenia, held together more by will than by joy. Yet alive, still connected to the mountains, the sea, still capable of those hard pragmatic pioneering skills which some day soon may be what we most need.

PREFACE TO *FOUR PARTS SAND* (1972)

EARLE BIRNEY

drawing outlines of birds & beasts in
such a way as to express emotions as
well   that is to be human   the earliest
marks put on cavewalls by men in
europe   or on stone cliffs in africa and
canada   are more than picturenames
    they are ways of telling us about
how they felt having to hunt deer and
mammoth and wild horses and bulls
how they feared the brute power   how
they craved the animal beauty   the art
of writing began in the pictures themselves   pictures to pictographs to
ideographs   developing into the great
writing-systems of the Egyptians   of the
Chinese
modern man has become so machine-
trapped he has forgotten how to make
those magic picturetraps   his tenyard
curves on the cavern roofs have become
tiny and rigid and linear   the excitement and fear of the alpha betas have
been shoved aside by the dumb march
of the letters   there's no emotion
running out of the shapes in the linotype
    not even a glimpse of the thing or the
idea of it   to see a mammoth on a page
of english we must put seven letters
together each in a set shape and all in
an exact order   and after doing that
most carefully and ingeniously it still
doesn't look like a mammoth   but it's
not the machine's fault   it does what
we tell it

Preface by Earle Birney reprinted from *Four Parts Sand* by Earle Birney with Bill Bissett, Judith Copithorne and Andrew Suknaski (Ottawa: Oberon Press, 1972) by permission of Oberon Press.

let's tell it to adjust to our hands once
more   to our freehands   so we can
get close again to the ideas and the
sounds behind the deadletter shapes
let the photo-offset solemnly assist our
doodles   our solemn doodles   our
spontaneous leaps into magical play   it
is true that traditional typefaces can be
beautiful   but only monotonously
like football*queen*faces   poets need
the lost freedom to make speechsigns
as varied and tough and cunning as
football*player*faces   writing poems is
also a game   a serious one of course
      but what game isnt?   and most of all
                                    wordball

THE COURAGE TO BE

D. G. JONES

Earle Birney is also a poet who would single out courage as a chief virtue. Yet in Birney's case it is frequently if not finally of a different stamp. It tends to be a stoic or a pagan variety, as opposed to Pratt or Smith's distinctly more Canadian courage. In all this argument Birney presents an illuminating, if at times ambiguous, example.

From "David" to "ARRIVALS Wolfville," Birney is preoccupied with the problem posed by death, with the meaning or justice of a world that moves with such power and such magnificence towards obscure destinations, indifferent in its progress to the carnage left behind in its wake. In both the above poems, the hand of the dead or dying, whether the victim has been smashed on the mountain's rock or on a locomotive's steel, hooks into Birney's conscience like the hand of Job. However we may forget the details of the accident, surely, he says in the latter poem, we must remember:

> the longfingered hand
> stretched in some arresting habit of eloquence
> to the last irrational judgement
> roaring in from the storm
> Or is it only in me that the hand hooked
> and I who must manage it now like a third?[1]

It is the lawyer's hand, here, which appeals for justice before the "last irrational judgement" of the God of Job.

When Birney looks at nature he is struck by "the cobra sea and the mongoose wind," and by the great flint of the mountain which come singing into the heart. The human situation is imaged in "Mappemounde" as that of a man voyaging in a frail ark through a hostile sea, a sea hardly distinguishable from the devouring Leviathan who swims there. At best, life is an exploration and adventure. But, like Captain Cook, each man sinks to explore his last reef with the spear in his back. The awareness of final annihilation permeates Birney's poetry.

"November Walk Near False Creek Mouth" is one of the longest

From *Butterfly on Rock,* by D. G. Jones (Toronto: University of Toronto Press, 1970), pages 123-128, 135-137. By permission of University of Toronto Press.

[1] Earle Birney, *Selected Poems* (McClelland and Stewart 1966), 100.

of the meditations on the human condition, and it is focussed precisely on the nothingness that lies behind the whole vast process and that appears to await all things. As in Roberts' "Tantramar Revisited," the moment is poised between winter and summer, day and night; it is a period of inactivity and relaxation. During the lull in the perpetual struggle to defend and create, the speaker pauses to contemplate, in a larger perspective than usual, the process in which he and the city, here between the mountains and the sea, are inevitably caught. What strikes him most is that even in this moment of quiet there is no security; no final victory over the forces of time can be hoped for. Even now the tide is slipping "its long soft fingers into the tense/joints of the trapped seawall." The last leaves of the alders have turned the lawns into "a battlefield bright with their bodies" The city apartments may be "aseptic penthouse hillforts," but nothing can stop the dissolving sea. On the highest ledge of all, beyond the apartment antennae, the pylons marching over the peaks, the jetstream of planes and the farthest galaxies, "lies the unreached unreachable nothing/whose winds wash down to the human shores," where they slip, shoving into each of his thoughts, nudging his footsteps, driving him back to his own "brief night's ledge."[2]

Before this final oblivion, Birney here adopts a tone of quiet acceptance, and upon his fellow man, who wittingly or unwittingly must share this fate, he appears to look with an ironic or wry compassion. But Birney's attitude towards a destructive or hostile universe, as expressed throughout much of his work, is neither the withdrawal of Roberts nor the affirmation of Pratt; it is rather a vigorous defiance. When Desmond Pacey declared that the principal virtues celebrated in the poems of E. J. Pratt were courage, courtesy, and compassion, Birney cried no. They were courage, loyalty and defiance. Or perhaps, they were the Anglo-Saxon virtues of loyalty, initiative, and endurance. For the world of Birney's poems is an Anglo-Saxon world, in spirit and not only in diction and rhythmic device. Akin to the world of "The Wanderer" or "The Seafarer," it is grim, full of menace, where life is the flight of a sparrow through the hall—but where nonetheless one endures and fights to the last, though the end is certain. "Come then," he says, in "Pacific Door":

> Come then on the waves of desire that well forever
> and think no more than you must

[2]*Ibid.*, 133-41.

of the simple unhuman truth of this emptiness
that down deep below the lowest pulsing of primal cell
tar-dark and still
lie the bleak and forever capacious tombs of the sea[3]

With courage and initiative man may even tackle Jehovah on his own terms. At one point Birney allies himself with Promethean man and throws his defiance in the face of a malevolent universe. Know, he proclaims in "Vancouver Lights":

These rays were ours
we made and unmade them   Not the shudder of continents
doused us   the moon's passion   nor crash of comets
In the fathomless heat of our dwarfdom   our dream's combustion
we contrived the power   the blast that snuffed us
No one bound Prometheus   Himself he chained
and consumed his own bright liver   O stranger
Plutonian   descendant   or beast in the stretching night—
there was light[4]

Yet to have outwitted Leviathan by destroying oneself is a dubious virtue indeed, though one consistent with Birney's frequently sardonic view of man. That view emerges in "Hands," as he remarks on man's obvious superiority to the rest of nature. The hands of the cedar are cold and unskilled and shall neither focus on a bombsight nor sew up a bayoneted bowel. "We are not of these woods." No, we are worse, "our roots are in autumn and store for no spring."[5] Nature may be hostile but "Man is a snow that cracks/the trees' red resinous arches/and winters the cabined heart . . . till frost like ferns of the world that is lost/unfurls on the darkening window."[6] No more to be trusted than the cobra sea, he is more to be feared. The iron rain of the bombs in "Vancouver Dusk" moves with the inevitability of natural forces towards the sleeping city, but with a directness and purpose that is human alone.

Birney cannot, in the end, ally himself with the aggressive Promethean man any more than with the encroaching sea. Even if he doesn't destroy himself, the Promethean man creates an infernal city, the Sudbury of "Way to the West." In the "skull of a hill," the "dumps of cans," the Pandaemonium and "20 miles of deserted battlefield" that the city presents to the travellers we find a real-life

[3]*Ibid.*, 142.
[4]*Ibid.*, 77.
[5]*Ibid.*, 75.
[6]*Ibid.*, 148.

version of Lampman's City of the End of Things. Like Satan's kingdom it is a miserable imitation of heaven. The wilderness, by contrast, is a welcome relief. There in the dark woods, the travellers suddenly realize the river still flows. After Air Canada's night jet passes, "we begin to realize/we'd been hearing the river too."[7]

It is Vancouver with its many lights that is put on trial in a later drama and very nearly doomed or damned. Its promoter, the aggressive Mr Legion, is charged with misrepresentation and dematerialized by Birney's spokesman, Mrs A. With him Birney rejects the Promethean "Advance."

Still, distrustful of man and distrustful of nature, Birney tends to walk with vigilance through a world of strangers, where courage and ingenuity are primarily defensive. "Meeting of Strangers" is the epic in miniature of a world of every man for himself. When a black figure approaches him in a deserted street, with a knife in his hand, saying, "Nice jacket you got dere, man," the speaker makes a spectacular leap into the intersection, where he is lucky enough to encounter a taxi. He even wins the admiration of his would-be attacker, who calls out, "dat a nice jump you got too.[8]

As long as his world is one in which men go armed against nature and against each other, Birney can truly say:

> men are isled in ocean or in ice
> and only joined by long endeavour to be joined.[9]

Real communion is rare in Birney's poetry. In the poem "For George Lamming," he is surprised, for example, to discover that he has temporarily lost his identity as a white man, and with it his isolation; he has become one with a dark circle of friends whose goodwill or acceptance has allowed him for a time to forget himself. It is only later, when he looks in the mirror, that he remembers his difference and realizes their generosity, their charity or love.

As often as not, the courage displayed in Birney's poems is a stoic courage which defies death rather than a Christian courage which accepts it. It is not, except in a few poems, the courage of Gethsemane. "El Greco: Espolio" is instructive. It is not accidental that in looking at this crucifixion scene, Birney found his eye drawn to the carpenter preparing the cross, rather than to the carpenter's son who is to hang there. Concentrating on the job, on doing it well, the carpenter does not take sides in the issue in which he is involved. As a result he will live long.

[7]*Ibid.*, 111.
[8]*Ibid.*, 56-7.
[9]*Ibid.*, 142.

> To construct with hands knee-weight braced thigh
> keeps the back turned from death.

He is not ready to explore his last reef. Yet, though he may observe with truth that it is too late for the other carpenter's boy to avoid death, he cannot say with anything but a superficial truth that it is too late for Him "to return to this peace before the nails are hammered."[10] For having accepted His death and further forgiven His executioners, He presumably carries His peace within Him. The words are those of the carpenter, and Birney attributes the whole emphasis of the painting to El Greco; yet the tone cannot be wholly ironic for the man who advised us to think no more than we must of the simple unhuman truth of the emptiness that presumably attends us all.

Indeed, the man who sails so warily through Birney's mappemounde invites the question posed by Jay Macpherson's "Ark Astonished."

> Why did your spirit
> Strive so long with me?
> Will you wring love from deserts,
> Comfort from the sea?
>
> Your dove and raven speed,
> The carrion and the kind.
> Man, I know your need,
> But not your mind.[11]

As long as his defiance is radical, man shall remain an isolated voyager, a moving point on the map, surrounded by the threatening waves. Only when he is prepared to accept his final, if not immediate engulfment, shall he find comfort, love, communion. To escape from his defensive position in his frail ark he must embrace the sea. This is the burden of Miss Macpherson's "Ark Overwhelmed."

> When the four quarters shall
> Turn in and make one whole,
> Then I who wall your body,
> Which is to me a soul,
> Shall swim circled by you
> And cradled on your tide,
> Who was not even, not ever,
> Taken from your side[12]

[10]*Ibid.*, 18.
[11]Jay Macpherson, *The Boatman* (Oxford University Press 1957), 51.
[12]*Ibid.*, 52.

Leviathan, the sea, all nature, and all time become one in Eve, in Adam's rib. It is more a question of attitude than fact. In the decision to embrace her, man would recognize that he has always embraced her. And in doing so he would discover that he embraced himself.

The solution lies in a feminine inclusiveness. A masculine exclusiveness leads only to despair. In Birney's trial of a city the masculine witnesses whom Mr Legion calls on for the prosecution all serve to ensure the damnation of Vancouver. Neither explorer, geologist, nor Indian chief, not even the tavern-keeper, can justify the city's continued existence. Before the law it is doomed. Of William Langland, perhaps the most exclusive because the most righteous of the witnesses, Mrs A. remarks, "His eyes were on the sins he loved to hate." It is Mrs A. who succeeds where the others failed, and it is her feminine inclusiveness that underlies her argument and gives her case its strength.

> For all mankind is matted so within me
> Despair can find no earth-room tall to grow.

Her argument proceeds from love, not law. She can affirm the life of the city, as she says she had affirmed it that very morning, "However my world had sinned."[13]

We may recall that in the nineteenth century Isabella Valancy Crawford also affirmed life against the threat of inexorable death in the name of love, her pioneer hero proclaiming that love had its own peculiar sky, "All one great daffodil, on which do lie/The sun, the moon, the stars, all seen at once,/And never setting . . . ."[14] Yet between Bliss Carman and Irving Layton, Canadian verse is not remarkable for its love poetry. There is little of love or woman in E. J. Pratt, or even in Earle Birney. Still, it is in the experience of love that man has most readily abandoned his separate identity in favour of a larger whole, exchanging his isolated existence for that communion with the human race embodied in Mrs A. or with the whole of creation embodied in Miss Macpherson's Eve.

Something of this theme is evident in Earle Birney's "This Page My Pigeon." And in another war poem, "The Road to Nijmégen," he writes:

> December my dear on the road to Nijmégen
> between the stones and the bitten sky was your face
> ...

---

[13]Earle Birney, *Selected Poems*, 206.
[14]Isabella Valancy Crawford, "Malcolm's Katie," *The Collected Poems* (William Briggs 1905), 203.

> I thought that only the living of others assures us
> the gentle and true we remember as trees walking
> Their arms reach down from the light of kindness
> into this Lazarus tomb.[15]

In the context, however, it is not the memory of love that primarily serves to persuade us to go on with the struggle. More convincingly, it is the spectacle of the old man hacking at roots, of the children groping for knobs of coal, of the women "wheeling into the wind on the tireless rims of their cycles/like tattered sailboats tossing over the cobbles" that argues a further affirmation of life. It is the living of others here in the blasted landscape rather than the memories of those far away, however beloved, that really inspires us.

Romantic love, the hyacinth girl in the garden, the personal relationship of two lovers—as a justification of life this type of thing has lost much of its force in the twentieth century, with its mass destruction and mass dislocation of people. But a more diffused love, a general solidarity and, above all, the courage of those who in the midst of devastation continue to show an affirming flame—these have become more pronounced and more important, in Birney's work as in others. There is a real question whether such courage is not prior to love as the ground of our continued affirmation.

....

In "The Damnation of Vancouver" Mrs A. remarks, "How could I know, without the threat of death, I lived?"[16] We may also recall the lines of A. J. M. Smith. " 'Nothing' depends on 'Thing', which is or was:/So death makes life or makes life's worth." Similarly, for Tillich it is death or non-Being at the heart of reality that makes the world a dynamic world and God a living God: "non-being drives being out of its seclusion, it forces it to affirm itself dynamically."[17] And that affirmation can only be made through individual beings in all their uniqueness. It is on this point that Birney ends his "Damnation of Vancouver."

Ultimately Birney's defiance becomes less bitter, more in fact that necessary self-affirmation against death and doubt we have called the courage to be. No longer an absolute defiance, it is characterized by that complicity a player shows when in a game he must assume

---
[15] Earle Birney, *Selected Poems*, 89.
[16] *Ibid.*, 212.
[17] Paul Tillich, *The Courage to Be*, 179.

a role, as hero or as villain, and maintain it to the end, for otherwise the game could not exist, could not be played at all. All this is made explicit in the final dialogue between Mrs A. and Mr Powers, who is the embodiment of fate and of the inevitable doom the future will pronounce on Mrs A. and her world. Mr Powers reminds her that she has won only a brief reprieve, her doom is still pending. She replies:

> Mrs A.: How could I know, without the threat of death, I lived?
> Powers: But do you know why you defy me?
> Mrs A.: (*Looking up almost tenderly at him.*)
>   That you might also be.
>   Without my longer will, my stubborn boon,
>   You'd have no mate to check with but the cornered moon.
>   (*Slowly*) It's my defiant fear keeps green this whirling world.[18]

Mr Powers congratulates the lady on her insight and, shaking hands, reminds her that they will meet or mate again, on Judgement Day. Mrs A. is content, but insists that meanwhile she will keep the key. To which Mr Powers punningly replies: he shall have the skeleton. The important thing for both, however, as Mrs A. points out in the final line, is that she will have had *a life*.

To the question, What shall we do with Leviathan? the answer would appear to be, Swallow him. Or, as John Newlove says of death in "Resources, Certain Earths," "Let me swallow it whole and be strong."[19] Among these poets, from Isabella Crawford through D. C. Scott, E. J. Pratt, A. J. M. Smith, Earle Birney, and Irving Layton to such younger writers as Jay Macpherson or John Newlove, there is a very real unanimity in their awareness and in the resolution of the problem of Job. All, in their fashion, abandon the garrison of an exclusive culture and go into the wilderness, where they experience, not a greater sense of alienation, but a greater sense of vitality and community. Implicitly or explicitly, each may be said to accept the fellowship of death, to lie down with the grass snake among all the other skeletons of badgers and raccoons and men, only to discover that the one great serpent has crept out upon the sky and coiled about his head like a crown of power. The night is transfigured, and a menacing world takes on the beauty of strength broken by strength and still strong.

Death may be viewed here as a positive good, as revelatory, as

---

[18]Earle Birney, *Selected Poems,* 212.
[19]John Newlove, *Moving in Alone,* 74.

driving life to manifest itself, its worth. But there is no attempt to gloss over its essential reality and individuality, to say that because life in general continues, death in effect does not exist. It is life in general that does not exist. It is the individual life, and individual death, that are immediately real. Though such a view may "justify" death, it does not justify the taking of life beyond that necessary for each creature's authentic self-affirmation. It does not justify the destruction of anything in the universe on the ground that it is by nature evil. Rather, it suggests that man, with his peculiar human awareness, ought to conserve as much of the varied individual life of the universe as possible.

MADNESS AND EXORCISM OF POETRY

EARLE BIRNEY

One comes down eventually to the only surety: one's knowledge of one's own little craft. My experiences are all I have to be certain about. Let me be honest. There are times when I've sat down and merely whittled a piece of verse, to hear a shape come, then throw it away; or times when I've been piano-practising, only trying to get the hang of the form of a sestina, or the breath-accent and the heart-beat of a Black Mountain line-series. But mostly I've been impelled—impelled sometimes merely by one acute sense impression, which started a chain of recalls back to an experience which, I could now apprehend, was emotionally important for me. Or perhaps a phrase in an old diary stabbed me with a memory of October in the Kootenays, and brought me a rhythm I must always have wanted to sing, if only to myself. Most of the time these impulses have had to be suppressed in the interests of making a living. The bulk of my early poems were written in army hospitals, on buses, or in a beach shack in holiday time. But it's not always possible to suppress. The poem nags and whimpers, like one of Samuel Butler's unborn children, to be given life. In the summer of 1958 I had a glimpse of a bear and two Kashmiri men on a roadside in northern India—seen from my passing car. It was a strange sight, of course, but it haunted me for reasons far beyond oddness. The bear was huge, shaggy, Himalayan. It must have been captured high up in the cool mountains and purchased by these men with perhaps the savings of their lifetime, and they had been walking with it hundreds of miles though mountain passes down to the terrible mid-summer hot plains, brutally training it for dancing as they went, so they could make a living exhibiting it in Delhi. But it wasn't just the bear's wretchedness, it was the two men's; it was their fearful, dumb hopping around the bear. Bear and men pursued me for fourteen months till I could find the leisure on a Mediterranean Island, and the mood,—and then in two hours the words came and the bearish rhythm and the images with which to lay those three ghosts, which were I think also the ghosts of my own multitudinous guilt feelings, as a well-fed western tourist in a world of unimaginable poverty and heat and dusty slaving. Even then it

From *The Creative Writer* by Earle Birney (Toronto: Canadian Broadcasting Corporation, 1966), pp. 15-16, 17-23. By permission of Earle Birney.

took a dozen later sessions of tinkering and touching to get it said well enough for these special spectres to stop spooking me. And now all that's left is a very different desire, a very mild and fading one, to use my personal spell to raise those ghosts among others. . . .

....

Although I have been emphasizing the seriously compulsive nature of poetry-writing, I wouldn't be honest with myself or my subject if I didn't also admit that poetry is, as well, a kind of intricate and infinite play. A hard exhausting one, maybe, but so are many games. Like mountaineering it requires endurance and an apparently crazy, pointless daring, an ability to perform in a kind of vacuum while aiming for a peak we're never sure we'll reach. Or I'd call it a kind of complicated hockey performed with a purely imaginative stick with which, however, we must dribble and shoot real pucks, thousands of them, made of words encasing ideas and emotions. And we must play all positions. A one-man Lewis-Carroll-hockey. Still a sport, not a job. For work, surely, is what you have to do.

True, lots of people have to write for a living, or in the process of making a living—reports, précis, lectures, themes, speeches, scripts, advertisements, letters. But that's prose. Poetry is something you never have to write for a living,—who would give you one?—though it may well be something you have to write to live, really live, if you happen to be built that way. However, that's a different sort of "have to", an internal one. *External* pressures to write lead to prose, and prose, if you think about it, is a very inhibited way of writing.

Consider all the rules we expect the freshman to learn, the codified handbooks of rhetoric. Linguisticists tell us that we can't even say, in modern English prose, "The cat kills the mouse". Or at least, we wouldn't. We'd say "The cat's killing the mouse" or "The cat killed (or, the cat will kill) the mouse". Just as we'd avoid such constructions as "cat kills mouse", except in telegrams—if you can imagine the need for such a telegram.

But in poetry you can say it any way you want. In poetry you can lean on context, rhythm, on the tone of voice (since poetry, if it's any good, is speakable, and comes out fully only when spoken) and you can demand closer attention from your readers, subtler understanding. This is, if you like, one of the ground-rules of poetry; this is the way it is. Moreover, people who enjoy poetry, who really love a good poem, will want to hear it more than once, may listen to it a dozen times, fifty maybe. (How many even great novels do we read more than twice in a lifetime?) So in poetry it's theoretically possible to say "The cat kills the mouse", and in almost *any* order of the words, and eventually be understood. Poets have freedom, freedom to be different, to surprise, shock, challenge —and of course freedom to hang themselves, to spoil everything and be only confused and confusing. But no poetry lover will blame them for trying to be different, trying to make him say goodbye to his inhibitions and shoot off in a moon-probe of the imagination.

In verse we could even say "The mouse killed the cat" and make it stick. For as Dylan Thomas kept reminding us, living is a slow act of dying; every organic thing begins to wear itself away from the moment of its birth. Chaucer put it that death turns on the tap of life at birth. Men can't just sit; neither can cats. They chase mice. Even if they're fed the best old Dr. Whoozit's Half-and-half Canned Pussy Food, their ancient sabretooth instincts drive them into the elaborate activity of hunting and killing; if they haven't birds or mice, they'll even invent them, out of a ball of wool or a shadow. Eventually they grow old killing mice, and so in a sense they die of it. And why can't we put all this together into an embryo verse?

> The cat kills the mouse
> and kills mouse again
> Cat kills mouse
> for it cannot kill men
> But the mouse the cat quelled
> and the mouse cat must kill
> are the grey fates that will
> fray the catty cells
> break his killing will
> Then still lies the cat
> though there is still mouse.
> The mouse killed the cat.

That isn't a poem, of course; it's not much more than a jingle, a piece of doggerel or catterel, but it could be the start of a lot of fun, trying to make a real poem out of it. The start, because the poem could go anywhere. Poems can; they are utterly free things. If two lawyers sat down separately to draft a law about cats, (say, about allowing apartment dwellers to keep them), the more efficiently, the more legally, they phrased their law the more alike their words would be. But if two poets sat down to write about cats, the greater artists they were the more *un*like their poems would be.

Of course there are rules, but they are rules the poet sets, that he makes up or borrows from other poet's games. If most poets follow a few regulations in common, it's only because otherwise it becomes a little too confusing for that spectator of his game, the reader, poor fellow. For example, in the piece I made up, I observed a few very ancient traditions of conventional verse writing. A fairly regular rhythm, each line with three natural voice stresses. The cát kills the móuse. Why all poetry has some kind of rhythm is a question, of course, that goes beyond game and play, something to do with this mystery of spell and exorcism, and with madness. My jingle had rhyme; *kill, will*; *again, men*; but rhyme has been used to any extent only for the last thousand years, whereas rhythm, regular or irregular, may be as old as spoken language itself,—a million years? Also I used some other jugglings with sound, mainly to break monotony, get musical variety. Half-rhyme—*quelled, cells*; consonance—*quelled, killed*. Alliteration or head-rhyme; a pun on *still*; internal rhyme and sound-echoing:

> are the *grey* fates that *will*
> *fray* the catty cells
> brea*k* his *k*illing *will*.

But enough of this embroidering on such wretched lines; it's just that a simple verse jingle can sometimes be more helpful than a serious finished poem to reveal some basic things about poetry, as a painter's rough pencil sketch can sometimes illuminate for us the way he paints. I'll turn now to another piece of mine about cats, which I think *is* nearer to being a poem than a jingle, (though that's just what *I* think. Perhaps it will show something more about my rules of poetic play. I'll read it bit by bit, though this may well be a way to ruin any total effect the poem might possibly have.

It's called "Aluroid". Which means cat-like, pertaining to the cat family. And why then didn't I call it "Catlike"? Because I want "Aluroid", and it's a word in good standing—at least in the *Unabridged Webster's*. Sure, most people who aren't biologists or Latinists or word-hoarding writers might have to look it up. But I regard all the million words in the English language as available to poets, and for this particular poem I've made a rule that I want readers willing to look up a word they don't know. For this poem, I'm cheerfully and deliberately limiting my spectators. To me *aluroid* calls up not only the domestic cat but all wild sorts too, from tigers down. And there's a favourite word of science-fiction writers, *humanoid,* often used to describe human-like inhabitants of other planets visited by scy-fy heroes. So my title could be psychological preparation for a cat which is not quite a normal pussy, a feline domestic but weird, even slightly human, and more than a little wild. I need a "loaded" title because the cat in my poem is going to be a Siamese, and this is how I want you to start feeling about her. "Aluroid" even sounds like her meiow, to me.

First stanza:

> Blurred in a blot
> of laburnum leaves
> panther taut
> the small Siamese
> has willed even her tail's
> tip to an Egyptian frieze . . .

By now I'm hoping you have the cat placed, crouched tensely up in a laburnum tree, a backyard summer kind of tree, trying to lie absolutely quiet and concealed in the leaves. If you haven't, it's because part of my game is to be devilishly brief, and I'm relying, of course, on your seeing the lines on a page, or being able to hear them more than once. These are further rules of the game, of all poet's games, for which, therefore, I make no apologies. Concentration is what you must expect in a poem, and what ultimately is one of its pleasures. The stanza ended with *frieze*. If you thought for a moment I meant *freeze,* that's fine, I did, too. I wanted you to think *both* of the frozen stillness of a cat waiting to spring and the sculptured image of a deified cat, the classical Egyptian species it's true, but that was a rather Siamese-looking breed. Then "frieze" is a pun? Of course. And again no apologies. In prose, puns may be the lowest form of wit; in poetry they may be a highly functional form of play, helping the reader to keep two images or thoughts simultaneously in mind.

The next verse:

> but not her two
> sapphire burning blue
> pools whose planetary bale
> to the topmost wren glares through.

More playing with images, though now for different reasons. I want this poem to be at the same time visually precise and as wide as I can make it in its imaginative suggestions. Siamese don't have just blue eyes; even the same Siamese will gaze with a different blueness according to its mood. At the moment before a kill, they are glittering and hard as gems, wild and unearthly as a blue star seen through a telescope. And of course they're the one piece of a cat's anatomy she can't conceal from birds, who aren't always so dumb, not even wrens.

As I hope we see in the next stanza:

> The silent ritual she brings
> they shatter, by their shrill
> profanities deny
> her lethal godhead till
> Bast in anguish springs
> her tawny grace at nothing

So the wrens in the treetop set up a warning chatter and the cat springs too late. My prose paraphrase seems briefer, but really isn't, unless I've muffed it, because in the poem I'm trying to say a lot of other things besides that, in the same breath; for instance, that we've been watching a kind of death ritual, that the cat acts like an appointed goddess of death in relation to the birds, one they're quick enough this time to repudiate. And I try to remind you again, by giving the cat now a name, Bast, that cats were once indeed thought of as deities, Bast being one of the Egyptian Catgoddesses.

Now the next stanza, still in the same sentence (since poetry can break up sentences anyway it wants) and still about the cat:

> drops unfelicitous upon
> the power-mowed lawn
> a staring failure
> chittering.

Anticlimax, irony; the cat abandons its temporary role of a fearful death goddess for its more normal one of domestic pet. So I stress the banality of the scene: it falls from the tree not into jungle reeds but onto machine-clipped turf. It looks silly now, unhappy, unfelicitous (un-felix-like), and it's making a frustrated, wet, chattering animal sound with its teeth for which I allow myself to invent a word chittering.

Next stanza:

> Dish clinks
> and in a breath
> she is a fawn
> cat, house-intent
> Bast's thirty teeth are masked
> The terrible fires
> sink to almond innocence.

So—dish clinks—it may not be lunch time in the kitchen across the back lawn where all this (we can now see) has been happening, but then again it may be, and cats take no chances about losing out on food. If there's no live wren for the moment, there may be a dead chicken liver, who knows; let's be a nice tame pussy again, adjust those eyes to deal with human beings, and get back to the house. Aren't cats wonderful and crazy and superb?

But that isn't really what the poem's about. It needs a last statement. One line, perhaps, set off by itself:

> The wrens fly off to other deaths . . .

Well, I must leave it to you: if that sentence doesn't add another dimension, the poem has failed. What I'm trying to do, in a sudden final little kick, is to surprise you into thinking back now over the whole poem as a statement about inevitable death, about the way it lurks in all creation, waits for us, finally gets us one way or another.

But even if I put it over, isn't that a terrifically obvious remark about life? Of course; but surely all art is only trying to look closer, with the fully personal eye, at what we think we already know. If my way of talking about a cat and wrens and death has turned out to be in some way stimulating to your own imagination, then wasn't the game worth it for you, even though you had to play my rules? If so, it was certainly worth it for me—though the odd, the real crazy thing, remains, that the game was one I already *had* to play.

Why? Why did I write about this trivial experience, and not about a million others that come to me in the course of daily living? Why is the poet not haunted by everything? And why by the things that do hex him? My cat sneaks up a tree, springs at some wrens, fails to catch any. The birds fly away. It then occurs to me that for each of those wrens there'll be a day when she or some other cat will be faster, or some owl or hawk more sudden; one by one they will fly into plate glass, or eat something with a killing parasite or virus in it, or freeze to death, or grow too old to fly, and starve. So what? So why didn't I just think that and forget it? I don't really know, of course, what goes on in my subconscious. It had something to do with the feeling of the chain of life and death suddenly linking us all, cat and wren and me, inescapably. More than that, this cat and those wrens and I had suddenly arranged ourselves to make an immediate living symbol of this universal theme. It was almost as if, in the blue air, a voice had suddenly said to me, "In the midst of life you are in death"; a cliché was suddenly invested, for me, with meaning and life.

THE WRITER-CREATOR IN TODAY'S WORLD

EARLE BIRNEY

Whether we are artists or politicians, we are human, we have the human striving to *belong* to society, to shed the loneliness of the Outsider, and enjoy the immediate pleasure of acceptance, popularity, the sweets of conforming. As John le Carré puts it, the writer "heeds the warmth of human contact, he looks at the heath fires like a tramp from a distant hill".[1] But if he comes down from that hill and settles into gregarious comfort, he must pay the price. In Canada, at the moment, that price may be only the sham approval, or the benevolent apathy, which our so-called "cultured" English middleclass bestow on him, on say, Irving Layton and other contemporary Canadian poets when they launch satiric assaults on the hypocrisy of Canadian political or sexual mores. Even popularity may be a defeat for the writer, if it means that *he* is taken seriously, but what he *says* is not. And those who muffle the artist-rebel today with empty laughter or condescending tolerance, may be succeeded by those who, like the cultural commissars of Soviet Russia, drove Mayakovsky to quick suicide in preference to slow death in the Arctic, and today seems to be reducing Yevtushenko to writing compromising failures, and has until recently kept the uncompromising and brilliant young Leningrad poet Joseph Brodsky a silenced satirist and a prisoner at hard labour in Siberia.

Do not believe it impossible to have a Canadian society which exiles its best writers permanently to Baffin, even though last year it gave one of our best poets a return ticket to visit and write a book there. This year [1965] in Toronto, in the centre of whatever artistic culture English Canada possesses, the paintings of three established serious artists were confiscated and judged legally obscene, and a prominent gallery owner who exhibited them was handed the alternative of a fine or jailing. The magistrate decided that the paintings suggested "sexual intercourse", a subject which he said "is of course discussed in the community" but is "not an accepted matter to be portrayed by an artist, and exposed to public view". The law did not question that the paintings were pleasing to the eye and finely executed, and without cheap or pornographic

---

From *The Creative Writer* by Earle Birney (Toronto: Canadian Broadcasting Corporation, 1966), pp 67-70. By permission of Earle Birney.

[1] John le Carré, "What every writer wants", *Harper's Magazine,* November, 1965.

intent. They were judged obscene because they were concerned with a human activity which Canada's intolerant Puritanism will not allow the artist to hint at, even though it is that act which not only creates both the Puritans and the artists, but which can offer the most beautiful and powerful physical experience occurring in the life of man and woman. Murder may be, and is, portrayed daily and realistically on television; sex, no. Today Canada forbids its artists to celebrate the joys of love. Tomorrow it may prohibit the celebration of the joys of peace, or freedom.

Can this sinister progression be stopped? Can we preserve and expand the liberties of our artists? A few years ago a number of British and American writers contributed a symposium to the London *Times* on this subject. They included Laurence Durrell, Saul Bellow, Arnold Toynbee, Stephen Spender and Cyril Connolly. For Connolly the issue was essentially simple. For him, only masterpieces of literature in the end justify the artist's existence; only masterpieces contribute permanently, he says, to the enlargement of the human spirit. And, for Connolly, masterpieces simply don't and can't be written in a country whose political conditions force the artist to compromise. Let the state keep its hands off the artist, and great art will eventually flourish. But for others, for most of these writers, the dangers ahead lie with the audience, with the mass reader who, say these writers, is already even in our western society, so regimented that he won't accept anything that does not have on it the seal of herd approval; and it is this taste for universal pap which prepares the common man to accept, even to love, dictatorship. The genuine artist, they say, will not capitulate, but he will be left with no one to whom he can communicate the spirit of his independence.

I believe the writer will go on trying, anarchically protesting. But it's one thing to use your abilities as a writer to make your own protest, and it's another to turn yourself into a 24-hour-a-day protesting machine. This is as bad as being a 24-hour-a-day conforming machine. And it's exactly these two extremes into which the communist writer is thrown. In capitalist countries he is the protester, in communist ones the conformist. Either way is the way of literary suicide even before physical death. As a writer I don't feel compelled to write only against war and for peace. If I find I've written something, out of inner need, which seems to have some possible effectiveness in this vein for others, I seek to publish it. And I admit I'm more and more innerly compelled to write in such a vein, since I agree with Arnold Toynbee that this is indeed an age when the fate of mankind hangs in a balance of finer hair than has ever suspended it before, in any human history about which we know anything. However, I also believe, with Herbert Muller and many others, that man is threatened today not only by an infectious epidemic of aggressiveness, but also, in this age of preventive and curative medicine, by his own fertility, and that this threat is in turn increased by his irrationally "frozen" religions, which encourage him to destroy his own earth in his blind fecundity. He's also bedevilled by another mass malaise of his creating, an urge to turn himself from a human being into a mere worker-ant or emasculated drone in a beehive. Personally, I want to be a creative man, not a bee nor a rat nor a grizzly nor a mouse. Which means that I strive, in this herding age, to remain a cayuse, an unbroken horse, who will have to be dragged, or ridden and broken to arrive at the roundup or the horse butcher's. I'll even settle for the role of the coyote, that lonely yapping ornery stinking enduring snooty creature, that wild-to-hell-with-conformity dog, that prototype of the damn-you-general critter we call a writer—howling alone, yet hoping at least to hear one other yip-yip start up over the next hill.

But there's more to writing than howling. There's singing. And isn't there lots still to sing about too? Isn't there, in a sense, everything?

The human race. Maybe it is a breed of killers, of pack-hunting carnivores and territory-defenders and leader-followers and social peckers, as the anthropologist Robert Ardrey contended in his book, *African Genesis*. Still, as Ardrey conceded, we are also a species capable of transforming itself into a better one. So long as we are alive we are the leadership of life, and we can still lead ourselves towards more and more brilliant (*and* peaceful) living as well as towards death. But we must know ourselves before we can better ourselves. And the achievement of greater self-knowledge is the achievement that all the poets and all the artists work toward more consistently and powerfully than do even the creative scientists. For when the best poems and the best novels and the best plays are dropped on the world they kill nothing but ignorance, destroy only man's hate of other men.

Yes, there is man still to be *sung* about as well as *howled* at, man to be hammered and cajoled into being mankind. And there is all life, waiting to flow. November trees in Canada are bare and icy, but we know the old earth under them waits and stores and renews her power to send the juice of creation sprouting up into April leaves.

EPILOGUE

EARLE BIRNEY

Now that thirty-four critics have praised and damned, and hopefully cancelled each other out, and I have been allowed repeated interruptions, who needs an epilogue? Not those who have actually read through faithfully to this point; they would be better off reading the text and making up their own minds—or reading somebody else's poems. The truth is, I want it: I want the fun of the last word, even though it won't be the last the instant the first review of this book appears.

The Literary Game is tennis-without-a-rule-book. Anybody can play, including the author; the score never gets beyond deuce; and the only referee is Time. Reading through Bruce Nesbitt's skillful arrangement of servings and receivings has been a wry sort of fun for me. I've been consoled, for example, by Northrop Frye's approval of "Damnation of Vancouver" and especially of Will Langland's role. There would have been ten performances of that play at the B.C. Centennial Festival if I'd been willing to scrap Long Will and replace him with Centennial Sam (a cardboard cutout of the Honest Pioneer suggested by a Festival sub-committee). And I might have seen the "Damnation" on the boards of Ontario's Stratford if I'd let Tony Guthrie cut Langland's part entirely. I thought, and I still think, with Frye that "in all English culture no better spokesman could have been found for the conservative-radical opposition to oligarchy" in this drama. Even if it's never performed again, I have the consolation that a good critic understood why Long Will was in my play and what the play is about.

"Simon Paynter", whoever he/she was, understood nothing. He couldn't grasp even such obvious patterns as the matching of style to content or period, and saw no aptness in using an adaptation of early English metrics in passages telling the story of the pre-human periods of life on earth. I wonder at the malice which urged this anonymous criticaster into a long review of a poetic drama, a form which he evidently detested; in fact, I get the feeling he hated poetry in general, hated any experimentalism or "play" in language. He never went along with the concept of Gabriel Powers as a Death Principle leaning out from the future, his "Joyce-cum-Fry double-talk" at least a plausible futuritive idiom—though what Powers is saying about a "think of booty" in the passage Simple Simon quoted was an inserted piece of "portmanteau" I wrote long before Christopher Fry's advent, and based obviously on the "thing of beauty" passage from Keats' *Endymion*!

There was no end to "Simon Paynter"'s rigidity. He couldn't sense even the relevance for including "Fire and Ice" in speculations about the fate of this world and our species. He is my candidate for the most boring critic in this book, for not only was he "pseudanonymous" and dull-witted, he couldn't write. A master of cliché and archaism, often "tempted to say" and full of "one fears", he is the "reviewer [whose] flesh creeps" in every paragraph, who is "startled to find", but never finds anything. In fact he is determined not to discover, for he writes out of a set of dogmas and prejudices which render my work simply an object for anathema. He warns the public there is no real satire in the first "41 of the 47 pages" of my play, for he has examined each, and found no "positive standard". There are, he says, only two things approaching "positive standards" in "Damnation" and they won't do. One is "landscape" and the other—something quite different, it seems—is "nature". What's wrong with them is that they are not really "standards", only "standbys", and outmoded concepts peculiar to British Columbians, of whom "Simon" presumably is not one. This sort of epithetic twaddle goes on and on: the play lacks "satire" but somehow has "comedy"—as different from satire, probably, as landscape from nature? And the comedy is "obvious", whatever that means; Simon is too instinctively the un-critic to offer an example or a definition of anything.

To belabour with vague terms and condemn without offering evidence are, however, habits not confined to the young or anonymous among Cancritics. Even the early Northrop Frye, I notice, did it when reviewing my first book. "Satire makes him relapse into an idiom more suitable for prose." That's the pithy sort of putdown which undergrad Englit students love to copy out, and use later in their own Cancritbooks (and one of them has recently done just that!) but it's strictly a non-statement; Professor Frye nowhere in his review indicates which of my poems he takes to be "satires", or gives an example of a "prose" lapse in the book. Professor Frye would serve me better today, if he chose to notice a book of mine. Others with lesser reputations but louder voices continue the game of generic tags and trial without evidence. Robin Skelton can be heard shouting sharp warnings in these pages that my lines "have a glossy avant-garde surface but little else", and my poems in general only "veneer and marquetry". It's particularly unkind of

Professor Skelton to withhold examples of what he means, since from what little I have been able to bear reading of his own verse I think him the slickest master of all Ireland and Vancouver Island in patchwork and surface, and though his work is never never *avant garde,* it shines with a particular gloss *en derrière.* (Thirty-all, Professor Skelton?)

There is often condescension and subjective judgement-out-of-hand even in a good European or American commentator dealing with Commonwealthian efforts. The subjectivity is most evident when the critic resorts to quotation. Just as Professor Skelton "proves" that my poetry is "meretricious" merely by setting two lines of it against a pair from "real work" by Wallace Stevens— an often-quoted Stevens couplet I have always thought highly artificial, and which is certainly irrelevant in content to mine—so Paul West, for whose criticism in general I have considerable respect, becomes equally unhelpful and unconvincing when he cites a few lines from Eliot *vis à vis* a passage from "David". For Professor West, Eliot's trip over a Swiss lake has "suggestive power"; my account of passing "time on a knife edge" in the Rockies has not. Byron's Childe Harold fascinates him; my Salish Chief is "fusty, if not fustian"; Appollinaire and e.e. cummings are O.K., but my "chaotic typography" is almost pointless. I find this sort of thing mere critics' tennis again, and I can only return the subjective ball with equal speed and egoism. I think Eliot's lines about "coming over the Starnbergersee" flat and dull, and West's remarks about my typography Philistine as well as fustian.

The most conscienceless practitioner to be found, in this book, of the undefined term, the insult by comparison, and literary snobbism in general, is undoubtedly the late Hayden Carruth. What is for me one of my best poems, "November Walk near False Creek Mouth", is dismissed as "too long and a good deal too imitative". Imitative of whom? And how long is too long? Other poems, unnamed, are damned for being on "set themes" (what themes? set by whom?) or "sermons-from-stones", or mere "rhetoric" or "absurd hyperbole". My work in general is described as being without "poetic seriousness" or "poetic faith". Hayden Carruth departed this earth without leaving definitions or examples of these portentous qualities, but he did suggest a measure for evaluating my work and by implication that of the "English-Canadian culture" of which he pronounced me so "very profoundly a product". His measure is the contrasting excellence of American poets. Compared with theirs, my poems are "third-rate Eberhart, fifth-rate Tate". Even my use of space for punctuation is unsuccessful simply because it is different from the manner of Gary Snyder and Robert Duncan, of whom I "seem unaware". Old-fashioned Yankee arrogance, carried this far, fails from its own silliness, particularly from someone as minor in the ranks of his own country's poets as was Carruth. He was an ignoramus to boot or he would not have argued that Canadian poets were unaware of American ones simply because we sometimes failed to imitate them. His criticism was an unconscious reflection of imperialist attitudes to Canadians in general, a hostility towards whatever is stubbornly different in our culture, and a contempt for what cannot be evaluated in American terms.

Not that Canadian critics are innocent of the *argumentum ad hominem* or avoid similar value judgements based on place. I am thinking of sentences like these in the present book:

> In 1929, when all the young and serious writers went to Paris Earle Birney was in San Francisco teaching at the relatively quiet Berkeley campus. (Andy Wainwright)

> *Campus Theatre Steps* . . . one is not apt to understand unless he comes from Eugene, Oregon. I come from Fredericton, New Brunswick. (Fred Cogswell)

> He has been supported for years and years by the universities [despite his] offensive condescension towards the entire academic corps. (Carruth)

> He has travelled a good deal . . . and his poems have the traveller's superficiality . . . Something arrests Mr. Birney's eye—old ladies on a summer verandah—it can be almost anything. (Carruth)

What to say about "so what?" In 1929 I wasn't teaching, I was marking freshman themes at subsistence pay; I worked my way to London and Paris five years later on a lumberboat. So what? . . . *Campus Theatre Steps* contains no references which could apply only to the Eugene, Oregon, scene (Cogswell's clue comes from my footnote) and its key allusions are to the titles of plays well known in the contemporary theatre. To my knowledge, the poem has never given problems of understanding to anyone except Professor Cogswell. . . . *In this verandah,* which Carruth uses to instance a habit of superficial travel-reporting, was written at home in Toronto during the early days of the Second World War, when it was unknown even to Carruth that the Americans would "win", or even fight in it. The poem is about the chanciness and fatality of all wars. The three "old ladies on a summer verandah" are the Fates, the *Parcae*; two of them, Clotho and Lachesis, are mentioned by name in the poem. It seems that Carruth had never heard of them. . . . As for my attitude to "the academic corps", I think professors much like anybody else—no better, certainly, nor do I condescend to them. The universities never supported me. As an overworked and nearly always underpaid professor of philology-anglosaxon-mediaeval-canadian-american-world-literature at all levels to the doctorate, I was one of those who, through most of my life, supported the universities.

Somewhat kindred, though better intentioned, are the attempts in this book to read my mind, mood, or intent when I wrote a particular verse or even a group of poems. Professor Fredeman, to whom I am indebted for one of the first serious considerations of my work in general, nevertheless finds that my "satirical poems, most of which are topical, fail . . . because of their embarrassment to the poet, who, throughout, is making a nervous attempt at objectivity". The two pieces he names, *Restricted Area* and *The Monarch of the Id,* were composed at different times and certainly not in nervousness (a state I could never write in) but in righteous contempt; the first, at the antisemites who posted a *Gentiles Only* sign on a Lake Huron beach; the second, at the law which gave one Puritanical civil servant in Ottawa the power to ban whatever books he personally thought sinful from entering Canada, without even reporting his actions to Parliament. They were certainly "topical" verses, and already faded. But they packed a punch when they first appeared, were reprinted in newspapers, quoted on radio and by politicians, and helped in their small way to enact a law forbidding racist signs in Ontario, and to repeal an authoritarian section of the Customs Act. All this happened before Professor Fredeman came to Canada. He could see that these satires were dead, but he did not know that they had died from their success, not their failure.

Again with the best of intentions, Professor Jones misinterprets mine, in *El Greco: Espolio,* when he remarks that the carpenter "will live long" because he "does not take sides in the issue in which he is involved". The poem says only that he will "have carpenter sons/God willing". He could have those and still die young. My point is that, whatever the length of his life, his concentration on doing well an allotted job allows him to live on a level above mere staying alive, a plane of socially accepted craftsmanship.

The "source" of a poem is another subject as fascinating for the critic as "intent"—and as precarious, if the rules of evidence are ignored. A. J. M. Smith declares three of my most anthologized early poems—*Hands, Vancouver Lights, Dusk on the Bay*— to be speaking "with the voices of Auden, Rex Warner, or Stephen Spender". To my ear, these poets have very different "voices", and one of them, Warner's, I hadn't even heard when I wrote those poems. Auden and Spender were admittedly early influences on my style, though Professor Smith furnishes no examples, but my speech is as different from theirs as theirs from each other. On the other hand, Smith is perfectly right to point out the interweaving of phrases from literary classics which goes on in my *North of Superior,* because these are deliberate interruptions I make (and which he can and does document); they are asides to my own voice, to underline the contrast between the storied landscapes of Britain and the traditionless wild of the Laurentian Shield. Smith understood what I was trying to do, but he wrongly suggests the influence of Pound—I learned my *Seafarer* the hard way—and he seems not to spot at least half my buried loot. Where is Wordsworth? Where lie Burns, Shakespeare, *The Golden Bough,* the King James *Bible?* Let's keep the rally going.

I am also a little piqued that none of these 34 judges took note of the trail of mythic references I laid in my "November Walk . . .". Even Kingsley Weatherhead, otherwise so alert and responsive to my work, finds only "trivial conversation" in the talk about the Lockeys of Outgarden. There is a Loki in that Utgarth, and more than "childish fragments that tourists have" in my contemporary equivalents for the Gifts of the Magi.

Better perhaps to be silent than to be wrong, however, on the subject of influences. *Anglo-Saxon Street* is written in Anglo-Saxon metre of a vintage six hundred years earlier than *The Canterbury Tales*; it cannot possibly have "the flavour of Chaucer" (Paul West). And certainly it is better for a critic to be silent about influences if he cannot distinguish between indebtedness openly and cheerfully admitted, and plagiarism. It seems to be the latter which Professor Cogswell, in a bumbling sort of way, is accusing me of, in his review of my *Rag & Bone Shop*: "He poaches on the preserves of writers as various in time and style as the author of Beowulf and bp nichol, adding little new in the way of thought or form." Poaching is an ugly property-minded word. It is also a misguided one when applied to the *Beowulf,* which is not a game preserve but a poem existing in the public domain for the last thirteen centuries. The one piece in my *Rag & Bone Shop* which employs Anglo-

Saxon metrics is original in thought and imagery, and the metre is functional to the theme. If I've stolen from barry nichol, who is happily not in the public domain, it has been unconsciously, and the theft is not one which has prevented him from complimenting me, as readers of this collection will have observed, for pioneering efforts in certain of the modes we have both employed. Cogswell is not only wrong, as well as rude; he is inconsistent—or else he has some sort of fixation about "poaching". For in his very next sentence he pronounces me "typical in thought and outlook of the average liberal-minded Canadian". I suddenly see ourselves, the horde of small-l libs across this nation, creeping like a pack of barren jackals at night into the conserves of the conservatives, to ravage the fertile antelope and rend the thoughtful hippopotami.

I think Canadian poets have more to fear from small-c conservatism, especially of the dogmatic sort I sometimes encounter in this collection in the remarks, say, of A. J. M. Smith. He is so obsessed with some notion of "pure poetry", peculiar to the nineteenth century, that he disapproves even of my including stage directions in a poetic drama. "This is fine for the amateur actor and the inexperienced director, but the reader of poetry, I should think, would prefer to take his poetry neat." But does he? Does even A. J. M. S. object to the directions, equally interruptive, in Shakespeare's plays, or those supplied for translations of the Greek tragedies? I have proportionately fewer of them than Yeats has in his *Deirdre* or Marlowe in *Doctor Faustus,* about which no one has thought to object. In any case I did not publish my play solely for readers of poetry, but also for people who might want to perform it. Some of these could be quite professional actors or directors, and yet not feel condescended to by my stage whispers. What is implicit in Smith's criticism is an unbridging narrowness of approach to the *look* of the poem on the page. He wants everything so clean and left-right lineal he doesn't even like visual art in a book. The collages (necessarily reduced to flat black-and-whites) which Leonard Brooks, a leading Canadian artist, contributed to my *Selected Poems,* are dismissed as "illustrations [which] though good enough in themselves, seem to be competing with the poems. Poetry ought to be left to speak for itself." If poetry had been, we would have lost many centuries of magnificent illuminated manuscripts, not to speak of the great intermedic art of William Blake.

His watertight approach to the arts inevitably leads Smith to condemn what he calls my "typographical gimmicks". In this judgement he is supported by Wainwright, who considers the "linear aspect of poetry" sacrosanct. It is a peculiarly provincial and uninventive approach to an art whose medium is that ever-changing thing, language. Writing, all writing, is a pictorial agreement about signs and other gimmicks. A page was, and is, a place to put markings. The "linear aspect of poetry" is neither a universal nor an immortal necessity, except for linotypers. Chinese poetry moves from top to bottom and right to left, and sometimes both ways at once. Appollinaire and Finlay move in any direction. Wainwright continues to clump in heavy-booted prose from false premises left-right to false conclusions. "Concrete poems", he says, "contain the assumption that the linear aspect of poetry is not alive." I've never heard of any poet taking that either-or position; I certainly don't. I accept the best technology of the world I live in, which allows my publisher to offset my poems straight or crooked, slanting like rain or curving like balloons, and to print them in black, green, red, or whatever colour of ink I choose for a word or a page. The "concrete" poet is not alone in "making pictures with words"; a page in a book is itself a visual experience, however conventionally it is laid out. But some critics see with only half an eye.

Some are not good at hearing either, especially those who haven't trained their ears to listen the way a poet must. I think Pratt sensed the rhythms of *David* better than Frye; the run-on lines do have somewhere "to run to", and Ned showed where. I don't think Frye fully understands the strange music that Anglo-Saxon prosody makes, either. He complains that my rhythms are not "fluent enough", the alliteration is "over-elaborate", and "the diction sounds spiky and self-conscious." I know Anglo-Saxon better than Frye does; I know I have not exaggerated its alliterative emphasis and strenuous rhythms. And I intended the diction to sound spiky and formal. It is simply that Frye, as is his right, prefers the fluidities of later poetry. So do I sometimes, *depending on the subject*—a point which none of my critics takes time to consider.

I feel equally certain that my ear is better than Milton Wilson's for "North American cliché and vulgarity." Naturally some of the poems in question were written some years before he criticized them, and do not sound "fresh" now because the slang and the bromides have already suffered changes. Such satires are dated, but that does not prove my ear was inaccurate. In any case, I know that *Toronto Board of Trade* . . ., *Billboards* . . ., and *Appeal to a Lady* . . ., are not considered by North American *listeners* to be the "unimaginative and tiresome work" he describes. I have been a professional reader of these and other poems to audiences all over North America, and for that matter the rest of the English-speaking world, for the last twenty-five years, and I know that these and similar poems are still listened to and liked. Critics who judge such work without hearing how an audience reacts to it should not expect the poet, at least, to listen very seriously to them.

Opinions about *Turvey* also appear in the present collection, along with my reactions to them—except in the case of Professor Dooley, whose critique had not come to my notice when I wrote "Turvey and the Critics". His possesses at least the merit of novelty. Nobody else has made such a determined effort to put *Turvey* down. No one else ever found it "bookish", or satirically invalid or "suffer[ing] from the Canadian novelist's usual difficulties with plot."

It's not clear what problems Dooley thinks we Canadians have had with plot, but it's evident to me that he had some of his own when he wrote about *Turvey*. One was an undergraduate sort of determination to steer a set course, whatever the weather, guided only by the most elementary of charts. He is out to prove *Turvey* a bad novel and he has instant categories for what's "first-rate". Novels should be "disciplined", for one thing (like Dostoevsky's?). If the hero is "the little man" buffeted by a system, then the novelist shouldn't give him any breaks. Turvey is therefore unconvincing, because I sometimes allow him to be "the lucky fellow who lands on his feet, the man who finds a friend just when he needs help most"—an annoying habit shared by Don Quixote and Falstaff and Joseph Andrews, as I recall—and like them too— "Turvey is greatly to blame for his own misfortunes". Professor Dooley's charts, it seems, can't locate Turvey at all; he is off on some amoral island, where the guilty are not always punished—the Island of Humour, I hope, many degrees south of the rocky coast of Satire.

The latter is home ground for Professor Dooley; he has published a book about it, very systematic and, like his examination of the humour in *Turvey,* quite humourless. The humour of my book, he writes, "derives from a rather small number of types of situations— most of them involving sex, drink, medical treatment, army discipline, or personnel selection methods". I'd think that was God's plenty in "number of types of situations", especially if arranged in that order, but Dooley finds sex, drink and the like pretty pallid stuff. The trouble is, he says, that "the author seems to put comic effect ahead of satire. In many [of the situations] no one is being attacked. . . . The interest lies in the comic development of Private Turvey." It never seems to occur to Professor Dooley that this was exactly my intent, and a clue to what he should really be talking about.

But Dooley has his Procrustean bed of definitions, and he's willing to kill Turvey by dismemberment if he won't fit the bed. Turvey, he mutters, is not a Schweik after all, because he isn't "consistently outwitting those in high position". Right! And again as I intended. Wrong! says Dooley: he is only partly like Schweik; he should be entirely like him, or not at all. At times the narrator gives us Turvey's thoughts, sometimes his own. Something else you can't do in Dooley's bed. And you can't shift to "less worthy models" of style, even if it's to burlesque a Victorian Happy Ending, because this is confusing to Professor Dooley, and distracts him from the contemplation of "thorough-going satires", which is what *Turvey* isn't. But what *is* it? Well, Professor Dooley's President, Claude Bissell, had said it was "a succession of fabliaux . . . a collection of broad army stories". So let's play it safe and agree with the President. But Dooley's experience of the Canadian Army obviously wasn't as broad as Claude Bissell's, for he mistakes Mac's RAF and Commando slang for a base imitation of Dickens' Mr. Jingle. (We begin to see why the Professor is the only critic who thought *Turvey* was too bookish.)

If only Dooley could have spared some of his super-sensitivity to Sources for one gleam of interest in Comedy! When Turvey, recovering from prolonged goosing by a sterophagoscope, looks out his hospital window and sees a typical Flanders cart-horse with its tail "docked cruelly short", he winces in sympathy. Surely that's an understandable reaction from someone who still feels he has a 2-foot telescope encased in his rear. But Professor Dooley earnestly disagrees. It's a reaction "more refined" than "it ought to be" for Turvey, and proves that I am a bad novelist who can't create a consistent character.

So anxious is ex-Captain Dooley to demote Private Turvey that he makes statements about the book which are not true. "The combatant part of the army does not come in . . . since Turvey never really reaches it." Either Dooley never reached whatever he thinks was "the combatant part" or he never got to the climax of my novel, since that occurs when Turvey reaches the Sharp End at the tip of the Canadian salient near Arnhem and, in the midst of mortar fire, learns of the death of Mac a few hours before. For that matter, most of the novel is laid either in England under air raids or in the Lines of Communications within Belgium and Holland, during the height of V-1 and V-2 attacks in the last and worst winter of the war. It does seem that Captain Dooley's military experience was considerably less than Private Turvey's.

I find his ignorance in another matter less understandable. It was predicted, he says, that the book would enjoy "popularity" but "such has not proved to be the case". What is his "proof"?—that *Turvey* was out-sold by "the official history of the second world war"! This may be—Dooley cites neither the "official" title or its sales—but *Turvey* was scarcely written to compete, and has had for twenty-four years a wide library and bookstore circulation among two generations of veterans, students and general readers. By the time Dooley's review appears, it has already reached a third printing in a Canadian "hardback" and sold out a separate British one from Abelard-Schuman and a paperback from Collins. It had also been pirated and peddled illegally in various parts of the world under the title of *The Kootenay Highlander*; nationally broadcast as a radio serial; and enjoyed a seven-weeks run as a stage play in Toronto. These are facts which Dooley could readily have acquired, and should have considered before denying even some "popularity" to this misfit *Turvey*. Truncated and cast out from Dooley's bed, the book has since managed to carry on through three editions in the New Canadian Library series, and two musical versions with full summer runs in national theatres. Small successes, it's true, but successes with the sort of audience very precious to me—with people who don't wait for a professor of satire to tell them when to laugh.

As for *Down the Long Table,* I'm quite willing to concede it's not my best effort, somewhat of a curate's egg in fact. I certainly agree with Arnold Edinborough that its "topicality is unfortunate", if he means, as I think he does, that the framework device tying the novel in with the McCarthy Senatorial hearings of the Fifties was a mistake. There's a whole new generation of readers for whom McCarthy is the name of a Good Senator, mild if inept, and a Senate Investigation Committee is a collection of even Better Senators out to repair the dykes of democracy flooded by Watergate. When I wrote *Down the Long Table,* most liberal-minded persons in positions of trust or authority in North America felt actually under threat of loss of job and reputation from the long hands of the McCarthy committee shuffling the cards of their pasts to find one that could be coloured pink. My framework had point then, however artificial it was, but little now, and I am proposing to my publishers that the opening and closing frames simply be eliminated when they reissue the book next year as a paperback. Freed of the McCarthy albatross, I think the book can stand and will have something to say to those born after the Thirties who did not experience what it was like to live and move about Canada in the Depression, poor and jobless and virtually without government aid. There is a good deal also in it about what it was like to risk jail and physical assault for the ideals of Marxist-Leninism and at the same time to be denounced as a fascist, and attacked and isolated from the working masses by those who were themselves the equals of the Nazis, the Stalinist supporters of a new Russian autocracy as murderous in the long run as Hitler's.

And yet I must admit the book has other faults. The London *Observer's* reviewer found between "a spattering of buoyantly satirical hits" some "rather prolix jokes about inter-party tiffs", and other commentators have been slightly put off by my adaptation of the Dos Passos interchapter of headlines. I am willing to defend the latter because I use his "gimmick" functionally by integrating the story line with the news clips. More serious is George Woodcock's criticism that *Down the Long Table* is "divided by the conflict between the historical impulse to reconstruct authentically time past, and the fictional impulse to establish a self-consistent imaginary world." Certainly I tried to fuse authenticity with the world of the imagination. I think all novelists have to do this. If a reader feels the elements do not fuse then the book is a failure for him.

Professor Dooley objects that Gordon, like Turvey, is not exactly one classifiable thing or another. He should be a Don Quixote but he isn't, because he tilts at windmills not from idealism but "out of perversity". (The word suggests more about Dooley's political bias than about the motivations of revolutionaries in that decade when Professor Dooley was too young to care.) Above all Gordon, like Turvey, is prone to "moral failures", a Quixote whose "first Dulcinea is another man's wife". Professor Dooley withholds his "sympathy for a character who doesn't deserve it".

Deserved or not, Gordon has had warmer sympathy extended from shrewder critics both in Britain and in Canada. The London *Tribune* thought his story rang true and "the Trotskyists in Canada a much more interesting bunch than the Stalinists". *Books and Bookmen* called the satire "Orwellian", and the *Times Literary Supplement* predicted a new generation would "be interested in . . . the years of awaiting the revolution that never came". The Toronto

Star found "hilarious episodes in the efforts to work up a revolution in a strictly non-inflammable land"—and so on across Canada. However, the literary journals disliked or ignored it, and the public didn't buy. It was my only book to be remaindered. Next year it reappears, and a new team of critics will play their own kind of tennis with it once more. I hope I'll be there again, trying to keep the score at deuce.

7 September 1973   EARLE BIRNEY

SELECTED BIBLIOGRAPHY

A. BOOKS BY EARLE BIRNEY

I. Poetry

David and Other Poems. Toronto: Ryerson, 1942.
Now Is Time. Toronto: Ryerson, 1945.
The Strait of Anian: Selected Poems. Toronto: Ryerson, 1948.
Trial of a City and Other Verse. Toronto: Ryerson, 1952.
Ice Cod Bell or Stone. Toronto: McClelland and Stewart, 1962.
Near False Creek Mouth. Toronto: McClelland and Stewart, 1964.
Selected Poems: 1940-1966. Toronto: McClelland and Stewart, 1966.
Memory No Servant. Trumansburg, New York: New Books, 1968.
The Poems of Earle Birney. Toronto: McClelland and Stewart, 1969.
Pnomes Jukollages and other Stunzas. grOnk, ser. 4, no. 3. Toronto: Ganglia Press, 1969.
Rag & Bone Shop. Toronto: McClelland and Stewart, 1971.
Four Parts Sand. With Bill Bissett, Judith Copithorne and Andrew Suknaski. Ottawa: Oberon, 1972.
What's So Big About Green? Toronto: McClelland and Stewart, 1973.
The Bear on the Delhi Road. London: Chatto and Windus, 1973.

II. Novels

Turvey. Toronto: McClelland and Stewart, 1949; Toronto: Collins, 1952; London and New York: Abelard-Schuman, 1959. With an introduction by George Woodcock; Toronto: McClelland and Stewart, 1963.
    As *The Kootenay Highlander*; London: Four Square, 1960.
Down the Long Table. Toronto: McClelland and Stewart, 1955; London: Abelard-Schuman, 1959.

III. Criticism

Chaucer's Irony. University of Toronto: unpublished Ph.D. thesis, 1936.
The Creative Writer. Toronto: CBC Publications, 1966.
The Cow Jumped Over the Moon: The Writing and Reading of Poetry. Toronto: Holt, Rinehart and Winston, 1972.

IV. Editions

Twentieth Century Canadian Poetry. Toronto: Ryerson, 1953.
Record of Service in the Second World War. A supplement to the University of British Columbia War Memorial Manuscript Record. Vancouver: U.B.C., 1955.
New Voices. With Ira Dilworth, Desmond Pacey, Jean-Charles Bonenfant and Roger Duhamel. Toronto: Dent, 1956.
Selected Poems of Malcolm Lowry. San Francisco: City Lights, 1962. 2nd revised edition, 1963.
Lunar Caustic, by Malcolm Lowry. With Margerie Lowry. London: Cape, 1968.

B. PAMPHLETS

Conversations with Trotsky, by E. Robertson (pseudonym). Processed London: E. Robertson, [1935].
Canada Calling. Montreal: CBC International Service, 1946.
Convocation Address. Calgary: University of Alberta, 1965.

C. RECORDINGS

David. Read by Earle Birney. Disc no. QC-86, 15 minutes. Creston, British Columbia: Photofolios, 1964.
Birney/Layton. Poems read by Earle Birney and Irving Layton. Canadian Poets on Tape, no. 1, 60 minutes. Toronto: Ontario Institute for Studies in Education, 1969.
David. Read by René Auberjonois. Disc. New York: Scott, Foresman, 1969.
Earle Birney. Poems and commentary by Earle Birney. Cassettes, no. 1. Toronto: High Barnet, 1970.

D. SHORT STORIES

"The Reverend Eastham Discovers Life", *The Ubyssey*, annual literary supplement, March 1924.
"Bird in the Bush", *Mademoiselle,* May 1948, pp. 143, 236-239.
"Mickey Was a Swell Guy", *National Home Monthly,* 49 (November 1948), 16-17, 26-27.
"The Levin Bolt", *Canadian Life,* 1 (March-April 1949), 7, 31, 38; as "A London Sketch" in Ralph Gustafson, ed., *Canadian Accent* (London: Penguin, 1951).
"The Strange Smile of Thos. Turvey", *Here and Now,* 2 (June 1949), 38-45.
"Turvey Engages a Paratrooper", *Saturday Night,* 64 (9 August 1949), 21.
"What's This Agoosto", *Montreal Standard,* 29 July 1950, pp. 14-15, 21.
"Private Turvey Becomes Acting Senior Officer", in John Robins, ed., *A Book of Canadian Humour* (Toronto: Ryerson, 1951, pp. 49-56.
"Enigma in Ebony", *Maclean's,* 15 October 1953, pp. 16-17, 104, 106-108.

E. SELECTED ARTICLES, ESSAYS AND REVIEWS

This chronological list of Birney's more important shorter work includes less than one-third of the total he has written; a more complete record is available in the bibliography by Peter C. Noel-Bentley and Earle Birney, listed below in section F, and in the Bibliography to Noel-Bentley's thesis up-dated by the staff of the University of Toronto's Rare Book Department, where Birney's papers are housed as the Birney Collection. References to material reprinted in the text have not been listed here.

"Aldous Huxley", in Pelham Edgar, ed., *The Art of the Novel* (New York: Macmillan, 1933), pp. 280-290.
"Personal Experiences in Nazi Germany", *New Leader,* 13 December 1935.
"English Irony before Chaucer", *University of Toronto Quarterly,* VI (1937), 538-557.
"Proletarian Literature: Theory and Practice", *Canadian Forum,* XVII (May 1937), 58-60.

"Canada and World Politics" by E. Robertson (pseudonym), *New International*, September 1938, pp. 261-264.
"Is French-Canada Going Fascist?" by E. Robertson (pseudonym), *New International*, October 1938, pp. 304-307.
"The Beginnings of Chaucer's Irony", *PMLA*, LIV, (1939), 637-655.
"The Two Worlds of Geoffrey Chaucer", *Manitoba Arts Review*, II (Winter 1941), 3-16.
"Advice to Anthologists: Some Rude Reflections on Canadian Verse", *Canadian Forum*, XXI (1942), 338-340.
"Is Chaucer's Irony a Modern Discovery?" *Journal of English and Germanic Philology*, XLI (1942), 303-319.
"Has Poetry a Future in Canada?", *Manitoba Arts Review*, V (Spring 1946), 7-15.
"Age Shall Not Wither Thee", *Here and Now*, I (January 1949), 86-87.
"On Being a Canadian Author", *Canadian Library Association Bulletin*, IX (November 1952), 77-79.
"The Writer and the H-Bomb: Why Create?", *Queen's Quarterly*, LXII (1955), 37-44.
"North American Drama Today: A Popular Art?" *Transactions of the Royal Society of Canada*, Section II, 3rd series, LI (1957), 31-42.
" 'After His Ymage'—The Central Ironies of the Friar's Tale", *Mediaeval Studies*, XXI (1959), 17-35.
"The Franklin's 'Sop in Wyn' ", *Notes & Queries*, n.s., VI (1959), 345-347.
"E. J. Pratt and His Critics", in R. L. McDougall, ed., *Our Living Tradition*, 2nd and 3rd series (Toronto: University of Toronto Press, 1959), pp. 123-147.
"The Modern Face of Hubris", in J. Alan Ross, ed., *Hubris, Man and Education* (Bellingham, Washington: Union, 1959), pp. 46-60.
"The Inhibited and the Uninhibited: Ironic Structure in the 'Miller's Tale' ", *Neophilologus*, XLIV (1960), 333-338.
"The Squire's Yeoman", *Review of English Literature*, I (1960), 9-18.
"Structural Irony within the 'Summoner's Tale' ", *Anglia*, LXXVIII (1960), 204-218.
"The Unknown Poetry of Malcolm Lowry", *British Columbia Library Quarterly*, XXIV (April 1961), 33-40.
"A Malcolm Lowry Bibliography", *Canadian Literature*, no. 8 (1961), pp. 81-88; no. 9 (1961), pp. 80-84.
"First Supplement to Malcolm Lowry Bibliography", *Canadian Literature*, no. 11 (1962), pp. 90-95.
"A. J. M. S.", *Canadian Literature*, no. 15 (1963), pp. 4-6.
"Second Supplement to Malcolm Lowry Bibliography", *Canadian Literature*, no. 19 (1964), pp. 83-89.
"The Canadian Writer vs. the Canadian Education", *Evidence*, no. 10 (1967), pp. 97-113.

F. CRITICISM

References to criticism reprinted in the text have not been recorded in this list, which includes all other major articles devoted exclusively to Birney, and selected reviews of Birney's work for which space was not available in this collection.

Beattie, Munro. "Poetry (1935-1950)", in Carl F. Klinck, *et al.*, eds., *Literary History of Canada* (Toronto: University of Toronto Press, 1965), pp. 761-765.
Brown, E. K. *On Canadian Poetry* (Toronto: Ryerson, 1943), pp. 76-78.

Burns, Gerald. Review of *Memory No Servant*, *Southwest Review*, LIV (1969), 95.
Candelaria, F. H. Review of *The Creative Writer*, *West Coast Review*, I, 1 (Winter 1967), 54-55.
Clay, Charles. "Earle Birney", in W. P. Percival, ed., *Leading Canadian Poets* (Toronto: Ryerson, 1948), pp. 23-29.
Davey, Frank. *Earle Birney*. Toronto: Copp Clark, 1971.
Drake, Albert. Review of *Memory No Servant*. *Western Humantities Review*, XXIII (1969), 179-180.
Dudek, Louis. Review of *Twentieth Century Canadian Poetry*, *Canadian Forum*, XXXIII (1954), 280.
Elliott, Brian. "Earle Birney: Canadian Poet", *Meanjin*, XVIII (1959), 338-347.
New, W. H. "Maker of Order, Prisoner of Dreams: The Poetry of Earle Birney" in *Articulating West, Essays on Purpose and Form in Modern Canadian Literature*. Toronto: new press, 1973.
Noel-Bentley, Peter C. *A Study of the Poetry of Earle Birney*. University of Toronto: unpublished M.A. thesis, 1966.
——— and Earle Birney. "Earle Birney: A Bibliography in Progress, 1923-1969". *West Coast Review*, V, 2 (October 1970), 45-53.
Pacey, Desmond. "Earle Birney", in *Ten Canadian Poets* (Toronto: Ryerson, 1958), pp. 293-326.
———. Review of *Twentieth Century Canadian Poetry*, *Fiddlehead*, no. 20 (1954), pp. 17, 19.
Purdy, Alfred W. Review of *The Creative Writer*, *Canadian Literature*, no. 31 (1967), pp. 61-64.
Robillard, Richard. *Earl Birney*. Toronto: McClelland and Stewart, 1971.
Rowland, Beryl, ed. *Companion to Chaucer Studies* (London: Oxford University Press, 1968), *passim* [includes commentary on Birney's Chaucer scholarship].
Stainsbury, Donald. Review of *Pnomes Jukollages and other Stunzas*, Leisure magazine supplement, *The Sun* (Vancouver), 20 November 1970.
Woodcock, George. "Earle Birney", in Rosalie Murphy, ed., *Contemporary Poets of the English Language* (London: St. James Press, 1970), pp. 94-97.